P9-EDT-787

"English Canada"
speaks out

"English Canada" speaks out

edited by
J.L. Granatstein
and
Kenneth McNaught

Doubleday Canada

Canadian Cataloguing in Publication Data
Main entry under title:

"English Canada" speaks out

ISBN 0-385 25342-7

1. Federal government – Canada. 2. Canada – Constitutional
law – Amendments. 3. Quebec (Province) – History –
Autonomy and independence movements. I. Granatstein, J.L.,
1939– II. McNaught, Kenneth, 1918 – .

FC630.E54 1991   971.064'7   C91–094444-X
F1034.2.E54 1991   73634

Cover design by Danielle Koch
Printed and bound by Gagné in Quebec
Published in Canada by
Doubleday Canada Limited
105 Bond Street
Toronto, Ontario
M5B 1Y3

Contents

Part II: The Regions

Part III: Citizenship and Rights

Part IV: The Future

Introduction

In 1965 the interim report of the Royal Commission on Bilingualism and Biculturalism proclaimed, "Canada, without being fully conscious of the fact, is passing through the greatest crisis in its history." If there were good grounds for alarm in 1965, how much greater reason is there for concern about the condition of Canada today?

We believe that the essays in this volume demonstrate decisively that our present crisis is not only deeper but more genuinely perilous than that of which the 1965 commissioners warned. Today Canadians are fully conscious of the threat to their national existence. At the same time they know that the issue to be decided is by no means as simple as that depicted in the Bi and Bi report. The solitudes of the "two founding nations" may still hover around interminable commissions of inquiry and theatrical takings of the public pulse; but both solitudes — the French and the English — have been penetrated by recently minted concerns that run every bit as deep as those of thirty years ago. Our contributors from across the country talk now of the rights of native peoples in all the provinces, of more than two "founding nations."

They speak also of an imperilled environment, of a precarious North, of the contrapuntal relationship between citizenship and multiculturalism.

There are many voices in this book, but there is also a common commitment — to the worth of the Canadian experiment. As that experiment is challenged from within we are, perforce, required to assess it both historically and within the context of contemporary comparisons.

Historically, the essays concur that, with all its mistakes and shortfalls, Canada has retained its attachment to the ideals of a tolerant, accommodating federalism and an evolving, independent democracy. Sometimes implicit and now explicit in the Canadian political enterprise is the assertion of national purposes. Such purposes have included equitable distribution of the product of economic growth; equity among provinces and regions; equity among social classes. Those national purposes have included, too, maintenance of the different identities of provinces, religions, languages, cultural groups. Exactly 100 years before the 1965 interim report, Sir John A. Macdonald enunciated much of this. In a speech predicting the purposes of the nascent federal state he stressed the "individuality" of the provinces and the "nationality" of French Canada. He was confident that "we shall have a strong central government under which we can work out constitutional liberty as opposed to democracy, and be able to protect the minority." Macdonald's reference to democracy was to the United States, which was just then concluding its tragic civil war to assert the absolute right of the majority to rule. Canadians have remained suspicious of simple majorities. Our contributors reflect this concern while also underlining the need of a strong central government to ensure equity among our multiple identities and the effective evolution of national purposes.

If the perspective of history endorses this kind of accommodating political nationality, a contemporary, comparative perspective on Canada's malaise does so in spades. As "failed" nation-states around the world disintegrate or endure bloody internecine struggle, foreign observers look with disbelief on our myopic antics. Readers will find in this book serious, unblinking analyses of the costs — social and cultural as well as economic — of the secessionist option, which is the most immediate and active agent in our deepening crisis. They will observe as well repudiation of the angry mythology wielded so effectively by Québécois nationalists in and beyond the Parti Québécois: the myth that defeat of Meech Lake was English Canada's personal rejection of Quebec; that, as Léon Dion told the Bélanger–Campeau hearings, accommodation of his province will be achieved only when Quebec puts a knife to the Canadian throat.

In this colloquium, then, English Canadians reassert their commitment to a flexible federalism and a political community that abjures any nationalism founded upon racial-linguistic tests. Implicit throughout the essays is the sense that francophone Quebeckers have become, to a quite remarkable degree, masters of their own house; that admitted injustices of the past have been largely undone. Our authors concur, in varying degrees, that satisfying still further nationalist demands by emasculating the federal government would be a far more serious threat to their conceptions of Canada than outright secession of Quebec would be. As the several authors consider how best to resolve the present impasse — the political mechanics, the constitutional options — they reveal a strong, historically rooted appreciation of Quebec's importance to the "idea of Canada." Unmistakably, throughout the book runs recognition of the immense complexity of the "Canadian question" of today as compared with the relatively simplistic formulation of 1965. The need to consider anew the structure and purpose of Canada grows only in part out of the "Quebec question." The need would be there even without the challenge of séparatism, without the proximity of Professor Dion's knife.

Whether Canadian federalism begs for basic "restructuring" or whether it can more profitably continue on its traditional course of patient, pragmatic adjustment is the question considered herein. The answers proposed are various, reflecting the many facets of our country. They do unite in a basic endorsement of Sir John A.'s anticipation of a nation devoted to working out "constitutional liberty."

Our title, *"English Canada" Speaks Out*, frankly caused some difficulty. There is no doubt that it conveys the sense of the contributions in this volume that those of us in "the rest of Canada" are one people and a nation in almost every sense that *indépendantistes* in Quebec think of themselves. We too have been formed by our country's history, by the knowledge of great events accomplished together and by the desire to build worthwhile lives here for ourselves and our children. Unfortunately, the title will also convey to some, we realize, that only the English-speaking or those of British origin are entitled to speak out on the question of the country's future. This is most definitely not what we intended, and no one who consults our list of contributors will be able to believe that we sought to exclude some 40 per cent of Canadians from our consideration. The simple fact is that those who live outside Quebec have no name other than Canadians. If Quebec becomes independent, then we will undoubtedly continue to call ourselves Canadians, pure and simple; but so long as Quebec is an integral part of Canada, we lack a name. *"English Canada" Speaks Out*, for all its potential for misinterpretation, conveys the desired message.

The impetus for this volume came from Ronald St. J. Macdonald, whose distinguished career as teacher and dean of law in Toronto and Halifax, and as an international jurist, reinforces his cherished Canadianism. Our contributors have written to no prescription save that of approving the Canadian adventure. They exhibit variety in discussing that commitment; no greater divergence, however, than that which is almost daily more evident among Quebeckers. And in view of that apparent fluidity they would all wish to have us stress that their contributions were written in April and May to meet a rigorous deadline of May 31, 1991. The only alterations we have allowed since then have been those necessitated by changing events.

We wish to acknowledge especially Doubleday's ready response to our original proposal. John Pearce's willingness to put the book on the "fast track" has minimized the risks of writing within a milieu where many apparent focal points are far from fixed. Linda McKnight laboured mightly on our behalf as well.

J.L. Granatstein
Kenneth McNaught

June 1991

Part I

The Issues

With or Without Quebec?

Reg Whitaker

Reg Whitaker is author of many books, including the forthcoming A Sovereign Idea: Essays on Canada as a Democratic Community. *He teaches political science at York University.*

Early in 1991, Prime Minister Brian Mulroney made an important speech to the Empire and Canadian Clubs of Toronto on the subject of Canadian unity. The subtext of his remarks was an assertion of faith. Mr. Mulroney, in prime-ministerial fashion, was preaching from the pulpit of the Church of National Unity.

As a faith, National Unity must never be scrutinized rationally. "Let me be clear: Canada is not up for grabs. Either you have a country or you don't. You can't have it both ways. My country is Canada. . . . The issue that confronts us today is not Quebec and not the 'rest of Canada.' The issue is Canada. Period."

By definition, "Canada" *includes Quebec.* Anyone who speaks of the possible separation of Quebec is speaking of the "break-up of the country." There is an oddity here. Mr. Mulroney reluctantly explored the metaphor of Canada as a marriage facing possible divorce. Of course he cautioned against contemplating the "expensive, corrosive and bitter" divorce option and spoke hopefully instead about "reconciliation." But a marriage, or a divorce for that matter, involves two partners. Mr. Mulroney recognizes only one partner, Quebec. "Canada" refers not to a partner but to the marriage itself.

This is a strange marriage indeed. But how else should we interpret Mr. Mulroney's stern admonition that "the government of Canada does not speak for what some mistakenly refer to as English Canada"? "The government of Canada," he insists, "refers to all Canadians, including Quebeckers." The closest Mr. Mulroney can come to naming Quebec's putative partner in Confederation is to refer distantly and sceptically to "what some people call the 'rest of Canada.'" He stretches his imagination to encompass the idea of just who or what would remain were Quebec to leave. "To conceive of Canada without Quebec's vibrancy and uniqueness is to envisage a greatly diminished nation." Here at least is the notion that there could be a "nation," however "greatly diminished," but Mr. Mulroney's broken-record premise of "a strong and united Canada" prevents him from any serious examination of the identity of the mystery spouse — the counterpart to Quebec.

The current constitutional crisis, sparked by the failure of the Meech Lake Accord and the militant initiatives Quebec has expressed through the Allaire report and the Bélanger–Campeau commission, is undoubtedly the most serious one yet in Canadian constitutional history. Crises present both danger and opportunity. The more desperate the crisis, the greater the opportunity. The crisis may do us all a great favour by making English Canada think seriously about itself. For decades Quebec intellectuals, academics, politicians, poets, singers, even on occasion bureaucrats have debated what kind of Quebec they wish to create. Now they are saying to us, the "rest of Canada": Get your act together; tell us what your bottom line is; then let's see if we can get along together or must part company.

This is an invitation to the rest of Canada to find its own authentic voice. We should be grateful to Quebec sovereigntists for forcing this opportunity. And we should be extremely wary of the Ottawa National Unity industry, which has already gone into high gear to derail the debate before it can get rolling. Mr. Mulroney and opposition leader Jean Chrétien — federalist Quebeckers both — have a vested interest in stifling the development of an authentic English-Canadian voice. The gospel of National Unity will be preached in stern and scolding tones by the Mulroney–Chrétien cartel, on the unbending assumption that there is a Canada, which by definition includes Quebec, but that English Canada has no legitimate existence. English Canadians should ignore these admonitions and get on with the task of defining themselves as a community, with or without Quebec

There are only three broad possibilities for a constitutional response that would clearly meet Quebec requirements while maintaining the shell of a Canadian federation: asymmetrical federalism (extreme special status for Quebec); radical decentralization (every province becomes Quebec); and suprafederalism (a European-style parliament for Canada–Quebec matters).

All these options have major drawbacks that make them unattractive to many Canadians. The most profound objection to all of them is that they constitute in the first instance reactions or responses to a constitutional objective set by Quebec.

The decentralization option is superficially more attractive in that it entails no special advantages for Quebec. But would it be to the advantage of the rest of Canada? Certainly there is a substantial right-wing lobby, led by the Business Council on National Issues, neo-conservative economists and perhaps by the federal Tory government, that sees radical decentralization as a solution answering not only to the Quebec problem but to a markets-over-politics, dismantle-the-national-state agenda as well. However, no general movement has emerged spontaneously out of English Canada calling for a one-way transfer of power from Ottawa to the provinces. No doubt there would be support for some decentralization, and almost certainly for a rationalization of federalism to eliminate duplication and waste in overlapping jurisdictions. But this makes sense to most Canadians only if it is, as even Brian Mulroney has admitted, a two-way street — that is, some powers would devolve downward, but some might better be sent upward.

From the perspective of Quebec nationalism, of course, all such qualifications of decentralization are simply beside the point. Any transfer of power from Quebec City to Ottawa is unacceptable because it constitutes diminution of Quebec sovereignty. But why should the rest of Canada always be a prisoner of a Quebec-driven agenda? In one sense, the past thirty years of constitutional discussion have been driven by a Quebec agenda. This is not to say that Quebec has always received what it wanted. But what is striking in retrospect is the degree to which the rhythm, the dynamic, the context of constitutional debate has been shaped by perceptions of what Quebec wants and what would allegedly satisfy Quebec. For sixteen years, Canada was governed by a Quebecker who was obsessed by a mission to maintain Quebec within Confederation. Trudeau's answers have now proven unacceptable to Quebec opinion, but that only makes the years of Quebec-fetishism imposed upon the rest of the country even more deeply ironic. Similarly, the discussions surrounding

Mulroney's major constitutional initiative, Meech Lake, are referred to as the "Quebec Round."

So long as the likes of Mulroney and Chrétien continue to dominate national politics, and so long as the gospel of National Unity continues to be churned out by the propaganda machinery of Ottawa, the response to the latest, and gravest, Quebec challenge will continue to be one of reaction, recoupment, applying grease to the squeakiest wheel — in short, variations of the tail wagging the dog. This will no longer do.

With the Allaire report and the report of the Bélanger–Campeau commission, Quebec has clarified the alternatives and put the ball squarely in the court of English Canada. We must now respond to them. Their positions were arrived at by Quebec debate among Quebec voices, cast in the terms of Quebec national interests and articulated as a Quebec option. The participation of English Canadians from outside Quebec was neither sought nor welcomed. Moreover, the government of Quebec has reiterated that it will refuse on principle to take part in any process for constitutional change initiated among the governments of the rest of Canada. By insisting that Quebec will speak only to the federal government, one on one, and will boycott multilateral federal-provincial negotiations, or even a constituent assembly, Quebec is in effect demanding that the rest of the country speak with one voice.

The Mulroney government cannot possibly be that voice, led as it is by a Quebecker and supported as it is by a mere splinter group outside Quebec. What Quebec's boycott of the provincial initiatives or a constituent assembly really amounts to then is a refusal to become involved in articulating an English-Canadian constitutional voice, with which Quebec could then negotiate at a later stage.

This is, I firmly believe, an extremely positive development. It is no accident that both Mulroney and Chrétien have denounced the idea of a constituent assembly without Quebec participation. Bourassa and Company are in this instance better friends of English Canada than these two so-called "national" politicians who would effectively deny a voice to English Canadians under the deceptive rhetoric of National Unity.

If English Canada is to find a mechanism for articulating its own authentic voice — or, if one wishes to be pessimistic, to determine whether such a voice exists — it must confront what the preachers of National Unity seek to avoid at all costs. We must explore the idea of a Canada without Quebec. This is not to predetermine the outcome, as some would have it. Just because we think about a Canada without Quebec need not mean that it will inevitably come about. It does mean that we must think through the consequences of setting a negotiating agenda that states clearly that some things are negotiable, and some things are not. In entering negotiations, one must be aware that they may fail to find mutually acceptable terrain for agreement. The advantage of a process that initially excludes Quebec is that if negotiations fail, Canadians will have already debated and in part determined what their fate will be without Quebec. If we do not allow such a process to take place in the first instance, as Mulroney and Chrétien would have it, Canadians will be left without any maps if a rupture takes place. This is not only unfair to English Canadians, it is potentially very dangerous.

An English-Canadian equivalent to Quebec's current stance would presume only one thing: Canada is made up of two nations. From the Quebec perspective that proposition is simply axiomatic, even if Trudeau and his acolytes continue to deny the obvious. From the other side, the truth seems less clear. Does "English Canada" or the "rest of Canada" constitute a national community with sufficient coherence to come to a common bargaining position for negotiations within Confederation, or to contemplate life as a nation if Quebec departs? I incline rather strongly to the affirmative answer. If I am wrong, then Canada does not deserve to exist anyway. If the answer is no, then Canada is nothing more than nine provinces parasitically sucking on Quebec's lifeblood to maintain an artificial existence. Let us at least find out if Canada is a real thing, or if English Canada has no more than a vampire existence that will vanish into dust when the constitutional coffin is opened to the bright sunlight.

If the federal government will not co-operate with an English Canada–only process, perhaps the provinces should simply ignore Ottawa and proceed with the first stage, inviting federal participation once it is under way. Why not a constituent assembly created by the nine provinces and the territories, made up, as Premier Bob Rae of Ontario has suggested, of legislators and representatives of the major elements of civil society from outside the legislatures? Politicians (who are elected by the people, after all, and who must in the end carry out any deals) would be joined by representatives of aboriginal peoples, women, labour, business, ethnic Canadians, environmentalists, and so on. The political and social delegates would be charged with the task of hammering out a constitutional agenda reflective of the larger society. At the end of this process (or of some alternative like it), three broad alternatives would be conceivable:

• There might be a position that does, after all, provide common ground for compromise with Quebec — a

"National Unity" solution. Especially if ratified by a national referendum, such a solution would be much stronger and more lasting than Meech could have hoped to be (even if it had been ratified by all the provinces), because it would have authentic support from English Canada.

• A position might develop that was unacceptable to Quebec, and the two nations would come to a parting of the ways, at least in the common political superstructure. In this eventuality, the groundwork for a common basis for a vital Canadian nationality (without Quebec) would have been forged.

• No common position might be squeezed out. Quebec would presumably shake off the corpse, and the rest of Canada would fall apart or be absorbed into the United States — a richly deserved punishment for failure.

A ticking clock concentrates the mind (perhaps even the collective mind) most wonderfully. With Quebec's referendum on sovereignty looming over the horizon, I think that the first two alternatives are more likely than the third. The first, the National Unity outcome, may happen because Quebec gets cold feet about following through on the high economic risks and uncertainty of sovereignty. But it is imperative that the rest of Canada formulate its bottom line in advance, so that even if Quebec eventually stays, we are not bluffed out of defending interests that are essential to us. Such a deal would simply lay the groundwork for a later populist backlash against Quebec.

It is imperative that English Canada not be bulldozed by fear of separation. What is offered in the Allaire report is a "deal" in which Quebec stands to have its cake and eat it too; there are no obvious advantages to be gained by the rest of Canada, save one — that the trauma of a public divorce is avoided in favour of maintaining a fictional cover story for the world. Allaire is attempting to play on a psychological weakness induced by decades of National Unity rhetoric in which English Canada's autonomy and identity have been systematically denied.

Although the metaphor of the marriage/divorce is one that insistently slips into English-Canadian discussions of the Quebec question, it is notable for its relative absence from Quebec discourse. Quebeckers rarely reach for this metaphor because they rarely think of Canada as an institution in which they have sufficient emotional investment to justify talk of marriage or divorce. They are more apt to think of Confederation in contractual terms, as an arrangement that justifies or fails to justify itself in dollars and cents. Allaire and Bélanger–Campeau have concluded that the arrangement is not working in these terms from Quebec's point of view: ergo, either the contract is changed or it should be terminated. It is English Canadians who talk about the pain and anguish of divorce, of the need for compelling emotional appeals to the other party to move back from the brink. I doubt that in the present circumstances such appeals will be perceived as anything more than signs of weakness to be exploited to exact a better deal.

It is noteworthy that among francophone representations made to the Bélanger–Campeau hearings, the only hesitations expressed about sovereignty, and the only favourable points made about federalism, were couched in the cold, hard terms of money. Perhaps, some big-business representatives suggested, federalism has been more profitable for Quebec than the sovereigntists claim; perhaps the sovereignty road would be too risky, raising the interest rates too high, scaring away investment, saddling the Quebec government with too high a fiscal burden. Here is a hidden parallel to English Canada's weakness: there is fear on the sovereigntist side too, fear of the economic consequences of separation. Since the sovereignty project is today very much under business leadership (it is symbolic that Messrs. Bélanger and Campeau are both prominent Quebec businessmen), it is well to remember that those who live by the bottom line also die by the bottom line.

I think that it would be a grave error for English Canada to play upon this weakness by threatening dire consequences. As we know from the late 1970s, scare tactics are counter-productive. Moreover, if Quebec does follow through with sovereignty and Canada must follow through on its threats, the post-independence economic relationship between Quebec and Canada may be poisoned to nobody's advantage.

What I suggest is something rather different and less invidious. English Canada should enter into negotiations within federalism with a firm sense of its own non-negotiable items and a clear recognition that fear may well come into play in constraining both sides. If a National Unity deal can be struck on these terms, it will be a genuine compromise, in which essential interests of both sides are safeguarded, while less essential interests are conceded. But English Canada must also be prepared to take a walk if it is getting nowhere in negotiating an honourable compromise. So we must give serious consideration to the option of Canada-without-Quebec.

Would a Canada-without-Quebec be such an unthinkable alternative to an unacceptable deal made on Quebec's terms? We have never tried it before, so we can hardly render a definitively negative judgement. We have tried an artificial Canada-with-Quebec papered together with the official rhetoric of National Unity. National bilingualism, ostensibly at the behest of Quebec but actually as an answer to a question Quebec never asked, has created an ersatz Ottawa-driven national identity in which few Canadians can recognize themselves. To avoid granting special status to the province of Quebec, Trudeau created nine special statuses for often tiny francophone minorities outside Quebec and considerable resentment among anglophones (of all ethnic origins) denied symbols appropriate to their own sense of themselves.

The 1988 election signalled a groundswell of English-Canadian nationalism, generally identified with the moderate left of the political spectrum: the idea of Canada as a "kinder, gentler America" — which was washed away by pro–free trade votes in Quebec. Present concern about maintaining national standards in social programs is a reflection of this same left-nationalism. Freed of the rhetoric of National Unity, there are elements in English Canada that could offer a stronger, rather than weaker, basis for national identification in a Canada-without-Quebec.

There is an English-Canadian constitutional agenda, but it has been consistently blocked or side-tracked by the Quebec-driven agenda. There is a swelling demand for a more democratic and responsive political system, a demand reflected in the growing support for the Reform Party, in the deep cynicism towards politicians and the political process glimpsed in every opinion survey and open-line radio show and in the sour English-Canadian reaction to the Meech Lake process. The West demands a more regionally responsive set of central institutions, embodied in the idea of a triple-E Senate. Such aspirations are rudely shoved aside by Quebec, which has no intention of limiting its own power in the existing institutions and which is concerned only about the transfer of powers to the government of Quebec.

Also on the agenda is a drive for egalitarianism and individual rights, which runs headlong into Quebec's concern for collective rights in the preservation of its own distinct society. Similarly, the hope for an increasingly multicultural and multi-ethnic Canada collides with Quebec's primary goal: promotion of the French language and Quebec culture. Looming over the entire debate is the question of the aboriginal peoples; it will be difficult to come to terms with native self-government and sovereignty when Quebec insists upon the primacy of its own sovereignty claims. This Canadian constitutional agenda will be unblocked only when English Canada and the aboriginal peoples insist firmly on the inclusion of their concerns at the same table with those of Quebec, or when Quebec leaves.

There is another reason for firmness and resolve in negotiating with Quebec, arising, paradoxically, from the same logic that has emboldened Quebec to advance its claims so confidently today. In 1980, Quebec sovereignty hinged upon the idea of an economic association with Canada. Such an association was conceived as a bureaucratic overlay of shared administration, undemocratically selected and unaccountable to the voters of either nation. It was a repulsive notion and, if it had been put to the test, would probably have been rejected by Canadians.

The Bélanger–Campeau commission is inspired by a different ethos, that of the era of free trade. Quebec–Canada economic relations could be governed not by bureaucratic regulation but by a fundamental treaty establishing a Canadian common market with unhindered movement of capital, goods and people across the borders. Such a common market could rest within a wider North American free trade zone. None of this denies the very real risks and costs of an open rupture, in the short term. But it does suggest that the longer-term consequences of separation are much lower than they might have been counted a decade earlier.

Quebec has taken the free trade context as empowering it to take greater risks in constitutional bargaining. But the same holds true for English Canada; discounting the considerable but short-term transition costs, English Canada can bargain from a certain position of confidence as well. Free trade and economic globalization suggest that sovereignty may be for the most part a political matter, with economics not directly at stake.

The future is always obscure and the outcome of the present crisis cannot be predicted. Perhaps Quebec will depart, perhaps it will not. But in either event, there is the real possibility that for the first time English Canada will find its own authentic voice. One way or the other, the escalation of the demands for Quebec sovereignty may stimulate the birth of two nations — another irony of Canadian history.

The Road to Meech Lake

Robert Sheppard

Robert Sheppard, formerly a Montrealer, is a columnist with The Globe and Mail.

To a teenager, Montreal in 1967 was the place to be. It was still Canada's largest and most vibrant city. And Expo 67, the international fair timed to celebrate the nation's centenary, brought the world and some of its most stunning architecture to our door.

By day, we could see first hand the competing technological prowess of the industrial countries. And by night, almost as soon as the moist Montreal darkness fell, we were drawn in the tens of thousands, like moths to a flame, to the cavernous concrete amphitheatre of Place des Nations, where the real power lay: the throbbing dance music of Motown or Sam Cooke. Even the French girls, dark-eyed and exotic, from the part of the city you tended more to drive around rather than through, would sometimes follow your smile and shrug onto the dance floor. They might have thought we were Americans.

Of course, 1967 was also the year that French president Charles de Gaulle shouted "Vive le Québec libre" from a balcony in Montreal. That Pierre Trudeau began to shine as a potential prime minister. That René Lévesque published his manifesto on sovereignty-association — *Option Québec* — and was drummed out of the provincial Liberal Party for his pains.

Lévesque was that other Quebecker, a rumpled ball of a man, idiomatic, rambling, discursive, who wore all his insecurities on his sleeve as, of course, Pierre Trudeau did not. Lévesque had been the undisputed star of the Lesage government, which had gone down to unexpected defeat the previous year at the hands of Daniel Johnson's more nationalistic —"Equality or Independence"— Union Nationale. And sovereignty-association, cobbled together in Robert Bourassa's basement rec room, was being put about by Lévesque and some of his followers as a rallying cry for a then dispirited Quebec Liberal Party — the Allaire report of its day.

English Canada, too, was imbibing its own nationalist treatise at about this time; it would also require time to jell. Philosopher George Grant's *Lament for a Nation*, a ninety-seven-page *cri de coeur* chronicling our love-hate relationship with American technology and popular culture and the forfeiture of old loyalist values, had a profound impact on a generation of Red Tories (whether or not they even realized that is what they were). Its central themes would be played out time and again — during debates over energy policy, school curriculums, the entrenchment of a charter of rights — right up to the moment of reckoning: the 1989 Free Trade Agreement with the United States, which happened along at roughly the same time as Meech Lake.

When you look for the beginning of the current dilemma, you can find it almost anywhere in Canadian history: Lord Durham's Report. Riel. Conscription. The War Measures Act. Even the attempt by some of the provincial governments soon after 1867 to make the federal government their vassal, through some of the more outlandish confederal theories of the day. That, too, has been around before.

But history is just one player in this drama. Circumstances have a role, as do ideas and personalities. Then there is the political two-step — one to propose and one to oppose (Canadian politicians, with very few exceptions, do not boogaloo). And the cumulative numbing effect of decades of constitutional gamesmanship.

Robert Bourassa, a government economist, turned thirty-four in the summer of 1967; he had been serving in the National Assembly as a Liberal for a year. Within three years he would be premier of Quebec, the youngest in its history, and about to be broken, the first time around, on the hard rocks of hostage takings, constitutional debate and language strife in Montreal's immigrant suburbs. Brian Mulroney was twenty-eight that summer, a young up-and-coming lawyer in an established firm, earning less than $10,000 a year, his biographer says, but with a ski chalet in the Laurentians and a fast car. In the federal election the next year, he would take on his first major organizational job for the Conservatives — he was the high-level connector between the federal party and the Union Nationale organizers who ran the Tory campaign in Quebec.

The centennial year was still a time of innocence. Yes, bombs had gone off in mailboxes in Montreal and the Royal Commission on Bilingualism and Biculturalism had just reported that its members "have been driven to the conclusion that Canada, without being fully conscious of the fact, is passing through the greatest crisis in its history." But French Quebeckers of exceptional skill and intelligence were still being drawn to Ottawa to defend and champion the federal spirit. Medicare had been enacted the previous year, marking what many felt to be the birth of modern Canada. The Official Languages Act and liberating social changes were in the wings. Divorce, among other things, would soon be easier.

The centennial year also gave us the first real flexing, in modern times, of provincial powers. Peter Lougheed, a small, determined man who once ran back kicks for a professional football team, the first of a breed of Harvard Business School premiers, had just been elected to the Alberta legislature and was only a few years away from taking power for good and transforming the province and much of the West in his likeness. In Ontario, Premier John Robarts had achieved such public stature that he was able to reach out, through the force of his own personality, to Quebec's Daniel Johnson and convene the Confederation of Tomorrow conference, in which all the provinces participated and an affronted federal government attended merely as an observer.

In the quarter century between then and the second referendum on Quebec's future, now scheduled almost blithely for the spring or fall of 1992, much has changed. Sovereignty-association begat the election of the Parti Québécois in 1976, which begat Bill 101 (a response to Pierre Trudeau's Official Languages Act) and the Quebec referendum of May 1980, which begat Trudeau's patriation exercise in 1981–82, which begat the abortive Meech Lake Accord in 1987, which begat the Bélanger–Campeau commission in Quebec, the Allaire report of the provincial Liberal Party, the Spicer commission federally and any number of provincial imitators. And now, it seems, another time for choosing. With, for many Quebeckers (and others as well), the prospect of independence appearing about as mildly unpleasant as a trip to the dentist.

This twenty-five-year span has also brought about remarkable transformations in what are glibly called English and French Canada. Not only have Quebeckers become much more confident and businesslike about their future — they graduate more MBAs each year than all the other provinces combined and sovereignty, whatever that means, has become as comfortable for the bourgeoisie as a pair of old shoes — but there has also been a subtle exchange of psychological values between the two groups. Over this period it was English Canada that abandoned the classic British approach of "muddling through" its political relationships in favour of a more Cartesian response. It was the side that was demanding "certainty" of the Meech Lake Accord, insisting that all the eventualities be covered off. By the nineties, it was Quebeckers who had the sure-footedness to rally behind the more creatively ambiguous symbols of sovereignty and the distinct society.

Throughout it all, constitutional reform, indeed even comprehensive constitutional reform, has been held out to both sides as the key, almost the grail, to save us from ourselves. As a constitutional law professor, Pierre Trudeau had often warned against this strategy during the sixties, arguing that Quebec did not have the numbers to realign the federation to its standards and would come away with only scraps. "I said, and I remain convinced, that we would be wrong as Quebeckers and French Canadians to invest all our energy in this sphere," he said as a candidate for the Liberal leadership in 1968. But his advice was not taken, least of all by himself, and so constitutional reform became hostage to competitive partisan impulses on top of its built-in flaws.

The seventies were not a good decade for the nation's constitutional business. It was as though the numbing repetitiveness of the disco generation had gummed up the dance steps of first-minister politics. The failure of the artfully staged Victoria conference in 1971, in which Bourassa first agreed to patriation of the Constitution from Britain and other changes, and then changed his mind when he returned to Quebec City, put off constitutional reform for many years.

By 1978 and 1979, when Trudeau was of a mind to try again, René Lévesque and the Parti Québécois were in power in Quebec and there was a new and discouraging mood across the land. The seventies had brought inflation, huge increases in the value of oil and resulting fiscal imbalances in the Canadian federation. The western energy-producing provinces were suddenly floating in new-found wealth and were tired of being patronized in the central corridors of power. The West wanted in, or at least to be able to do things its way.

Ottawa's rather clumsy response was to pick a fight over oil prices, among other things. For a time, it appeared as though the feds were fighting on all fronts — against the West, against the separatists in Quebec, against some of the more peppery premiers from Atlantic Canada, against even the forces of complacency in Ontario. Before too long these groups would forge an alliance — the enemy of my enemy being my friend — and so the age of competitive federalism, the prince against the barons, was born.

Compounding the problem was Trudeau's unyielding nature and his own nationalism, forged in part by his experience of minority government at the mercy of the NDP from 1972 to 1974. In the early and mid-seventies, federal departments — multiculturalism, housing, urban affairs, the environment — grew like Topsy, increasing the grey areas where federal and provincial interests bumped up against each other. Prime Minister Trudeau variously described this as speaking for Canada, or the land being strong (even as it was being heavily mortgaged). But in the provincial arenas it created a mind-set of defensive federalism, like Lougheed's desire to "get the feds off the front porch," which meshed with the chess-like manoeuvres of the PQ. Ultimately this would change the nature of the whole debate and lead to a constitution where some of the central features were opting out and a notwithstanding clause.

Many felt that personality was at the heart of this problem. By the late seventies, Trudeau and Lévesque had been involved in their own private debating society for nearly twenty years. And Pierre Trudeau's prickly bearing was well known. But when the provincial premiers, even the Tory ones from Alberta and Newfoundland, continued to gang up on Prime Minister Joe Clark during the brief Tory interregnum in 1979, it certainly appeared as though a new demon had been unleashed upon the land.

So when the Trudeau Liberals were returned to power in February 1980, in the midst of the Quebec referendum on sovereignty-association, there was an equal determination on their part to give no quarter. As Marc Lalonde, a trusted lieutenant of Trudeau, told a magazine interviewer at the time: "It was quite clear in our minds that, if we came back, it would have to mean something. We got nickelled and dimed to death between '74 and '79, and we would not make the same mistake again."

Once again, perhaps even despite itself, constitutional reform became the centrepiece for dealing with the nation's ongoing communal anxieties. Trudeau promised Quebeckers during the referendum campaign that his MPs would put their seats on the line to find an honourable solution to the current dilemma. And this, along with vague threats about the potential loss of old age security payments under a sovereign Quebec, seemed enough to turn the tide.

The 1980 referendum was a traumatic experience for Quebeckers, ripping apart families and neighbours, often along generational lines. The best account is still Denys Arcand's remarkable documentary film *Le confort et l'indifférence* in which a gardener, an emotional supporter of sovereignty-association, tells an interviewer: "We were voting for our lives. I trembled as I marked my ballot."

It also brought with it two important psychological consequences that would linger after the votes were tallied. One was the ganging up on Quebec by Anglo premiers who trooped in one after the other to say there would be no special treatment for a sovereign Quebec. The other was the implicit recognition, despite the Anglo interference, that this was an internal matter for Quebeckers and that they would never again be captive to economic restraints.

In the immediate aftermath of the referendum, the PQ shed its child-of-the-sixties politics and became resolutely capitalist. Quebec Inc. was born, though the rest of the country did not fully realize this at the time because it had become caught up in trying to create its own new compact, through the politics of the Charter of Rights.

The Charter, linked solidly to the Constitution itself, was to be Trudeau's CPR — nation-building in the modern era that would, ultimately, direct the public's important concerns once again towards the central institutions, in this case the courts. Its development has to be seen as one facet of the federalist hubris of the times; in conjunction with a number of other initiatives, such as the National Energy Program and the curtailment of provincial transfer payments, it was designed to haul the pendulum of decentralization back towards the centre. At the time, the track seemed clear of opposition: the PQ was demoralized because of its referendum loss; Joe Clark's Tories were in disarray, having forfeited the reins of government after only nine months. The moment seemed right. Never again was there likely to be a French-Canadian prime minister with immense popularity in Quebec who would be willing to drag the stone sled of the country's Constitution over the objections of his home province.

Trudeau's "unilateral" attempt to patriate and reform the Constitution (he was actually supported throughout by two provinces, Ontario and New Brunswick) was a magnificent obsession — what someone called a *coup d'état* in slow motion. But it provoked a response of equal magnitude. For eighteen months, from the Quebec referendum to the national deal on November 5, 1981, the Constitution debate raged in Parliament and in the media, as the economy fell into recession. Before long, virtually every major institution and group in the land was drawn into the fray: the national political parties (torn by the conflicting demands made on them by their constituents), the business community (in a foretaste of its later involvement with free trade), provincial premiers (who faced angry mobs on the steps of their legislatures), the courts, the legal and academic communities, natives, women, handicapped and multicultural groups.

Years later, in retirement, Pierre Trudeau would blame the Supreme Court of Canada for overstepping its role in September 1981 and making a "political judgement." The Court's verdict that patriation without full provincial consent was legal but contrary to "convention" forced him back to the bargaining table for an eventual deal with nine of the ten provinces — Quebec being "abandoned" during a night of constitutional cut-and-paste — and sowed the seeds of future problems. But Trudeau's complaint about judicial interference misses a point: it took the combined forces of virtually every major institution in the country to force a legitimizing compromise. It was the Canadian Way, people assured one another, until it became almost a chant. The premiers just stepped forward at the end to snap shut the lock on the cage.

The most far-reaching political consequence of the patriation exercise was, of course, the abandonment of Quebec. Lévesque literally slept the night away while his allies in the Gang of Eight, the dissident provinces that had fought Trudeau's scheme, cobbled together a deal. No one (including most Quebeckers, it seemed) ever expected a separatist PQ government to clinch a deal with Pierre Trudeau. And Lévesque made a number of strategic errors in casting his lot in with the dissident provinces, including signing away his province's "historic" veto and even putting his signature on a newspaper ad resplendent with red maple leaves, the first of his *beaux gestes*.

But still, the sense within Quebec of being left in the lurch — not just by its provincial allies, but also by the Supreme Court judgement that said no one province, including Quebec, had what amounted to a constitutional veto — became lodged somewhere deep in the marrow. The opinion polls in the months following patriation continued to show a steep decline in popularity for the ruling Parti Québécois and the separatist option. But at the same time, a large majority — nearly 60 per cent, or about the same proportion that now adheres to something called sovereignty — said Lévesque was right not to sign the patriation deal.

For Quebeckers, the central duality of the country — its very bi-ness — had been tampered with. It had been tampered with already, probably irretrievably: with the rise of the West, and the tide of non-European immigration that was changing the face of most large Canadian cities, and Bill 101, which made it more difficult for many liberals outside Quebec to support that province's ambitions. But patriation, eventually celebrated with top hats and tails on Parliament Hill in April 1982, was what brought it all home. It was like a time bomb, observed Claude Morin, Lévesque's constitutional minister, in the immediate aftermath. "When the Charter of Rights is used against Bill 101, then people here will realize the daily influence on their lives and the whole thing will start again."

Flash forward six or seven years from Claude Morin's prediction — to when the Supreme Court of Canada disallowed the part of Bill 101 prohibiting English on signs and Bourassa used the Charter's notwithstanding clause to override the judgement, just as the Manitoba legislature was dealing with Meech Lake — and you see the truth of his argument. But just a few weeks after his comments — when seas of brown faces and women of all ages mounted impressive lobbies on the steps of various legislatures in western Canada to reinstate important Charter sections on women's and native rights that had been traded away by the first ministers — and you could see the weight of the argument on the other side.

In hindsight, what this outpouring of direct democracy demonstrated was that another element had been added to the constitutional brew of Quebec nationalism, namely provincial power-seekers and regional discontent. Populism is too quaint a term to define it; political consumerism, a bit too crass. But it combined elements of both, along with sophisticated interest-group politics like those dominating the U.S. scene and a good dollop of voter cynicism, which was right in keeping with the I'm-all-right-Jack sentiments of the roaring eighties.

At the public hearings that led to the final draft of the Charter of Rights in the fall of 1981, Trudeau's much-vaunted first effort was taken apart like a Tinker Toy and put back together by dozens of outside interest groups, many of them drinking from the sweet cup of political intrigue for the first time. And this contributed, as much as anything else, to the sea change that was under way in the old-line parties.

Trudeau's derring-do killed the Liberal Party as a national force. It rent the New Democrats along east-west lines, a division that was still apparent at the convention that chose Audrey McLaughlin as the party's new leader in fall of 1989. And it left the federal Conservative Party obsessed with Quebec. One of the handful of Tories who voted against the final patriation compromise was Senator Lowell Murray, the dour, bilingual Cape Bretoner who had been in the groom's party at Brian Mulroney's wedding in 1973 and then Joe Clark's chief political strategist. Senator Murray, who would go on to become Prime Minister Mulroney's minister of intergovernmental affairs during the Meech Lake negotiations, could not abide the thought of Quebec being abandoned again by the Conservative Party, as it had been in the time of Louis Riel and again in the conscription crisis of 1917. From this conviction grew the Tory alliances with a new generation of Quebec nationalists. It was a coalition that was first decried and then later absorbed by Brian Mulroney on his long march to the Tory leadership, and it reached its apotheosis in the troubled personage of Lucien Bouchard who eventually came to his own fork in the road. Bouchard, chose the path of René Lévesque.

Swept to power in 1984, the Mulroney Tories were determined to supplant the Liberals as the party of

Quebec (and the party of the business establishment). At the same time, political hubris not being limited to any one governing party or period in history, there was also a determination to supplant the ghost of Pierre Trudeau and better him at the constitutional game. It was an intoxicating challenge to a new generation of federal and provincial leaders that cannot be discounted from the politics of Meech Lake; if they played their cards right, they, too, could wear top hats on Parliament Hill.

The Conservatives' first moves were to sweep away the last remnants of the National Energy Program, administrative measures that appeared to satisfy, for a time anyway, the new provincial leaders in the West who were tired of the constitutional game. Then came the proposal for free trade with the United States and the cathartic release, for some of the regions anyway, of being able to gang up on fat-cat Ontario, whose new premier, Liberal David Peterson, was opposing it. Finally, the nod to Quebec.

It was probably inevitable that at some point the constitutional dossier would have to be opened again to bring Quebec back into the fold, though there was no compelling political reason to do this in 1986 and 1987 when the Meech Lake process began. At the time, though, everything looked right on paper. There was a federalist party back in power in Quebec, the Liberals under Robert Bourassa once more. The new government in Ottawa had made co-operative federalism its watchword. The West was still bruised by the recession of the early eighties, and Ontario was in an expansive, feel-good mood. Topping this off was the most modest set of demands from any Quebec government in living memory — only five short items. What could go wrong?

The short answer was that the élitism and secretiveness of the process, designed in the hope that it would let sleeping dogs lie, in the end achieved exactly the opposite effect. The accord became the symbol of an extremely unpopular federal government, and the implicit notion of special status for Quebec ran up against the new equality compact of the Charter of Rights.

When Brian Mulroney called the first ministers together in a room in an old government lodge at Meech Lake, a reedy, nondescript little body of water in the Gatineau Hills, few, even of those present, felt they would be emerging with a unanimous agreement. There was a brief feeling of euphoria across the nation that the first ministers had set aside their usual bickering and regional concerns for something that looked to be in the national interest.

Within a month, the Meech Lake Accord was back before the first ministers at the Langevin Block in Ottawa where, in an extraordinary all-night bargaining session, the agreement was put into legislative form and agreed to again, despite, at this point, the very real concerns of the premiers of Ontario and Manitoba. Three weeks later, June 23, 1987, the Quebec National Assembly passed the Meech resolution and the three-year constitutional clock began ticking.

By this point, there could be no more real debate about the actual merits of the accord. Some provinces and the federal Parliament held public hearings on the initiative, but it could not be amended without getting Premier Bourassa to agree to re-open the package in his legislature. He, of course, was determined not to compromise or show weakness in public.

Bourassa had already compromised, he insisted throughout the long debate that ensued. His contribution was in bringing such a small set of conditions to the bargaining table in the first place. And he had yielded a few points at the private first ministers' meetings, although he had gained some as well. The distinct society clause that was at the heart of much of the communal anxiety over Meech Lake was moved from the preamble to become a stronger interpretive clause, reportedly at the prime minister's offering.

But the groups that had no voice at that table felt their

concerns were being given short shrift. Key among them were the natives, who watched their constitutional hopes for self-government put on hold (and would find their champion in Elijah Harper), and those who wanted to uphold the primacy of the Charter of Rights and Freedoms.

There are three enduring images of the Meech Lake fiasco. B.C. premier Bill Vander Zalm, at a pay phone at the lodge at Meech Lake, fumbling in his pockets for change to call his constitutional adviser 3,000 miles away to see if he should sign on. The premiers and the prime minister emerging from the Langevin Block into the dawn, looking sheepish, as if they had been caught playing poker all night. The six days in June 1990, when the first ministers sequestered themselves on the top floor of the convention centre in Ottawa and treated the country to an emotional roller-coaster ride.

The six days in June, which seemed more like a political hostage taking than anything else, constituted the famous "roll of the dice," as the prime minister later referred to it in a *Globe and Mail* interview. He would argue that this phrase was taken out of context, but that was almost beside the point. That was the way the country, including the majority of Quebeckers (who saw other attributes in it as well), had come to feel about the entire gambit.

Like Pierre Trudeau's patriation scheme, Meech Lake lacked legitimacy. Trudeau won his prize by compromising in public with the premiers, securing his charter by accepting their amending formula. Bourassa had made it a badge of honour that he would *not* compromise in public; this was the new Bourassa, not the one who had been burned in effigy during his first terms in office. And those who had begun the enterprise with him, and who had raised the stakes enormously in the final months, could not conceive of abandoning Quebec a second time in a generation.

The longer explanation for the failure of the Meech

reforms is that they became caught up in the events and personalities and general messiness of Canadian politics. Twenty-five years of constitutional wrangling seemed to have created a batch of federal and provincial political institutions whose role it was to exaggerate the regional and cultural differences in the country.

In addition, the eighties were a time for the changing of the guard, as Canadians lined up new provincial champions to face off against the Tories in Ottawa. Those who came to the scene (Frank McKenna, Clyde Wells, Gary Filmon and Sharon Carstairs) were, to a greater or lesser extent, depending on their personalities, opposed to what their predecessors had agreed to, the classic two-step of parliamentary politics.

Moreover, as the constitutional initiative was going forward, so too was the proposal for free trade with the United States, which raised once again all the old hang-ups of English-Canadian nationalism, the lament of George Grant. Free trade was approved in the November 1988 federal election, essentially because of the votes of Quebec. English Canada was divided over the plan, emotionally and politically. And in the West, popular disillusionment with the ruling federal Conservatives — their party through thick and thin — had reached new lows. The Mulroney Tories were too beholden to Quebec, the West complained, almost with one voice; they were just Trudeau Liberals in plaid.

It did not help when Bourassa, one month after the federal election, used the notwithstanding clause of the Charter of Rights to override the Supreme Court decision on the language of signs. Is this the federalist face of Quebec? the rest of the country asked. Is this why we are sending our kids to French immersion schools?

For a time it appeared as though all the political events, big and small, were contriving to undermine whatever few remnants of trust were left in the system, especially in the central ambiguity — the distinct society clause — that was at the heart of Meech Lake. Was the distinction merely political window dressing, a statement of honour and welcome, and "nothing to worry about," as Prime Minister Mulroney intoned at one point? Or was it closer to Bourassa's view, as he told the National Assembly in 1987: "It cannot be stressed too strongly that the entire Constitution, including the Charter, will be interpreted and applied in light of the section proclaiming our distinctiveness as a society."

Faced with a Hobson's choice — Meech or nothing — English Canada demanded the latter. Bourassa wanted his ambiguity; the rest of the country wanted it spelled out. In the immediate aftermath, the two groups drifted back into their respective prejudices. Hopeful signs were few and far between, though there was still an impressive democratic component to the debate, to the almost balletic way the two solitudes would grope towards (and away from) each other in attempts to keep the dance alive.

The Meech process drove a stake through the heart of executive federalism, and Bourassa drove the final nail when he said he would never again deal with his provincial counterparts, only with Ottawa. A somewhat nostalgic assertion of the old English-French, Canadian duality. He never actually said "equality or independence." But that was his general drift.

Rolling the Dice

Ron Graham

Ron Graham is a freelance journalist and former associate editor of Saturday Night. *The author of* One-Eyed Kings *and* God's Dominion, *he is now writing a book about Quebec to appear in 1992.*

"If only Meech had passed," a very intelligent woman said at lunch the other day in Toronto, as a group of us contemplated the disintegration of Canada. It had been many months since the Meech Lake Accord had died, but she could still get furious remembering Clyde Wells's refusal to have a vote on it in the Newfoundland legislature.

"If only Meech had passed," a powerful and well-informed journalist repeated at dinner recently in Montreal. He clenched a fist, thinking about those who had killed it. "And not one of them has ever admitted for one instant that they just might have been wrong!"

This sentiment has enough currency within Quebec's political class and among English Canada's opinion makers that it's worth a few moments to try to demolish it once and for all — if only because it is hard to build a future on such a rotten construction of the past. In essence, it is a Big Misrepresentation based on several Little Misrepresentations (and, to be fair, a few naive hopes), and it has its source in knavery, stupidity and various combinations of both.

Brian Mulroney came to power in September 1984 with the ambition "to be remembered in history," according to his friendly biographer, and one of the ways was to reach a constitutional deal with Quebec. It would repair any harm done by the fact that the Quebec government had not signed the agreement leading to the Constitution Act of 1982 and the Charter of Rights and Freedoms; it would play to the Tory voters in Quebec and the Quebec nationalists in his own caucus; and it would be a personal triumph that would best Pierre Trudeau's historic achievement.

Quebec had not signed the agreement, of course, because the Parti Québécois was in office and could not have acquiesced in any deal that strengthened the province's commitment to Canada. Mulroney himself had recognized that obvious reality on numerous occasions before 1984, and far from arguing that Trudeau should not have proceeded without the Quebec government's approval, he supported both patriation and the Charter — as did nine premiers, almost all the Quebec MPs in Ottawa and most Quebeckers in the polls of the time. Severing the colonial tie to Britain and enshrining language rights had been traditional Quebec demands, after all.

Once in power, Mulroney soon encountered the same sort of obstructionism from the Parti Québécois government, even though he had begun to play footsie with separatists in order to win the election and build a Tory-nationalist alliance against the federalist Liberals. People who had voted yes in the 1980 Quebec referendum moved in as party advisers and government officials, and if anyone dared ask if Mulroney was being taken for a ride, he always responded indignantly that no one should be shunned if ready to give Canada another chance. I was one of those who raised an eyebrow when he appointed Lucien Bouchard as Canadian ambassador to France, and I have yet to hear the prime minister or his media claque admit that "they just might have been wrong" or that they had been taken for patsies.

That was the mentality when the PQ was defeated in 1985 by Robert Bourassa, Mulroney's old friend and tacit supporter, and a booster for "profitable federalism." Though Bourassa himself saw no need to rush into a deal, Quebec came back to the bargaining table with five crucial demands. There it met the other nine provinces, who were ready to satisfy Quebec in order to get to their own agendas, and Brian Mulroney, who was ready to concede almost anything in order to get into the history books. "We're fighting your battle," Ontario and Manitoba had to keep reminding him during the talks. "You should speak up."

To get the Meech Lake Accord from the premiers, and then to sell it to the public, Mulroney resorted to his familiar tactics of distortion and exaggeration. "We must never forget that, in 1982, Quebec was left alone, isolated and humiliated," he now claimed. "How could we, for a single moment, accept Quebec being excluded from national life? It was the worst injustice ever inflicted on Quebeckers." To which Robert Bourassa added, "Canada will be a country with an unfulfilled destiny, with a major partner not being part of the Constitution."

In truth, of course, Quebec was very much part of the Constitution. No province signed it *per se,* and no province was excluded from it. The Supreme Court proved that in law, and Bourassa himself proved it in politics with Bill 178, which used the notwithstanding clause of the Charter in December 1988 to protect Quebec's language legislation. Odd behaviour for a province that had been "left out" of the Patriation Round of 1981–82, I thought. Odder still for a premier who seemed so keen to have Meech, for he had been warned in no uncertain terms that overriding the Charter would mean the death of the accord in English Canada.

If most Quebeckers didn't know or care about the legal implications of the Constitution Act of 1982, they could be aroused by words such as "humiliation" and "injustice." Here were the prime minister of Canada and the premier of Quebec in concert telling them that they had been left out and humiliated by their national government and the rest of Canada in 1982. This was news, apparently, for the polls and the mood on the street had revealed little widespread unhappiness when the Queen herself showed up in Ottawa to celebrate patriation and the Charter. True, there had been some shame among the PQ leaders, who had negotiated incompetently and lost Quebec's veto power in the process, and among Quebec intellectuals and journalists who had witnessed the failure of their heroes. But the very victory of Robert Bourassa in 1985 demonstrated the support of the population for a pragmatic, business-oriented and federalist leadership.

Although it might have been appropriate for Bourassa to turn up the nationalist heat to get what he wanted from Ottawa, it was treacherous for Mulroney to do so for the sake of Meech. "If Queen's Park and the people of Ontario had said, 'We don't want this constitution,' do you think the Queen would have come over here and there would have been a party in front of Parliament Hill with everybody in striped pants celebrating a constitution without the industrial heartland of Ontario?" he went around asking. By implying that the people of Quebec had not wanted this constitution and had been left out of it, he further implied that Ottawa had deliberately shafted them in a way it wouldn't have done to anyone else. No wonder Quebeckers started to get indignant.

Their programmed rage was part of Mulroney's gamble. It allowed him to say to the premiers and English Canadians that Meech had to pass, as written, without a comma changed, or else Quebec would separate. In this argument, Meech became the very least that Quebec should receive to correct the heinous insult it had suffered. Quebec was asking for only five changes, after all, compared with the twenty-two demands the Parti Québécois had presented, and these changes had struck Mulroney as so reasonable and minimal that he gave away more than Bourassa had needed. Quebec was saying yes to Canada, Mulroney continued, and now Canada had to say yes to Quebec. Saying no to any morsel of Meech would mean saying no to Quebec. It would be another insult and another humiliation.

Having been alerted to the secret humiliation of 1982, Quebeckers understandably were on double alert to any new one, thanks to Mulroney, Bourassa, the PQ and their nationalist followers. It would come, they were told again and again, if English Canada rejected the accord's recognition of Quebec as a "distinct society." What could be more obvious or basic? Indeed, almost no one rejected its sociological truth or its place in a preamble. But when Meech put it in the body of the Constitution, with a provision for the "Government of Quebec to preserve and promote the distinct identity of Quebec," some of us began to question if this wasn't special status by another name. Would it mean new powers, or changes to the Charter?

Not only were the lawyers divided on the issue, but Mulroney told English Canadians that the phrase meant nothing, while Bourassa was telling Quebeckers that it meant "new ground" regarding language, culture and "our political, legal and economic institutions." Both agreed, however, that to question "distinct society" was to reject Quebec, though I never met an ordinary Quebecker who gave a damn about whether this symbol of pride was in the preamble or the law.

While Mulroney repeated to English Canada that Quebec would be back for much more unless it got Meech, Bourassa was assuring Quebeckers that Meech was only the first round. It was the old strategy of step-by-step consolidation, each step so modest and placatory but leading inevitably towards sovereignty. The game was openly revealed in the first paragraph of the infamous Allaire report, produced for the Quebec Liberal Party in January 1991. Its wild abuse of federalism and preposterous list of demands were supposed to be a response to the failure of Meech, and perhaps the "humiliation" myth explains the report's tone and extremism. But the committee made it clear that it had been set up in the spring of 1990 to prepare "the political content of a second round of negotiations in the event of ratification of the Meech Lake Accord."

So Meech wouldn't have bought peace after all. Within a year, Quebec would have been back for more — but under a new set of rules entrenched firmly in the Constitution and much more favourable to the Quebec government. Meech wasn't a case of giving Quebec five points instead of twenty-two or more. It was a case of changing the process in order to increase Quebec's chances of getting the substantial changes that were coming tomorrow. That's why the Quebec government was willing to settle for the minimum in Meech and why Meech became so crucial to it. And if Meech didn't work as planned, if "distinct society" didn't mean new powers, or if the Supreme Court didn't serve the province's interests, then the Quebec government could raise the cry of injustice, humiliation and separation once again.

That cry was used by Mulroney and Bourassa to beat

the premiers and the population into accepting Meech without public input or the slightest modification. To work, the threat had to be real, which meant that Quebeckers had to be whipped into a lather about Meech as a symbol. Journalists, academics, business leaders, union chiefs were all pressured by offers and threats from Ottawa and Quebec City to speak up as one in defence of Meech. There was no room for opposition or amendment, they were told, because failure would mean either the status quo or the break-up of Canada. Quickly, of course, this transformed into a self-fulfilling prophecy. Months before Meech collapsed, the polls showed a majority of Quebeckers in favour of independence, driven by the humiliation rhetoric and the anti-French backlash stirred up in English Canada.

Even then, Mulroney didn't calm the waters or prepare for life without Meech. To do so would have raised his odds once he decided to "roll all the dice" and lock the premiers into the old railway station in Ottawa for a week in June 1990. Despite the many compromises suggested by the parliamentary committee under Jean Charest, Mulroney couldn't or wouldn't negotiate. It was Meech or chaos, he maintained, and he sided with Bourassa in insisting that Quebec should not have to give an inch to salvage the accord. Quebec had already given up enough, they maintained, as though the other provinces hadn't given up anything and Quebec hadn't garnered more than its first demands. A deal was a deal, they kept repeating, although it was Quebec that had walked away from the Fulton–Favreau agreement on an amending formula in 1964.

It was high-stakes gambling at its scariest, with the future of Canada on the table. When it looked for a while as if Mulroney had won, he was quick to brag publicly about his prowess. When he lost, he was faster to blame somebody else. Such is human nature, one might say, but there is less excuse for intelligent people to let him get away with it.

While politicians and commentators ran around madly trying to fix blame on who or what killed Meech — Pierre Trudeau or Bill 178, Clyde Wells or Lucien Bouchard, Elijah Harper or the Brockville flag incident — they usually assumed that the killers were responsible for what happened next. In fact, all the evidence suggested that even if Meech had passed in the last-minute panic, the nationalist forces that had been more or less vanquished by 1982 were back stronger than ever before. Mulroney and Bourassa had let the tiger out of the cage in order to ride it in triumph, and now it was threatening to swallow them whole.

Whether Meech lived or died, its getting and selling opened wounds in both French and English Canada that the deal had been intended merely to bandage over for the sake of temporary appearance. Because of those wounds, most of us who opposed Meech recognized the political dangers that would follow its death, though we argued that in the long run and with better leadership a satisfactory deal could be found and most Quebeckers would choose to remain in Canada. That is precisely what Mulroney and Bourassa (most days, at least) are now saying — though, if things should turn around in 1992, the thanks will be due less to them than to the common sense and emotional attachments of the Quebec people.

If things don't turn around, the Meech fiasco will have exposed sensitive nerves and revealed fundamental conflicts that Meech itself could not have covered up any longer. At that point Mulroney will find himself in history, certainly — as the single person most responsible for the end of Canada.

The Folly of
Constitutional Reform

Nelson Wiseman

Nelson Wiseman is a Manitoban now teaching political science at the University of Toronto.

The 1960s spawned a thriving constitutional reform industry in Canada. In 1991 it is still with us, apparently immune to economic recessions and the comings and goings of governments. Unlike much else in the federal Conservative agenda since 1984, this public sector industry has not endured cut-backs, deregulation, privatization, downsizing or capping. It is, rather, a hyperventilated growth industry.

Historical evidence suggests that constitutional revitalization is better produced by political will and administrative imagination than by changes to the black letter of constitutional law. Constitutional renewal has been the product of evolutionary and periodic adjustments, policy flexibility and continual experimentation. Unfortunately this lesson of the past appears forgotten; perhaps it was poorly learned and not well grasped in the first place. The leading political classes — English-speaking and French — in Ottawa, Quebec, on Indian reserves and elsewhere have become preoccupied with constitution writing and rewriting rather than with constitution making. Perhaps they seek too eagerly their places in history books as constitutional statesmen.

In preaching the virtues of constitutional reform, the politicians have been aided and abetted by packs of policy advisers, lawyers, pollsters and political scientists. The mass media have been so obsessed with reporting confrontation and conflict that they are helping to stir them up. Those in the constitution business are determined and headstrong. (Where else but Canada did the leading political class complain that its constitutional crisis was being kept off newscasts and front pages by the Persian Gulf War?) Paradoxically, the greater the efforts of politicians and their advisers to remedy alleged constitutional ills, the larger and less controllable the sickness becomes.

The political class has become so frustrated, if not exasperated and exhausted, with constitutional politics that it has turned to pleading with the public to answer questions many people might never have considered. Alas for the constitutional reform industry, there is little stomach among the public for constitutional squabbling. Constitutional negotiations are hopelessly misunderstood by the media and the public. That is natural and forgivable since the constitutional experts themselves engage in fervid disputes over what the wording in this or that proposed formulation means or might come to mean in practice.

There is no popular imperative for constitutional politics. It is an élite pleasure industry. When the Meech Lake Accord died in June 1990, more than four in ten Canadians thought of the Constitution and national unity as the most important issues facing the country; but less than four months later, only one in twenty thought so. This did not deter the captains of the constitution industry from new investments and expansion. Before 1990 ended, five provincial governments had committees studying future constitutional scenarios, and the federal government had created one group to plumb the thoughts of all and sundry "ordinary" Canadians and another to assault the constitutional amending formula.

Yet another group, Network on the Constitution — led by a former clerk of the Privy Council and a veteran of the industry — emerged to monitor the dozens of other private groups studying constitutional proposals. It qualifies as a research lobby for the industry. This contagious activism contradicts the predictions of first ministers and their support groups in the industry (such as Canadians for a Unifying Constitution and Friends of Meech Lake) who had insisted in the first half of 1990 that if Meech died the curtain would be drawn on further constitutional negotiations.

The obsession with legalistic constitutional tinkering represents a flight from creative politics. Rather than tackling the material and concrete problems of people, the politicians and their constitutional advisers are fixated on an effort to accommodate irreconcilable and competing constitutional visions. They are soliciting and marketing structural formulas that are the stuff of constitutionalized institutions. They are struggling as well to formulate noble abstractions dealing with individual and group rights as well as government powers. The leading political and administrative classes, those in cabinets and in the upper echelons of parallel federal and provincial departments — from environment and energy to agriculture and finance — need to keep focused on the substance of good public policy rather than be diverted by constitutional turf wars. Good public policy, as in the creation of the CBC by the federal government, of the Caisse de dépôt by the Quebec government and of medicare by Saskatchewan's government, should be the principal objective.

The leading political class refuses to acknowledge the very real and substantial costs of pursuing constitutional reform. Constitutional reform is a false messiah. It does not deliver on its promise. (Are Canadians more united or freer because of their newly beloved Charter?) It causes more unintended, unexpected and uncontrollable problems than it solves. (Support for sovereignty in

Quebec increased rather than decreased with the hatching and smothering of Meech.) And it sets in motion a locomotive process headed for yet more constitutional reform and bickering. (That is what all the first ministers promised in June 1990 as an immediate by-product of Meech's ratification.) In brief, the pursuit of constitutional reform produces problems, not solutions. The Constitution needs a respite from the politicians and more time to bask, in its current incarnation, in the courts and the classrooms.

More Canadians are concerned with employment, housing, social and environmental issues than with the question of who has jurisdiction in these policy areas. The courts have sensibly pursued a course that facilitates concurrent non-competing legislation. Before 1982, formal constitutional change came occasionally in small doses and was helpful to all parties: amendments in 1940, 1951 and 1964, for example, transferred jurisdiction over unemployment insurance and old age security benefits from the relatively poor provinces to relatively wealthy Ottawa.

Of much greater significance in effecting *de facto* constitutional change has been federal-provincial diplomacy driven by the needs of the administrators of bold and useful policy initiatives. During the Quiet Revolution, Quebec's nationalist objectives were achieved through the provision for "opting out" with compensation from more than two dozen federally sponsored programs, including the Canada Pension Plan. Protocol was developed to give Quebec a voice in Canadian delegations at international conferences in areas of provincial jurisdiction without constitutional tampering. Canadians and Québécois demonstrated the pliable and malleable character of the "living" constitution, so unlike its starchy large-C counterpart.

Canadians and Québécois have productively muddled through in a federal system that has been beneficial for both: francophones now occupy 80 per cent of all management jobs in Quebec, and the difference between per capita production in Ontario and in Quebec narrowed substantially between the early 1960s and the late 1980s. If "the real Constitution is the economy," as Bob Rae has so neatly put it, nothing much was wrong with it in the mid- to late 1980s when Canada's economy expanded at a rate substantially exceeding that of any of the G-7 states. Nevertheless, keen not to miss the reform train, Ontario's social democratic government has now joined the constitutional carping.

One of the virtues of the archaic, decrepit but remarkably resilient BNA Act has been that its inadequacies, ambiguities and contradictions were sufficiently glaring that governments were compelled to modify it creatively, to adjust and readjust as circumstances warranted and permitted. World wars, depression, technological changes, court decisions and the secularization and urbanization of society all forced changes. Most were small in themselves but they were revolutionary in their totality, producing popular and necessary public policies of which no founder of Confederation could have dreamed. Nowhere in the BNA Act are medicare, the CBC and equalization payments guaranteed, yet Canadian politicians and public administrators developed them without recourse to formal constitutional amendment. Canadians cite such policy, rather than constitutional innovations, in defining fundamental value differences between the Canadian and American ways of life. They were achieved through will, vision and the imaginative exercise of the substantial constitutional authority that both levels of government already possess rather than by formal constitutional adjustment.

What has all the meddling with the Constitution achieved? The 1982 Constitution was trumpeted by the constitutional reform merchants as the way of repaying Quebec for having kept the faith with Canada in the 1980 referendum. The federal Liberal government, led by

Québécois ministers in command of a party caucus a majority of which had been elected in Quebec, rammed the Constitution Act through Parliament and around the provinces, the courts and the British government — all in the honourable cause of addressing and solving the alleged constitutional and national unity problem. Quebec public opinion was soundly supportive and the revised Constitution came into effect in 1982 under the signatures of three Québécois (Pierre Trudeau, Jean Chrétien as minister of justice, and André Ouellet as registrar general) and the Queen. To harp on the alleged illegitimacy of the 1982 Constitution — as the Bélanger–Campeau commission and the Allaire report do because the Quebec National Assembly spurned it — is selective storytelling that needs challenging.

Although its rationale and substance was the accommodation of French Canada, the Constitution was soon assaulted by many of those in the reform industry such as Brian Mulroney who had just recently been singing its praises. They claimed that the new Constitution Act violated, humiliated, excluded and isolated the core of French Canada — Quebec. A reading of the act, however, reveals that there is scarcely anything in it — Section 23 on minority-language educational rights is all I can find — that abridges Quebec's pre-1982 powers. In this single case, Quebec is given special status to discriminate on the basis of national origin, something another part of the Charter tells us is *verboten*. Quebec did lose the veto it had developed through custom, rather than law, over further constitutional changes; it can, however, exempt itself from any changes to which it objects. Moreover, the Lévesque government had agreed to the current and much-maligned amending formula; it could hardly be some alien imposition.

Most Québécois considered sovereignty yesterday's issue; national unity was not a problem in the mid-1980s. Nevertheless, English Canada was called upon by Mulroney to join in a new Quebec round of constitutional

59

mischievousness — the Quebec Round, which yielded the Meech Lake Accord — to make amends for the alleged slights visited upon Quebec by other Québécois — Trudeau and his federalist caucus.

The rise and demise of Meech demonstrated that constitutional reform is impolitic for the participants and disintegrative for the polity. Trudeau, the architect of 1982, soon afterwards became the most unpopular politician in English Canada (if not Quebec) and would have been trounced had he not resigned in 1984. The price/earnings ratio in the constitution industry has been disastrous. Net returns have been negative and the dividends too meagre to relish (although pro-choicers succeeded in using the Charter to strike down abortion laws, tens of thousands of alleged criminals have used it to escape trials that are slow to begin and corporations have used it to shield anti-competitive behaviour).

The leading political classes — English, French and native — are naive about what constitutions actually accomplish. They underestimate the formidable non-constitutional impediments to achieving their policy objectives. Constitutional change is often irrelevant. In 1981, for example, Saskatchewan demanded and won greater constitutional control over natural resources, but that did nothing to keep the prices of those resources from melting on international commodity markets. In 1983, natives secured a constitutional amendment that incorporated land claims agreements into their entrenched treaty rights, but that did nothing to accelerate land claims settlements. Similarly, in Meech, Newfoundland secured a promise of future negotiations over fisheries jurisdiction, but that did nothing to increase fish stocks.

Quebec's society and economy have thrived and matured against the backdrop of a constitutional order that Quebec's nationalists have challenged unceasingly since the 1960s as hopelessly inadequate and beyond salvation. Are the complaints genuine or phantom grievances? A higher percentage of Quebeckers speak French today than at any time in decades. Quebec's labour force is no longer a culturally segmented one in which francophones earn relatively low incomes and occupy low-status jobs. French-speaking Québécois no longer qualify as an exploited ethnic class. The "white niggers of America"? Not quite. Rather, it is Quebec's anglophones of British stock who are the aging, declining, dispirited and less dynamic group.

The BNA Act did not succeed in perpetuating or consolidating Anglo supremacy in Quebec; it facilitated rather than deterred francophone ascendancy. If the preservation and prosperity of the French-Canadian fact is at stake, let us not ingenuously subscribe to the notion that the Constitution will assure it or deny it. Constitutional reform has not increased or decreased the fertility of francophones and will not do so. It will not prevent upwardly mobile francophones from deserting Montreal for the suburbs while simultaneously fretting over compromising the city's French visage. Nor will it secure the vitality of Quebec's cultural industries. There will always be English-French tensions in Canada as long as there are distinct French- and English-speaking cultures and as long as the legacy of the Conquest weighs on Quebec's intellectuals.

The Constitution is a glamorous but inadequate and inappropriate vehicle for preserving and promoting the distinctive French island that is Quebec in a surrounding Anglo-American sea. The well-spring of French Quebec's identity and vigour rests in the history, collective consciousness and internal dynamics of its society, not in what the Canadian and Quebec constitutions or other laws provide. The "control" of language and culture by any government — federal, provincial, English, French, Soviet or Islamic — is a worrisome and problematic concept.

The idea that legal "control" produces the intended results is questionable. Quebec's government resorted in the late 1980s to paying its residents for the production of babies, yet the provincial birth rate remains below the national and Ontario averages. Quebec's constitutional "control" over immigration, reinforced by successive administrative agreements between Ottawa and Quebec, has been of similarly questionable relevance to the unfolding of broader sociodemographic trends. In 1988 only 9 per cent of Quebec's immigrants had French as their first language (versus 6 per cent who had English and 20 per cent who had Arabic). No matter how the Constitution might again be amended, Quebec will not and cannot prohibit immigrants from moving on to other provinces nor can it compel European francophones to settle permanently in Quebec.

An example of the irrelevance of the Constitution in advancing minority cultural interests is the Franco-Manitoban experience. It is cited by both Quebec nationalists and federalists for the purposes of drawing quite different conclusions. The nationalists point to the treachery, bigotry and untrustworthiness of the English provinces and the federal government. Thus the need to rely on Quebec, and only Quebec, to defend French interests. Federalists point to the need to carve a respectable space and status for the official minorities wherever they live in officially bilingual Canada. Federalists vow never again to permit the trampling of constitutionally entrenched rights as occurred in Manitoba.

What both sides neglect or misrepresent is what actually happened to Franco-Manitobans when their constitutional rights were suppressed and then resurrected. After 1916, when French public schools were banished in Manitoba, the percentage of Manitobans claiming French as a first language actually increased. Beginning in the 1950s and accelerating since the 1960s — coincidently with the appearance of the federal Official Languages Act, the re-emergence of government-funded Franco-Manitoban schools and the Constitution

Act, 1982 — the percentage of Manitobans claiming French as a first language decreased. The reinforcement of the constitutional status of French by the Supreme Court in the 1985 Manitoba Language Reference case has been similarly irrelevant to the prospects of the French fact in Manitoba. The Franco-Manitoban story has had much more to do with the eclipse of parish life and schools than with the adherence to or the violation of constitutional "guarantees" or "powers." So too with Quebec's story.

What ought to be done to the Constitution? As little as possible. The current constitutional crisis, like those before and those to come, is fed by an irrepressible nationalism in Quebec. Rather than trying to finesse, manage or cater to it, let us give it the benign neglect and laissez-faire approach it deserves.

Canadian social scientists hail and celebrate John Porter's 1965 classic *The Vertical Mosaic,* but they are so caught up in the current crisis that they have repressed his analysis of "national unity" as a permanent, never-ending obsession: "The question which arises is whether the discord-unity dialogue has any real meaning in the lives of Canadians, or whether it has become, in the middle of the twentieth century, a political technique of conservatism." As in the 1960s, constitutional wrangling in the 1990s distracts from issues of privilege and equity, from the improvement of public welfare and from the amelioration of intolerable conditions of deprivation and injustice. Single mothers on welfare, the unemployed, food bank recipients — in Quebec as elsewhere — are more in need of keeping themselves and their families together than of abstract reformulations.

In stoking the fires of the constitutional reform industry, expectations are being raised by politicians only to be inevitably dashed. It is Utopian to believe that a new constitutional package satisfying everyone's competing demands will be unanimously ratified by eleven legislatures, which are flexing their newly discovered power to veto constitutional change. Political realists know that there will likely not be any more substantial formal changes to the BNA Act or the Constitution Act, 1982 (although there might still be some micro-amendments like the 1983 change respecting native rights).

Quebec must not be rejected or perceive itself to be once again rebuffed as it claims it was in 1981 and 1990. Rather than insisting on constitutional change that the rest of Canada is unwilling to accept, let Quebec continue to *behave* distinctly within the very broad constitutional powers it does possess. The exit from the current impasse lies where it began, in Quebec, not in the rest of Canada. If Quebec escalates tensions by voting for sovereignty, declaring independence or, more important, behaving unconstitutionally, this will be devastating for Quebec's government and for the province's welfare.

Canadians are not interested in the emasculation of the federal government as demanded by the Allaire report. Much of the response in the rest of Canada, therefore, is one of resentment if not contempt. Most Atlantic Canadians, Manitobans, Saskatchewanians and others, including many Québécois, want to maintain and promote the Canadian "social contract" in which the federal government assures comparable standards and levels of funding for a range of social welfare and regional economic programs — from medicare and pensions to regionally sensitive unemployment insurance and industrial development incentives.

In the aftermath of Meech, politicians and their constitutional advisers are an especially discredited lot, desperate for respect and resurrection. They were the spin doctors of pessimism and doomsday scenarios in the first half of 1990. Unless Canada did what they defined as necessary and did it their way — the way of constitutional reform — then Quebec would separate and Canada would disintegrate. This has not happened and it will likely not happen, even after referendums that might be milestones on a road that runs in a circle. Referendums will solve nothing. In retrospect, the 1980 referendum and the 1982 Constitution were no more victories for renewed federalism in Canada than Mikhail Gorbachev's 1991 referendum was a victory for renewed federalism in the Soviet Union.

There is good reason to be optimistic about Canada's prospects. So long as Quebec's government pursues Quebec's "superior interests," as its premier vows, Canada will continue with Quebec in it. The cost of separation would be substantial for both sides but especially for Quebec. Federalism has been too profitable for Canadians and Québécois to desert. Even the PQ's staunch sovereigntists plead to continue to share Canada's currency, and the waffling sovereigntists among the Liberals plead to continue to share in Canada's equalization payments. For Quebec's haute bourgeoisie, reason prevails over emotion and passion. Without this group firmly and almost universally aboard, the independence train is not leaving Quebec's station.

As always, it is a good time to talk and negotiate, but not about formal constitutional reform. Rather we must concentrate on reforming economic, social and environmental policies that really matter to people — from unemployment benefits to regional development to communications. Let politicians and public administrators develop and strengthen asymmetrical arrangements for Quebec if need be within the existing federal system. This could be accomplished non-controversially in immigration policy in 1991 only because it was achieved outside the ambit of constitutional change. Similarly, governments must negotiate with natives to allay their concerns — from self-government to land claims — without constitutionalizing the issues.

Constitutional politics are now too heavily laden with symbolic baggage to yield successful outcomes. Let the political class and its public servants resolve practical problems by striving for workable, down-to-earth and day-to-day solutions. The pursuit of constitutional reform is impractical, self-defeating and probably now impossible. Let us steer away from grand legal designs and the Utopian quest for definitive and comprehensive formulations and substitute instead specific, utilitarian and flexible instruments of policy. It is time, indeed overtime, to shut down the noxious constitutional reform industry before it wreaks any more havoc on the political environment.

Canada's Political and Constitutional Future: Reflections on the Bélanger–Campeau Report and Bill 150

J. Stefan Dupré

Born in Quebec City, Stefan Dupré teaches political science at the University of Toronto, where he writes on federalism.

Two myths and two leaders propelled the Report of the Commission on the Political and Constitutional Future of Quebec (the Bélanger–Campeau report) and are central to its sequels. The myths are Imposition and Rejection. The leaders are the premier of Quebec, Robert Bourassa, and the leader of its official opposition, Jacques Parizeau. The initial sequel is Bill 150, passed by the Quebec National Assembly in June 1991.

The Constitution Act of 1982 was imposed on Quebec against its will. The failure of the Meech Lake Accord embodies English Canada's rejection of Quebec's well-intentioned attempt to embrace the Canadian constitutional order. These statements, like all myths worthy of the name, are half-truths. In all honesty, the fact that the Quebec National Assembly branded the Constitution Act of 1982 as illegitimate must be balanced against the fact that this act was endorsed, indeed formulated, by the province's democratically elected representatives in the federal House of Commons. In all honesty, the fact that English-Canadian public opinion turned against the Meech Lake Accord by the substantial majorities recorded in various public opinion polls must be balanced against the recorded approval of the federal House of Commons and eight provincial legislatures. Sweeping such balance aside, Imposition and Rejection stand nakedly half-true: genuine myths that may yet become the founding myths of an independent Quebec and shatter the territorial integrity of Canada.

Enacted into being with bipartisan support, the Bélanger–Campeau commission was created by a statute whose very preamble nurtures the myths of Imposition and Rejection: "Whereas the Constitution Act, 1982, was proclaimed despite the opposition of the National Assembly; whereas the 1987 Agreement on the Constitution, the aim of which was to allow Quebec to become a party to the Constitution Act, 1982, has failed." As stipulated by the statute, the commission's membership was fundamentally determined by the Quebec premier and opposition leader. At the core of the membership of thirty-six were nine governing party MNAs appointed by the former and six opposition party MNAs appointed by the latter. The National Assembly's third party had one member. Eighteen other members, three from the federal House of Commons and fifteen non-parliamentarians (the two co-chairmen, four other business people, four trade unionists, two municipal representatives and one each from the co-operative, school board and cultural sectors), were all appointed by the premier in consultation with the opposition leader, and these two were themselves designated to sit on the commission as its thirty-fifth and thirty-sixth members.

This final feature of the membership in and of itself ensured that the Bélanger–Campeau commission would be a parliamentary emanation *pas du tout comme les autres*: it was in fact the Bourassa–Parizeau commission.

Another feature that distinguishes this commission from the garden variety of federal or provincial bodies that have examined constitutional matters is that it produced a single, stark recommendation. Notably, this recommendation focuses exclusively on process. On this score, the report loses its distinctiveness and instead faithfully partakes in the prevalent mood of post-Meech Canada.

What the conventional wisdom sees in the failure of the eminently substantive Meech Lake Accord is a failure in process. Constitutional change through the process of federal-provincial negotiation and agreement by the first ministers of the realm, now unmasked as a mere group of eleven men, is out. What is in? Anything that is not executive-dominated. The shopping list consists of a variety of items: consultative exercises, parliamentary and non-parliamentary commissions, constituent assemblies or constitutional conventions, referendums.

Focusing as it does on process, the Bélanger–Campeau commission's single recommendation picks and chooses from the list. The chosen instruments turn out to be parliamentary and plebiscitary. The commission's recommendation spells out precise instructions for the drafting of a bill to be passed by the National Assembly. The upshot is Bill 150. In line with the commission's instructions, the bill's preamble faithfully repeats the whereases of Imposition and Rejection. Bill 150 then spells out a statutory two-track process as stipulated by the commission's recommendation.

Track One can be called the undefined sovereignty-association track. It mandates a referendum on sovereignty, to be held in 1992 either between June 8 and 22 or between October 12 and 26. An affirmative outcome will, in the words of Bill 150, "constitute a proposal that Quebec acquire the status of a sovereign State one year to the day from the holding of the referendum." There is also to be a parliamentary committee to analyse all matters related to Quebec's accession to full sovereignty and, in the event that the government of Canada were to make "any formal offer of economic partnership," to make recommendations on its acceptability to the National Assembly. Because it is established upon the passing of Bill 150, the Track One committee is envisaged as playing an active role throughout the period leading up to the referendum.

Track Two can be called the passive constitutional renewal track. In line with the Bélanger–Campeau commission's recommendation, Bill 150 mandates the creation of a second parliamentary committee, this one to assess any offer of "a new partnership of constitutional nature" from the government of Canada, and to make recommendations about it to the National Assembly. It is specified that only an offer that "is formally binding on the Government of Canada and the other provinces" may be assessed by this parliamentary committee. Quebec will not again attempt to persuade whatever number of provincial legislatures may be necessary to secure the ratification of whatever constitutional amendments would be entailed by the offer received. Apparently, any offer examined by the Track Two parliamentary committee is to be a federal-provincial "done deal" whose ratification by the National Assembly, presumably on the recommendation of this committee, would be the last step necessary to translate this offer into Canadian constitutional law.

The Bélanger–Campeau report's otherwise precise

instructions for the drafting of Bill 150 were silent on the composition of the Track One and Track Two parliamentary committees. By referring to these as "commissions," Bélanger–Campeau may perhaps have envisaged a membership that, like its own, included non-parliamentarians. However, Bill 150 stipulates otherwise. The two entities created by Bill 150 are pointedly called committees and composed exclusively of MNAs, sixteen apiece in proportions that reflect party standings in the assembly.

Notably, as in the case of the Bélanger–Campeau commission, the premier and the leader of the opposition are named to each committee. It follows that each will in fact operate as a Bourassa–Parizeau committee, with a high likelihood of replicating the adversarial partisanship that prevails on the floor of the assembly. It is a safe proposition that such partisanship will be motivated as much by the provincial general election that must take place by 1994 as by the referendum, which is likely to take place first.

With the parliamentary instruments chosen and a plebiscite scheduled, Bill 150 duly reflects the Canadian post-Meech obsession with process. This much said, the particular version of process that Bill 150 brings into statutory existence offers the opportunity, hazardous though it may be, to reflect upon the future.

It is reasonable to begin such an exercise by examining the position in which Premier Bourassa finds himself, a position that he has himself endorsed. Having rejected executive-dominated processes, how much freedom does he have to manoeuvre in a procedural setting that is at once parliamentarized and on the brink of a plebiscite? Mr. Bourassa's influence over the Track One and Track Two parliamentary committees will be wielded through their membership. As leader of the governing party, he selects the Liberal MNAs who constitute the majority on each committee.

With respect to the Track One sovereignty-association committee, Mr. Bourassa holds several cards, assuming that normal governing party discipline will prevail. There is every potential of a majority report that would emphasize, were it his will, the disadvantages of full sovereignty, running from its implications for Quebec's credit rating to the acceptability of a Quebec currency, about which even Mr. Parizeau has expressed reservations.

Given federal government policy, what appears certain is that the Track One parliamentary committee will not receive a "formal offer of economic partnership" from Ottawa in 1992. It follows that within the time frame set for the sovereignty referendum, the issue of sovereignty cannot be clothed in the mantle of association.

As for the sovereignty referendum itself, Premier Bourassa is free to pick June or October 1992. Then there is the wording of the question. Is it to be recommended by the Track One parliamentary committee? It is here that the leader of the opposition, whose party scored a major victory in achieving the referendum on sovereignty, is at a disadvantage. Barring bipartisan consensus, which is up to Mr. Bourassa, the wording of the question can be either recommended by the Track One committee's Liberal majority or left for cabinet to decide. Either way, it is eminently safe to assume that private governing-party polls will be available to test any of a variety of wordings — including radical formulations of the question, which would give all but the most sovereigntist voters pause. If Premier Bourassa remains well disposed towards federalism, he may play, in the wording of the question, a card that might preordain a negative referendum result.

He holds other cards as well. Mr. Bourassa can always

use his majority on the floor of the National Assembly to cancel or postpone the sovereignty referendum. The political cost is whatever attaches to the passage of a bill that supersedes the Bill 150 clause mandating the 1992 referendum. Other options come at a political cost that Mr. Bourassa can also assess at the time he considers them. As Ghislain Dufour, one of the business signatories of the Bélanger–Campeau report, puts it in his vigorously worded addendum, an existing statute on public consultation provides authority for the government to hold a pre-emptive referendum on anything, including federalism. And with regard to the sovereignty referendum, the requisite majority remains to be defined. In Mr. Dufour's opinion, an outcome as consequential as Quebec's independence should require a 65 to 75 per cent majority.

In and of itself, Bill 150's Track One jeopardizes neither Canada's constitutional future nor its territorial integrity. Under the clothing of parliamentary and plebiscitary instruments, the premier's discretion is ample. But will this discretion remain alive and well? Here, of course, is where Track Two comes in.

In deference to the myths of Imposition and Rejection, the Track Two parliamentary committee is to be the passive recipient of constitutional offers. After all, it was Quebec, on which the Constitution Act of 1982 was imposed, that made the five-point offer that launched the Meech Lake Accord on its road to rejection. Under the Track Two approach, Quebec no longer makes offers; it only receives them. And here is where Track One is supposed to support Track Two. Among the Bélanger–Campeau commission's experts, it was the eminent political scientist Léon Dion — gentle, federalist Léon Dion — who delivered the show-stopping line that English Canada "will make concessions—and even that is not assured — only if it has a knife at its throat."

Just as Track One holds the knife, so does Track Two leave Robert Bourassa dangerously exposed. His restricted ability to manoeuvre on Track Two leaves him — and the future of the Canadian constitutional order — heavily dependent on the entities with the knife at their throat, namely Ottawa and the anglophone provinces. He has room for off-track manoeuvres, such as his party's Allaire report, which appeared a month before Bélanger–Campeau. Rather than an offer, here is a demand — in the language of labour-management relations, an opening demand. Transparently excessive, it does no more than issue a signal. Track Two does not eliminate the possibility of emitting further, possibly moderated, signals, as was done during the debate on Bill 150. But it seems to eliminate negotiation through the visible if closed channels of federal-provincial summitry, to say nothing of Quebec's participation in a constituent assembly. Barring sufficient reason for a dramatic about-face, Mr. Bourassa must leave the ball in the court occupied by Ottawa and the anglophone provinces.

In that court, three broad possibilities, not mutually exclusive, exist. One involves manufacturing, by a parliamentary committee, constituent assembly or whatever means, an offer that binds Ottawa and from six to nine provinces. The number must be nine if amendments to the amending formula or certain French-English language rights are included in the offer. The second possibility is a constitutional offer manufactured with the sole consent of the House of Commons; it would necessarily encompass only those constitutional changes that, under Section 43 of the Constitution Act of 1982, can be ratified by the House and the legislature of the province concerned, in this case the Quebec National Assembly. The third possibility involves progress towards an offer that would be sufficiently robust to permit Mr. Bourassa to use his Track One discretion either to cancel the 1992 referendum or doom it to defeat.

To speculate on these possibilities is not exactly a comforting exercise. Is a constituent assembly of federal and anglophone provincial representatives a realistic prospect by 1992, let alone one whose substantive outcome at a minimum comes within shouting distance of the failed Meech Lake Accord? Does the content of Meech not set the rock-bottom standard that an offer would have to meet in order to permit Mr. Bourassa to arrest the Track One process without the certainty of defeat in the Quebec election that must occur by 1994? What about a Meech-like offer that, by omitting an amendment to the amending formula and hence a Quebec veto, requires ratification by only six anglophone provinces? Might a powdered-up version of Meech (the distinct society clause, for instance, in a preamble) wash if it were coupled to something else?

That something, to continue this speculative exercise, might be the outcome of the second possibility, namely a Section 43 offer: changes to the Constitution that need ratification by Ottawa and Quebec only to enter the realm of law. Section 43 encompasses amendments involving "any provision that applies to one" province. It may offer the means of securing a different kind of distinct society clause, if the clause pinpoints Quebec as a province. Unlike the Meech version, it could not wander into the matter of constitutionalizing other fundamental characteristics of Canada.

Section 43 may have potential for something else as well. Consider the federal spending power, which arguably has never been explicitly outlined in the Constitution as applying to all provinces. Perhaps Section 43 could allow a constitutional amendment limiting the federal spending power in Quebec. The Allaire report offers a shopping list of limitations. One item, unemployment insurance, appears beyond the reach of Section 43 because this spending and revenue-raising matter was explicitly added to federal jurisdiction in 1940. But an impressive number of other listed items — workforce training, social assistance, hospital and medical services insurance, family allowances, to name the more striking — are covered by the non-specific spending power rather than by explicit constitutional clauses.

This invites the thought that opting out, worked out by Prime Minister Lester Pearson and Quebec premier Jean Lesage in 1964–65, might be resurrected, this time in a constitutionalized version. Remnants of opting out still exist. A Section 43 amendment might terminate designated federal spending programs in Quebec and compensate Quebec with federal tax room. But if that sounds reasonably simple, as fiscal matters go, the fact of the matter under current circumstances is that it is not.

In the Pearson–Lesage era, the federal budget was balanced. Accordingly, determining the right amount of tax room was a matter of calculating the proportion of the revenue collected by Ottawa from Quebec taxpayers that corresponded to the federal spending forgone. The exercise is now far more complicated, given the federal operating deficit and a budgetary situation where debt servicing charges exceed one-quarter of federal operating expenditures. Approximating the equivalent of any part of the federal spending effort becomes a matter of discerning the equivalent aggregate of tax revenue, debt-servicing charges and borrowing liabilities. It raises the very issues of apportioning debt that arise in a separation scenario.

A Section 43 approach to the federal spending power in Quebec may remain available as a possible Track Two offer. At the very minimum, however, it is likely that only strong federal leadership, perhaps resting on bipartisan or multipartisan support in the House of Commons, would have a chance of swaying the public opinion of an English Canada with a knife at its throat. Furthermore, the Section 43 approach would likely require politicians, obsessed for two generations with the law of the Constitution, to rediscover the other part of our constitutional order — the conventions of the Constitution. Opting out, particularly in a constitutionalized version, generates the hard question of the role that is to be played by Quebec's federal MPs vis-à-vis federal programs that would no longer be available in Quebec. The answer might be sought in a convention whereby Quebec MPs do not vote on such matters. If a particular government measure is defeated, the measure itself would fail but the government could nonetheless carry on, if it survived a confidence motion in which all MPs participated. Is the learning curve required by such a convention too slippery and steep for Canadian politicians, to say nothing of public opinion?

What remains along Track Two is the third possibility, that of substantial progress towards an offer or offers that involve some mixture of what has just been canvassed, including a non-constitutionalized limitation of the federal spending power. There will doubtless be no shortage of exhortations — from various political and business quarters and from commissions yet to report or still to be appointed — to the effect that offers are seriously in the making. In the absence of substantial progress, however, the myths of Imposition and Rejection can only be further invigorated and Track One will yield the referendum, over whose wording Mr. Bourassa retains a measure of discretion and which might require more than a simple majority to pass.

If this is to sketch an immediate future of substantial uncertainty, the scene gets even murkier in the slightly longer run. Consider the scenario of a 1992 referendum that yields a respectable pro-sovereignty majority. Under Track One, a unilateral declaration of independence will follow one year to the day after the referendum, in this instance June or October 1993. Meanwhile, Ottawa's own electoral clock mandates a federal election in that very year. Under the law of the Constitution, Quebec can neither exclude itself from this election nor be excluded from it. Will the election be fought over the issue of recognizing Quebec's independence so that a separation agreement can be negotiated as a matter of international law? What if actual or pending declarations of independence by Quebec aboriginals who have a territorial base cloud the issue? Which parties take what side on the issue? Will there be no federalist politicians left to run in Quebec?

Two of the three — there were only three — dissenters on the Bélanger–Campeau commission provide an unambiguous answer to the last question. They will exist. What is more, the representative of the Equality Party, Richard Holden, and federal Liberal MP André Ouellet mount, in their written addenda, a frontal assault on the myths of Imposition and Rejection. Ominously, however, these myths have developed to the point where such assaults may never amount to more than the proverbial whistle in a windstorm.

If the uncertainty of the immediate future is not to give way to the turbulence that lurks in the slightly longer run, offers, or at least substantial progress towards an offer, must be made. As for the "knife at the throat" analogy, there is good reason to set it aside. As myths, Imposition and Rejection are not lies; they are half-truths. But even half-truths create moral obligations for political action. Constitutional morality may yet explode the myths.

A Ghost at the Banquet: Could Quebec Secede Peacefully?

Kenneth McNaught

Kenneth McNaught is retired from the History Department at the University of Toronto. He is the author of the standard biography of J.S. Woodsworth and of The Penguin History of Canada.

"If a country wants to divide absolutely I am not on the side of those who say we will hold it by force." So spoke Pierre Trudeau in November 1976, shortly after René Lévesque's electoral triumph in Quebec. Beyond question he voiced a visceral, if unexamined, Canadian feeling. Even to raise the question of possible violence as a likely adjunct of Quebec secession is to court the charge of advocating resort to arms. I know, and it is not pleasant. However, if it is true that those who do not learn from the past are condemned to repeat it, it is equally true that we should learn from comparative observation of the world around us. Neither history nor the world today gives much cause to rely upon the mythology of a non-violent Canada. Can we really believe that we are somehow exempt from the experience of our own past as well as from the calamitous consequences experienced in the nation-breaking dramas of the present? Yet, among the competing and contradictory calculations of the costs of

Quebec secession, we find little attention paid to either the likelihood or the costs of violence.

Economists and ideological soothsayers scrutinize carefully the ramifications of a Quebec–Canada common market, a monetary union, division of the national debt, possible expensive agreements on control of the environment, boundary adjustments, compensation for federal property in Quebec. Most of the crystal-ball gazers lard their predictions with wobbly statistics. Their calculations, of course, lead inexorably to preordained conclusions. Unintended consequences, as opposed to pre-packaged scenarios, are usually left quite unconsidered. We have reason to demand a sprinkling of realism on this unhealthy dose of pablum.

A first portion of realism might be a brief review of our own track record. The signposts are all too numerous. Moreover, they form themselves into a fairly clear pattern. Canadians, from the earliest times, have had recourse to violence: to resist perceived injustice, to promote or defend economic interest or cultural security and, not infrequently, as a simple expression of bigotry. The country was, after all, born in violence — from the long struggle of New France against the Iroquois, the New Englanders and the British to the bloody but successful defence against American invasions in the 1770s, 1812–14 and 1866. The much celebrated rivalry between "the Bay" and the Nor'westers is replete with combative competition for economic advantage culminating in the Seven Oaks massacre of 1816. The rebellions of 1837, 1869–70 and 1885 may have been small and significantly unsuccessful but they do not bespeak a society immune from collective violence in support of political purpose. Violence was, too, an ever-present feature in the forest industries reaching from New Brunswick to the Ottawa Valley. In the timber-based communities, French-English and Canadian-American confrontations were supplemented by Orange-Green battling among Protestants and Catholics. As industrialization took root in towns and mines from Cape Breton to Nanaimo, desperate strikers were regularly suppressed by police and soldiers. Because the violence of murder and simple lawlessness have been less evident features of Canadian than of American history, Canadians are prone to believe that their society is less violent. In our present situation, it would be unwise to remain so blinkered.

In Canada the use of lethal force is legitimated not by appeal to a constitutional right to bear arms in pursuit of life, liberty and happiness, but by the need to support peace, order and good government; and this is no snappy academic abstraction. Although not often articulated, our conviction that real liberty and democracy depend upon order — that they cannot survive illegality or the political use of violence — is profoundly important. Not only have violent forays been quickly suppressed by state force, the state has not infrequently applied its power in anticipation of collective political violence. On such occasions, with the argument that "constituted authority" must be protected against perceived risks, the state has engendered violence by the application of its own force. Military suppression of massive strikes in Winnipeg (1919) and in Cape Breton's coal-steel towns in the early 1920s, and of the unemployed trekkers in Regina in 1935 provides but a few instances.

The pattern has not dissolved in more recent times. In Montreal deployment of the army in October of 1970, although preceded by several years of urban terrorism, was principally justified by "apprehension" of insurrection against constituted government. Also at Montreal, twenty years later, the army was summoned to suppress the Mohawk warriors' armed resistance to the constitutionally conveyed right of non-Indian townspeople to build a golf course on land claimed by the Indians. It is a sardonic feature of our Kafka-like situation that the man who called in the army on both these occasions was Robert Bourassa. At the time of writing, it is not surrealistic to imagine that the same premier may summon military assistance to suppress the Cree of northern Quebec who oppose the spoliation of their ancestral lands by Hydro-Québec.

To assess the risk and costs of violence in the future, we should consider closely the possible scenarios. More difficult, we should relate to those scenarios the experience of our own past as well as the insights to be gained from other states that have passed through, or are now enduring, similar crises.

The path of renewed constitutional negotiations is an obvious possible route. That path, however, is strewn with bitter wreckage. It is now blockaded by pre-emptive positions staked out by the Bélanger–Campeau commission and the Allaire report, by the lines drawn on the rocks by both the government and opposition parties in Quebec. Refusal by Robert Bourassa to sit down with Clyde Wells and all the other premiers to bargain about the twenty-two areas of jurisdiction claimed by his government seems as predictable as the failure of some semi-populist constitutional convention. The deadline set by Quebec is alone decisive. So a referendum in Quebec in late 1992 is more than probable.

An outside possibility is that the referendum question will centre upon an offer cobbled together by Ottawa and the provinces. In this unlikely event, a *non* majority is predictable. Much more likely, the referendum will ask Quebeckers: Should the government declare Quebec a sovereign state and negotiate with Ottawa the terms of a future relationship with Canada? A unilateral declaration of independence would become unavoidable; without it, even the possibility of negotiating with Canada would not exist.

Let us look at the least likely scenarios. In the event that Ottawa and nine provinces fashion and endorse a constitutional package that is then presented to Quebec and put to a referendum vote (all within the brief time frame prescribed as "Canada's last chance"), the chances of a peaceful campaign are much less than was the case during the Lévesque referendum in 1980. Speculating about what would follow upon a whisker-thin majority *oui* vote for a package that would certainly whittle away a good deal of Quebec's existing demands, one finds little reason for complacency. In 1980, with Lévesque still in office, the prospect of a second round kept the lid on. Now the second round has come and gone; the comparatively calm waters of Meech Lake have seeped away. Bourassa, having encouraged the highly personalized language of "rejection," of francophone *nationalisme,* would be faced with a replay of 1970 rather than of 1980. The processes of "constitutional democracy" that Lévesque managed to sustain would almost certainly give way to mass action in the streets.

In the more likely event of a referendum on sovereignty, a *non* majority is now virtually inconceivable. Endorsement of the sovereignty option should therefore be the focus of our concern. Moreover, if we think that the terminology of the constitutional debate has hitherto been obscure, we may look for instant clarification as this future unfolds.

For at the heart of the impending crisis lie terms that are very slippery indeed — and that mask a potential for violence that few of us have wished to confront. "Sovereignty," for example, has been given all the hues of the rainbow. By the time this is in print, the persiflage will have evaporated and "independence" will shine through. Again, the process of *étapisme* and "constitutional renewal" will be seen to have the precise goal of secession from the Canadian union. Likewise, the words employed by Bourassa when he introduced the Meech Lake Accord for adoption in Quebec's National Assembly will be seen as revealing Meech for what most anglophones suspected it was: the granting of a constitutional right of secession. In the assembly, the premier concluded that the accord granted Quebec the unrestricted right of "self-determination."

Well, the ambiguities of Meech caused its abortion. For the present purpose, it cannot be too strongly emphasized that within our framework of government there is no constitutional right of secession. To implement a referendum majority wish for sovereignty, the National Assembly would thus have to endorse a unilateral declaration of independence (UDI).

The reverberations of a Quebec UDI would be far more serious than most of us suspect. To begin with, it would at once be seen as illegal and revolutionary. Legally, constitutionally, the provinces of Canada have no independent legitimacy. In 1867 the British parliament passed an "Act for the Union of Canada [Ontario and Quebec], Nova Scotia and New Brunswick" with a preamble noting that the provinces "have expressed their desire to be united." This British North America Act is still the basic constitutional law of Canada — as amended from time to time and simply renamed the Constitution Act in 1982. Our present provinces thus exist as the end product of an unbroken constitutional evolution. That evolution includes wide federal jurisdiction in economic and foreign affairs, boundary delineation, civil liberties and criminal matters — in short, "peace, order and good government." Nevertheless, many people in Quebec, including the premier, argue that Quebec's "right of self-determination" is not limited either by Canadian constitutional law or by the favourite *séparatiste* argument that Confederation was a "compact" between equal founding nations. Indeed, constant reiteration of the right of self-determination, together with Quebec's refusal to endorse the 1982 Constitution Act, point to a clear *séparatiste* understanding of the revolutionary nature of their position. *Séparatistes* know, too, that most Canadians believe that in the final analysis, Quebec secession could be accomplished peacefully — just as many believed in 1939 that Canada could remain neutral if war broke out.

I suggested at the outset that our own history evidences an almost knee-jerk readiness to endorse quick military action to suppress "illegal" challenges to "constituted authority." Moreover, this apparent devotion to the rule of law and of existing constitutional structures is shared by anglophones and francophones — as shown, for example, by the 1970 October Crisis in Montreal, and the Oka–Mercier Bridge mess in 1990. But in addition to our own record, we would do well to look abroad. In any reconnaissance of foreign "models," we will find no exact comparisons. Yet rooting about for examples of secession from nation-states, real or apprehended, yields no encouraging comparisons.

A favourite *séparatiste* instance of a state dividing itself without violence is that of Norway–Sweden in 1905. In that year, the Norwegian parliament simply declared independence, ending the "union" with Sweden. The background of that Scandinavian union, however, renders meaningless any serious comparison. In 1815 the Congress of Vienna had transferred Norway from the Danish to the Swedish crown as penalty for Danish support of Napoleon. Since Norway had been a dependency of Denmark for 400 years, this bit of fancy diplomatic footwork in 1815 made little difference to Norwegian autonomy; by 1905 Swedish "rule" was virtually nominal.

More relevant foreign indicators are to be found in Switzerland, Nigeria–Biafra or the United States where secession attempts produced reunion through civil war. Nor does a glance at today's Europe (leaving aside the contestations in the Middle East and the near-anarchy in India) afford much comfort. In France, Spain and Italy, Basque and Sardinian secessionists cause chronic violence. The likely disintegration of Czechoslovakia, Yugoslavia and the Soviet Union, all multi-ethnic states, is accompanied by varying degrees of internecine violence. It requires no oracle to forecast escalation of that violence, as well as grave economic instability resulting from it.

Despite the passage of time, the aborted secession of the Southern Confederacy from the United States offers the most disturbing points of comparison. As Canadians do now, some 30 million Americans in the late 1850s agonized over the constitutional division of powers within a continental federation that also called itself a union. The South saw itself as a society distinct from that of the North, a society whose values and survival were imperilled by unconstitutional use of federal powers by northern majorities. A society based upon slave labour and cherishing a romantic ideal of chivalry, the South felt that the northern majority was about to impose high protective tariffs that would benefit northern industrial growth and westward expansion while increasing the production and living costs in the South's cotton-based economy. By prohibiting slavery in the western federal territories, the North would also deprive the South of the chance to preserve its distinctiveness by extending its economic organization westward in parallel with that of the North.

Inexorably, the South's concern with survival took on all the features of nationalism. Racial homogeneity of the southern nation (a myth sustained by excluding slaves from citizenship) became ever more important as southern leaders drew invidious comparisons between their distinct society and that of the North. As floods of immigrants, mostly "lower class" and many of them Catholic, poured into the North, the disproportionate influence of the South in Congress came more and more into question. While southern leaders denigrated the multi-ethnic and dubious character of the North's industrializing society, they grew ever more fearful of the worsening demographic imbalance.

As the "inter-sectional" crisis deepened in the late 1850s, fire-eating southern nationalists pushed hard for secession, for a sovereign confederacy. Others, such as Alexander Stephens, held cautiously to the federal union; but with actual secession Stephens became vice-president of the Confederate States. And secession, of course, followed close upon the heels of failed negotiations for constitutional amendments to curb federal power. That the "peculiar institution" of slavery underlay the disputes over the Constitution should not obscure the fact that the fundamental conflict was between two societies with sharply divergent views on population mix, "culture" and economic policy. Those societies disagreed, too, not only on the constitutional distribution of powers but on the nature of the Constitution itself. The dispute over that question brings our comparison into sharper focus.

Southerners today talk of the War Between the States. Northerners recall the Civil War. At the time, southerners pointed out that the Constitution referred to the states as "sovereign" entities who had delegated some of their powers to a central government — an argument similar to, but much more correct than the *séparatiste* "compact theory" of Canadian Confederation. Northerners countered that the Constitution was adopted specifically to overcome the weakness of a confederal government — in short, to establish a "more perfect union." The bottom line is that America's civil war was fought to maintain the union, to reassert that the whole was greater than its parts.

The intense devotion to the Union exhibited by a majority of today's Americans is, in large measure, an outcome of their civil war. What might well interest Canadians most about that conflict, however, are the differing assumptions made by opinion makers at the time. During the "secession crisis" of 1860–61, southern fire-eaters proclaimed the need to take back the powers delegated to the central government, to reclaim complete sovereignty. They also predicted confidently that the North would never fight merely to maintain the Union. In the North, the most influential Republican editor, Horace Greeley of the *New York Tribune*, wrote: "If the cotton states shall decide that they can do better out of the Union than in it we shall insist on letting them go in peace." At the same time, the Republican president-elect, Abraham Lincoln, appeared to vacillate. Right down to 1859, he was on record as believing in the "right of revolution," of unrestricted self-determination. He went so far as to assure the South that he would not interfere with slavery where it already existed. But at the same time, he revised his position on the right of revolution by adding the proviso that the cause must be just.

By the time of Lincoln's inauguration in March 1861, the Southern Confederacy had already been formed. In his inaugural address, while he declared the Union to be perpetual and denied any right of secession, Lincoln was also conciliatory: "Before entering upon so grave a matter as the destruction of our national fabric, with all its benefits, its memories and its hopes, would it not be wise to ascertain precisely why we do it. Will you hazard so desperate a step while there is any possibility that any portion of the ills you fly from have no real existence?" And this plea he reinforced, in terms instantly recognizable to Canadians: "Physically speaking, we cannot separate. We cannot remove our respective sections from each other nor build an impassable wall between them. A husband and wife may be divorced and go out of the presence and beyond the reach of each other; but the different parts of our country cannot do this." Then followed the poignant query: "Can allies make treaties easier than friends can make laws? Can treaties be more faithfully enforced between aliens than laws can among friends?"

Two other passages from Lincoln's 1861 address seem especially relevant. Anticipating the future troubles of a Confederate government, he observed that "if a minority will secede . . . they make a precedent which will in turn divide and ruin them." And, finally, the dilemma we seek to ignore: "The government will not assail you. You can have no conflict without being yourselves the aggressors. You have no oath registered in heaven to destroy the government, while I shall have the most solemn one to protect and defend it." In the end violence exploded because Lincoln believed that in a federal union there is no legal-constitutional right of unrestricted self-determination and because he was obliged to safeguard the rights and properties of citizens as well as federal property that was confiscated under authority of a UDI.

The two North American federal unions differ in a great many respects; they are also similar in many. There is no constitutional provision for secession in either. Most of the southern states were creations of the federal government; Quebec too is the creation of a central government — whether imperial or federal. In the event of a UDI, the problem of federal responsibilities within Quebec would be far more complex than was Lincoln's similar problem. There are infinitely more Canadian installations — governmental, commercial and military — in Quebec than there was federal property in the American South. Nor did southern secession divide the remaining American union geographically. Much of Canadian property in Quebec, both public and private, is the result of expensive federal policies designed to ensure a Québécois sense of participation in the Canadian union: museums, galleries, the National Film Board, CBC–Radio Canada, research facilities, air and rail systems, harbours and waterways, military institutions and defence industries — to name only the most obvious.

The federal government has an obligation to ensure the security of all these, but beyond that it has a clear responsibility to protect the liberty and security of individual Canadians, including those who oppose a UDI. How could any Canadian government accept a unilateral Quebec take-over of all these rights and properties and then simply sit down with no chips to negotiate possible compensation? Everything in our history says this wouldn't wash.

Beyond doubt a Quebec UDI would activate the deepest Canadian concerns about legality, continuity and constitutionality. The assumption that Canadians would accept unilateral definition of the boundaries of an independent state of Quebec lacks credibility; it minimizes our insistence on legality and, indeed, the very nature of the Canadian union. Quebec fire-eaters founded their *nationalisme* upon race, upon a national idea that is the antithesis of Canadian federalism. René Lévesque put it succinctly: to be Québécois it is not enough to speak French, you must *be* French. Because this rejects the very idea of Canada, a secessionist claim to northern territory that was given to Quebec as a province of Canada by the federal government in 1912 would likely be sharply contested — as would the *séparatiste* claim to much of Labrador, which was allotted to Newfoundland by the British Privy Council in 1927.

The whole question of Canadian responsibilities in the event of a Quebec UDI leads to the question: What might actually happen? Inside Quebec, emotions would certainly peak. Parades, demonstrations, spontaneous occupation of properties and clashes with those who opposed the UDI would make 1970 or 1990 pale by comparison. Even a Bourassa could not again summon the Canadian army to restore order. Yet could the government of Canada abnegate its legal-constitutional responsibilities pending a negotiated or arbitrated settlement? And the soldiers would have to be drawn from anglophone units beyond Quebec. The question of how francophone units of the Canadian Forces would respond to federal government orders in such circumstances need scarcely be posed.

Whatever the shape and extent of the violence that would accompany a UDI, the spectre should be exorcized. To allow it to hover among us would be to forswear the legacy of a nation dedicated not only to peace, order and good government but also to tolerance and flexible federalism. Political will and forthright leadership are to be preferred far above the destructive machinations of the "constitutional reform industry." It is that industry that has brought us to our hapless condition and that threatens further crippling of a *bonne entente*. Better, far, to put on the brakes and heed the sensitive reflections of columnist Lysiane Gagnon, who wrote in the spring of 1991: "Quebec may have her coat on, but her boots are still in the closet. And not only her boots: her wallet. And not only her wallet: family belongings, old pictures, love letters, cases and bags filled with history and emotion you can't easily leave behind."

Canada, Quebec and the World

J.L. Granatstein

J.L. Granatstein has written on defence and foreign policy, most recently as co-author of Pirouette: Pierre Trudeau and Canadian Foreign Policy. *He teaches at York University.*

FLASH: Washington, 1 July 1994: President George Bush told a White House press conference at 2 p.m. today that the United States has national interests in Canada and Quebec that have to be taken into account when Quebec independence comes into effect late this fall. "Our air defences make critical use of Canadian airspace and radar nets now," the president said, "and we expect both Canada and Quebec to continue to recognize this in the future." Moreover, Bush added, "if the stability of Canada and Quebec cannot be guaranteed," American troops "might have to be deployed" to protect U.S. economic, political and military interests. When reporters asked what leverage the United States government has over the incoming government of Quebec, Bush replied bluntly, "If they want to get a Free Trade Agreement with us, they had better hear what we say."

The world is frankly puzzled and disbelieving at the news coming from Canada these days. This country about to break up? One of the richest, most free societies of the world about to go the route of Yugoslavia or the Soviet Union? A country that has played a major and creditable role in the world for a half century about to split asunder? *Incroyable!* As a Toronto-based reporter for *Yomiuri Shimbun*, one of the major Japanese newspapers, has said, his editors in Tokyo simply won't print the stories he files about Quebec separation. "They just won't believe it until it happens." Much of the world, much of Canada, likely feels that way. And well they should.

The simple truth is that in terms of international affairs the independence of Quebec makes absolutely no sense at all; the presidents of both Mexico and the United States have made this clear in comments in Canada in spring 1991. At best, it will make Quebec once more the insulated, isolated province that it was in the years before the Quiet Revolution brought it out of its shell; at worst, it will leave it an economic ruin with a declining birth rate and few immigrants, far more tightly controlled from abroad than it ever was by Canada, and one of those pathetic nation-states that look to their representation at the United Nations — Quebec would be seated between Qatar and Romania, its fleur-de-lys flag flapping in the New York City breeze outside the UN building — as the solitary touchstone of their international identity. A mini-state like Quebec simply will not count for much in the world — except when Quebec's native peoples troop off to New York, as they almost certainly will, to demand that the United Nations act on their pleas for independence from Quebec.

Separation will also leave a truncated Canada greatly diminished, with its status as a middle power, a foremost nation or a principal power much reduced. The only undoubted benefit in the break-up of Canada will be that foreigners will no longer have to sit through speeches that last twice as long because Canadian dignitaries feel obliged to repeat their deathless words in both official languages. More seriously, no one should doubt that dissolution will have a great impact on the way Canada and Quebec deal with and relate to the United States. Predictably, independence for Quebec will likely leave both the new republic and a divided Canada under the thumb of the United States in a way that makes our present economic, military and political subordination seem negligible.

The end of the Cold War has created a series of opportunities for the world at the same time as it has posed new difficulties. The Gulf War of 1991, for example, demonstrated that the United States and the Soviet Union could work together and that the United Nations could act, thanks to U.S. pressure, against aggression. That was a hopeful sign, whatever the merits or demerits of the specific case in question. Similarly, the advent of *glasnost* and *perestroika*, the liberation of Eastern Europe and the reunification of Germany, the negotiation of significant arms-control agreements and the obvious preoccupation of Moscow with its desperate internal problems have eased superpower tensions dramatically in a way that was simply not foreseen just five years ago.

For Quebec, contemplating the possibility of independence, this new world situation must have seemed like manna from heaven. Had the 1990s been a difficult Cold War era, for example, defence would have loomed very large in Washington's eyes, and there would almost certainly have been demands from the United States for an independent Quebec to undertake an active defensive military role in the North. In the new world order, Jacques Parizeau, Lucien Bouchard and their hangers-on must think, such demands are unlikely and Quebec should be able to get away scot-free from

Canada's international treaty obligations with nothing more than insincere promises to uphold existing defence arrangements.

The Parti Québécois under René Lévesque in 1970 had adopted an out-and-out neutralist posture, one that called for an independent Quebec to opt out of NATO and NORAD and take up the isolationist posture long favoured along the banks of the St. Lawrence. But once the PQ leaders realized that such a position was doing them no good at all in Washington or Western Europe, there was an opportunistic shift in 1977 and 1979 to a stance of upholding Canadian treaty commitments in NATO and NORAD. Independentist Québécois now appear to believe that the change in global tensions has made this volte-face virtually painless. Troops from the new republic could be pledged to stay in NATO, an easy promise to make at the beginning of the 1990s when the prospects of Canadian and U.S. troops coming home look very good indeed. Quebec could also agree to participate actively in NORAD, again something simple to promise when the need for air defence in a world of détente is apparently nugatory. Whether anyone in Ottawa or Washington or NATO headquarters will believe these pledges is another question entirely.

Still, the easy assumptions in Quebec about the course of great power relations, like so many of the others being made there now, are pipe-dreams that simply misunderstand Washington's concerns. First and foremost, the Soviet Union's military still has a powerful air force, an array of ICBMs, and 25,000 nuclear warheads at its disposal. Secondly, the Kremlin and its powerful marshals continue to be reluctant to agree to the terms of the arms reduction treaties that were negotiated with such difficulty over a long period. In such a state of affairs, no American government can afford to neglect its defences and especially the air defence of North America and the United States.

There is yet more. So long as the Soviet Union is unstable, so long as the Estonians, Latvians, Lithuanians, Ukrainians, Georgians, Armenians and all the others seek independence, Washington, operating on the principle that superpower instability in and of itself is always dangerous, cannot afford to assume that the present era of relaxed tension will be permanent. And so long as there exists the prospect of a revolution against President Gorbachev, from either the left or the right, from either the army, the KGB or Boris Yeltsin, the peace of the world is bound to be fragile. In these circumstances, which seem certain to continue for at least the short-term future, the North Atlantic Treaty Organization and the North American Aerospace Defence Command are, in the estimation of the United States, necessary — and rightly so. There may be changes, there may be cuts in the defence budgets, but the West's guard will not come wholly down, and geography makes it clear that the United States will have to pay close attention to Quebec and Canada. And no one, neither American nor Canadian, consulting opinion polls taken during the Gulf War could have failed to notice the lack of support for the war in Quebec; the Americans are likely to remember this and weigh it in the balance in any negotiations with a new independent Quebec.

That includes talks on the Free Trade Agreement. The FTA between Canada and the United States demands close attention. The agreement, for which Quebec business pressed so hard during the run-up to the election of 1988, was without question designed to facilitate the operations of American business in Canada and to ensure access to the scarce resources Americans will need in the twenty-first century. Some of those resources are in Quebec, of course, and the *indépendantistes* have operated on another easy assumption — that Quebec, once liberated from Ottawa's yoke, could automatically pick up the FTA's terms and carry on happily trading as before.

But are they correct? The international lawyers have yet to pronounce definitively, but there is every reason to believe that a successor state, such as an independent Quebec, is not automatically covered by agreements such as the FTA. A new negotiation will be required, and there might be several surprises for Quebec in any such bargaining.

First, much would depend on just how the break-up of Canada was accomplished. If there were bitter feelings, as everyone should expect, Washington might be faced with choosing which of Canada or Quebec it would favour, and there can be scarcely any doubt that Ottawa, commanding 20 million people with the industrial heartland, the oil and most of the mineral resources would take preference over Quebec City and its six million.

Moreover, the level of government intervention and state support for industries in Quebec is very high, even by the standards of the rest of Canada. For example, the Quebec Pension Plan has been used very creatively and effectively to provide financing at below-market rates to Quebec firms, while the provincial utility Hydro-Québec has sold electricity below cost to aluminum smelters and other corporations in the province. In the long, difficult negotiation of the FTA, the U.S., Lord knows, looked on virtually everything the Canadian government did of this sort as an unfair subsidy and a gross violation of the sacred principles of free enterprise. "The whole of Quebec's manufacturing sector," Alan Rugman, a University of Toronto economist, has said, "could be subject to potential U.S. countervail cases.... Quebec would have to renegotiate the Free Trade Agreement with the United States." He adds, "It's obvious Quebec would not get as good a deal." (Canadians, too, might object to such unabashed subsidies when Quebec seeks a common market with them.) Charles Doran of Johns Hopkins University notes, "Once one becomes an independent entity, then one is bargaining directly against the full blast of Washington's negotiating ability and efforts.... That might be a different situation" for Quebec. Many Canadians and some Québécois thought the FTA's terms weren't exactly a sweetheart deal as they stood; what a Quebec–U.S. FTA, should one be negotiated, might look like is, of course, unknowable.

There should be no doubt, however, as to which party in those negotiations will hold the whip hand. The northeastern United States needs Quebec's hydro-electric power, the great newspapers need Quebec's paper and the mills of the Midwest require Quebec's iron ore; but none of those commodities is unobtainable elsewhere. The Americans can also get along without Quebec's manufactured goods — subway cars, after all, can be made elsewhere than by Bombardier in *la belle province.* Quebec, on the other hand, will be desperate for a FTA with the Americans, for without guaranteed access to the world's largest market its economic survival as an independent nation would be in serious doubt, especially if a truncated Canada bargained toughly and refused to offer the common currency, the common market and the open borders that Québécois also foolishly take as givens. What the Americans would want from Quebec City in economic and social terms can be left to the economists to ponder, though there can be no doubt that the United States will insist on its corporations having the right to operate in English; what Washington might demand in other areas, however, can be speculated upon.

The Americans are certain to link any FTA negotiations with Quebec to their defence requirements. Since the advent of the Cold War more than forty-five years ago, Pentagon planners have counted on the existence of a stable Canada to their north and one that, despite occasional hesitations and doubts, has shared American perceptions about the Communist threat to North America and Europe and helped in their defence. But if Quebec should become independent, that easy state of affairs will alter dramatically, and in place of political certainty will come a marked degree of political instability. In a world as unstable as ours is certain to be throughout the 1990s, in a Quebec–Canada environment that will be uneasy at best and might possibly be on the verge of civil war, the Americans will have a legitimate right to demand certain guarantees to ensure that their northern flank is not dangerously exposed and, no less legitimately, to test Quebec's commitment to the defence of North America. Defence over Quebec airspace must be maintained at least at the present (quite inadequate) level. That means that Quebec will have to pick up the commitments made by Canada under NORAD, commitments renewed for an additional five years in the spring of 1991, and in the North Warning System — including the maintenance of radar stations and fighter interceptors. Moreover, Quebec's membership in NORAD will have to be negotiated (though Quebec, unlike Canada, could scarcely expect to be given by treaty the right to have the post of deputy commander).

In all likelihood, the Pentagon will insist on overflight rights for Strategic Air Command bombers, on refuelling rights, and possibly even the right to test Cruise missiles over Quebec. In times of high international tension, the Americans could also demand the right to station aircraft, crews and nuclear weapons on bases in the newly independent country. The American government might also insist that Quebec maintain troops in NATO, a demand, however problematic it may be today at a time when Canada is preparing to withdraw most of its NATO contingent, that could well be possible two or three years hence when negotiations occur. These kinds of demands, all of which at various times have been made of — and conceded by — Canada, will not sit lightly on Quebec, but there will be no option other than to accept them if they are made conditions for a Quebec–United States FTA.

So difficult to swallow could the U.S. negotiating position be that some in Quebec are certain to react fiercely against it. The general public remains fundamentally isolationist and inward-looking, sure to be unhappy at being tightly bound into the American war machine. From the left, well represented still in the Parti Québécois, there will be insistent demands that Quebec go it alone; from the right, there will be equally persistent arguments that it might be easier to let Canada continue to handle defence and foreign policy. The Allaire report accepted by the Quebec Liberal Party in early 1991, for example, left defence to the federal government and proposed a shared jurisdiction over foreign affairs. Whether the federal government, not to say the Canadian people, could accept such a situation after a declaration of independence is most uncertain and would obviously depend on the conditions Quebec tried to attach to any such request; that Quebec could be truly sovereign and independent if Canada controlled its foreign policy seems highly unlikely.

The Americans, like Canadians, are also certain to demand that their ships have guaranteed free access along the St. Lawrence Seaway as it passes through Quebec.

Even if they cannot be certain that their investments in Quebec will flourish in a post-independence economic climate that is likely to be cool at best, they will demand guarantees that their investments be secured against expropriation. They will want something as close to a stable status quo as can be achieved, and they have every right to demand these things.

Canadians can also expect an increase in American demands of them in virtually all post–break-up scenarios. With two nations on their northern border, Washington will be able to play off one against the other, to whip-saw Quebec and Canada. Canada's bargaining power in the General Agreement on Tariffs and Trade is certain to diminish, precisely at the time when the European Community is moving towards integration, towards recreating itself. (How Quebec on its own will deal economically with Europe is virtually unimaginable, although PQ leader Jacques Parizeau airily assumes that France will sponsor Quebec in the EC.) Moreover, American firms and those of other countries thinking of locating in Canada or Quebec (should any still want to do that) will naturally seek concessions from one country and try to better them in the other.

If there is massive decentralization and an increase in regionalism in Canada after Quebec's departure, then, of course, the potential for playing off a fragment of Canada against the others also increases exponentially. The centrifugal forces in Canada will increase, without question, and that too will enhance American leverage. And Canada's weakness and instability, like Quebec's, will frighten planners at the Pentagon. What guarantees could there be that Canada, troubled and torn, will be able to maintain its air defence commitments? If the federal government gives away powers and revenues in an effort to placate the remaining provinces, how will Ottawa be able to pay its defence bills, now about $12.7 billion a year and, given the equipment needs of the Forces, unlikely to drop much in the near future even when personnel are cut drastically? In such circumstances, American demands to take over responsibility for continental air defence over Canadian territory seem far from unlikely in peacetime and almost certain in an emergency. And once control over our airspace and our defence has definitely passed to the United States Air Force, how much sovereignty could Canada retain? Many Canadians and especially those in the Maritimes and the far West may well conclude that the game is up and opt for absorption by the United States.

Bad as that is, this is far from the worst possible scenario for Canadians and Québécois. The late distinguished diplomat and scholar John Holmes wrote during the earlier secessionist crisis of the late 1970s that "the Basques and Kurds and Northern Irish are more murderous by far" while "our secessionists are very pacifistic." Happily that has been true up to now. Nonetheless, there is a very real possibility, despite our total unwillingness to contemplate it, for disputes over borders or, more likely still, for communal fighting after a Quebec declaration of independence. There are close to a million anglophones and allophones in Quebec, and hundreds of thousands of francophones living in virtually every province of Canada. In the atmosphere of high emotion, exultation and anger that would accompany the destruction of a united Canada, very little will be necessary for the first spark. A Montreal Anglo waving a placard at an independence celebration, for example, might be all that is needed to set the city afire. If fighting persisted, spread and escalated, the Americans could easily feel obliged — in the interests of peace, in the interests of preventing loss of life, in the interests of protecting their investments and strategic position — to send troops into Quebec and Canada to pacify the unruly inhabitants.

Unlikely? John Holmes, who knew the United States well, wrote that the "Americans, as the self-appointed vicars of the Western world, would probably feel that they had to do something" to stop the fighting. For years, they have had a well-equipped and powerful light division based at Fort Drum, N.Y., one that is trained in cold-weather operations; they have a major air base at Plattsburgh, N.Y.; and their airborne divisions are within a few hours' flying time of the border. And lest there still be readers who remember Richard Rohmer's now-prophetic (if dreadful) novels, there should be no doubt that the U.S. Army and Air Force could make short work of the attenuated forces of an independent Quebec or Canada.

Sir John A. Macdonald once said, "We are a great country, and shall become one of the greatest in the universe if we preserve it; we shall sink into insignificance and adversity if we suffer it to be broken." The grand old man was surely right, and it will be a tragedy beyond compare if Canadians and Québécois ever have to read a news bulletin like the following:

FLASH: Washington, 17 January 1995: President Dan Quayle announced this morning that he had ordered American troops into Quebec to "restore order" after fighting between Canadian and Quebec military units broke out last Sunday. Heavy American armored forces crossed into the territory of Quebec under cover of darkness and paratroops are already reported to have seized the grounds of the National Assembly in Quebec City despite scattered resistance by police and military units. The whereabouts of President Lucien Bouchard and his cabinet are unknown. At this point, no word has been released about any American actions in and around Ottawa. President Quayle said that the American people would understand the reasons that forced him to act, and he was sure that "God is on America's side." The president added that once order was restored, the troops were prepared to stay as long as necessary to ensure that "American interests are not disrupted or destroyed." How long that might be, the president did not say.

Part II

The Regions

The Regional Dynamics
of National Unity

Martin Cohn

Martin Cohn writes on national politics for The Toronto Star, *where he is a member of the newspaper's editorial board. This article is drawn from his research for a special series on the regional dynamics of national unity.*

"What does Quebec want?" The perennial constitutional question has fallen out of fashion in the post-Meech era. Another "Quebec Round" would be doomed to failure, so it has been superseded by a "Canada Round" to take account of all Canadians. But any attempt to give Quebec and the rest of Canada equal billing begs the question: "What does Canada want?"

More precisely, what do the regions want of Canada? What does the West really want? What will the East want next? What more could Quebec want? And does Ontario want for anything? As they put forward their individual agendas, the provinces are likely to emerge more divided than ever in their bid to stay together.

Behind the abstractions are real issues affecting real people: Should individual provinces be able to tamper with medicare programs, leaving Canadians with unequal access to health care, or should Ottawa enforce national standards? Are powers over immigration and citizenship a federal preserve or should they be parcelled out to the provinces? Does bilingualism mean two official languages from coast to coast, or only selectively in provinces with the political will to maintain it?

Provincial governments often prefer regional variations in programs and powers, because the hallmark of regionalism is a shared distrust of the centre. During past constitutional negotiations like-minded provinces routinely teamed up against Ottawa or other easy targets. For example, the western provinces together wanted control over their natural resources during the 1981 "Patriation Round." More recently, Newfoundland and the West have teamed up to fight for Senate reform that would give smaller provinces a bigger say in federal decision making. And Quebec has made common cause with Alberta in resisting minority-language rights — along with Saskatchewan and Manitoba.

Antipathy towards Toronto is still one of the country's great unifying characteristics, along with Ottawa-bashing. But shared hostility can't mask the reality that regional solidarity is an outdated myth in Canada, built on temporary and illusory alliances. Strip away the tactical imperative of the moment, and these bonds quickly dissolve. Distrust resurfaces and parochialism reappears. When the interlude of co-operation runs its course, the country is once again at cross purposes. The only difference is how unpredictable the provinces have become as they position themselves for the coming Canada round.

Quebec has lost its ability to shock. After the collapse of Meech Lake, nothing it says or does surprises. Canadians were braced for the worst when the governing Liberal Party approved the Allaire report as its new constitutional platform last March, with its two alternative courses for the province.

Under a "new Quebec–Canada structure," the province would have "full sovereignty" in most areas, and an "economic union" with Canada. Or, if the rest of Canada refused to go along, Quebec would go its own way by seeking "full sovereignty" in most areas, and an "economic association" with Canada. Either way, Quebec would have its way — sovereignty and an economic association. Or simple sovereignty-association.

The report calls for Quebec to assume full authority, or "sovereignty," over twenty-two constitutional powers ranging from agriculture to the environment, but also including unemployment insurance, workforce retraining, regional development, health and welfare, research and development, energy and most taxation powers. Indeed, the list is so long that it's easier to specify what Ottawa would be left with: defence, customs, currency, equalization and the national debt. These demands were quickly dismissed outside Quebec.

A few weeks later, the Bélanger–Campeau commission on Quebec's political future — with thirty-six influential members from business, politics and labour — came to a similar conclusion. Unlike Allaire, it presented no specific shopping list, but it set a similar, late-1992 referendum deadline. Quebeckers calculated that a precise time frame would persuade the rest of Canada to produce a timely response.

Quebec premier Robert Bourassa personally endorsed both documents, but committed himself to nothing. Reserving the final decisions for himself, he retained his *marge de manoeuvre*. He can call a referendum on independence, pre-empt it with a vote on renewed federalism or just wait until a general election in 1993.

A year after the Meech Lake débâcle, opinion polls showed a majority of Quebeckers still supporting some form of sovereignty-association, including outright independence. But the same surveys showed a solid majority also wanting to renegotiate a new constitutional deal with the rest of Canada. Somehow, most Quebeckers were supporting separation and national unity at the same time, while questioning the viability of both. Apparently, they wanted their premier to stand firm, but to stay flexible.

For all its flexibility, Quebec is firm on one point: it wants a changed Canada, according to Intergovernmental Affairs Minister Gil Rémillard: "A drastically changed partnership with the rest of Canada, or sovereignty by way of a referendum in the fall of 1992 — those are the options. The government is there to govern, and it has all the necessary room to manoeuvre."

The dynamic force driving Quebec politics is an unprecedented alliance between old-line cultural nationalists and a new generation of market nationalists in the business world. If a problem needs fixing — whether it's protection of the French language or the environment — they look to Quebec City for help, not Ottawa. Thus, when the province proposed controversial medical user fees, in violation of the Canada Health Act, separatist labour unions disdained the federal legislation and mobilized on their own. Federalist business executives also argued that Ottawa had no business in the hospital beds of the province. To reinforce its position, the Bourassa government pinned its hopes on its erstwhile allies out west, who had previously shared its resistance to federal incursions.

British Columbia could always be counted on to join Quebec's fight for greater autonomy. When the Allaire report came out, B.C. politicians — and not just then-premier Bill Vander Zalm — said "Bravo." Canada's westernmost province evinces a remarkable unity of purpose on the issue, a political cohesion similar to Québécois solidarity. Politicians in the province — both Socred and socialist — want a radically restructured country, with an agenda closely resembling Quebec's aspirations. "When we in government looked at the Allaire report, it was a gift — it appealed to us [because] we have a great deal in common with Quebec," Vander Zalm said at the time. "When the Allaire report comes out and says, 'Let's define what a federal responsibility [is] and what a provincial responsibility is,' we say: 'Hurrah! That's great.'"

However much the Socreds and the opposition New Democrats detest one another, they detest Ottawa even more. Which is why NDP leader Mike Harcourt, B.C.'s virtual premier-in-waiting, sounds much like his political opponents on the subject — and not at all the traditional NDP centralist. "I'm even more of an extreme decentralist than just federal and provincial [powers]. I've always been a grass-roots, community-based political person," he said. "I want a quite substantial restructuring of the way decisions are made in this country — back to the taxpayers, back to their communities, back to the regions of this country of ours. And I see the provinces as facilitators of that."

B.C.'s shopping list is almost as extensive as Quebec's, but instead of "sovereignty," its buzzword is "disentanglement." It wants greater power over education, workforce retraining, health care, immigration, child care and other services, without interference from Ottawa. At a meeting of western premiers in 1990, B.C. circulated a memo outlining its demands: "The federal government would withdraw from transferring cash to the provinces in respect of health care, post-secondary education and social assistance," and from any "new and expensive program areas such as day care." In return, the provinces would raise their own money and run their own programs without federal duplication. But if Ottawa gave up control of the financial strings, it could no longer dictate minimum national standards for medicare. And it is exactly that tangled web that B.C. seeks to disentangle. "Recognizing that Canada is large and diverse, it would be appropriate to dispense with most national standards, using instead standards developed by each province," the memo argued. But it said little about how the provinces would pay their own way. For rich provinces such as B.C. and Alberta, self-financing social programs would be easy enough. But for their poorer Prairie cousins in Saskatchewan and Manitoba, disentanglement might undermine vital equalization payments funnelled through

113

Ottawa. B.C.'s memo got mixed reviews, along with Quebec's Allaire report.

The Prairie provinces are usually portrayed as outsiders, railing away against Ottawa. But the stereotype is surprisingly out of date. After years of trying to cut the federal government down to size, the Prairies have had their fill of decentralization.

Alberta, the perennial crusader for provincial rights, still feels left out of the national power structure. But unlike Quebec, Alberta doesn't want out — it wants in. It's the same story in Saskatchewan and Manitoba, where slumping grain prices have hit the farm belt hard, and economic prospects are grim. As "have-not" provinces, they're in no hurry to take over greater responsibilities from the federal government. A decade ago, with resentment simmering over official bilingualism and the National Energy Program, the West made common cause with Quebec in attacking Ottawa. Today, regional alienation still flourishes, but people on the Prairies feel no kinship with Quebec nationalism. Instead, they want the centre to stay strong.

"I believe in having a strong central government to carry out the responsibilities assigned to it under the Constitution," said Alberta's deputy premier, Jim Horsman. "It has to have the ability to do that [or] you're going to weaken the country." While Quebec and B.C. want sovereignty and disentanglement, the Prairies want to maintain and even strengthen national standards for key social programs such as medicare, workforce retraining and even education. The old bogeyman of bilingualism has also receded, as people come to accept that "we're a bilingual country," according to Manitoba premier Gary Filmon. Even the grass-roots Reform Party is much misunderstood when it is caricatured as a separatist movement. In fact, it wants a stronger voice in Ottawa, underscored by the Prairie push for a triple-E Senate that is elected, equal and effective. Its purpose is to give the West a stronger voice in national politics in order to reinforce, not diminish, central institutions. In theory, a reformed Senate would take the spotlight off the premiers and their provincial agendas. But it would come at the expense of populous Ontario.

Ontario, the province that has never acted like one, is having an identity crisis. Until now, Canada's biggest, richest province played the role of honest broker in constitutional negotiations, while always promoting a pan-Canadian perspective. When Quebec complained and the West whined, Ontario always turned the other cheek. But under NDP premier Bob Rae, Canada's industrial heartland may be having a change of heart. His government is wondering whether Ontario, with a population of nearly 10 million, should become a province just like the others and start promoting its own provincial interests.

Ontario has traditionally been comfortable with the idea of a strong central government, because it seemed so close to home. Now Rae wants to reclaim some of those powers for his own provincial government. High on his agenda is wasteful duplication by both levels of government in areas such as workforce retraining. For Ontario's first social democratic premier, efficiency matters more than ideology, and proximity is the key to power. "I don't think there's anything either right wing or left wing about devolution," he says. "I've been at both levels, and provincial politics is closer to the parish pump, it's closer to how people are really feeling, it's closer to the ground." Rae would counter-balance decentralization by allowing Ottawa to foster "common standards" through a social charter, which would be less exacting than, say, the Canada Health Act.

Ontario is itself divided on how far to go. Big corporations on Bay Street with heavy investments in Quebec want to avoid a break-up at all costs. Their natural sympathy for deregulation and decentralization coincides with Quebec's constitutional ambitions, making them convenient allies. But labour wants to maintain a strong and active central government capable of intervening in social and economic areas. Reconciling those conflicting agendas won't be easy, but Rae is well positioned to try. He has kept all his options open and so far has antagonized no one.

Indeed, Rae has managed to preserve his reputation as a constitutional innocent. It's almost forgotten that he played a supporting role in Ontario's earlier endorsement of the Meech Lake Accord, that he defended it vigorously within the NDP and that he worked the corridors during the final negotiations in June 1990. "We came this close to getting Meech," he says, gesturing with his thumb and index finger an inch apart. "I have a hard time with the argument that says, 'Well, we didn't get Meech, so now it's the world.'" Meech may be behind him, but Rae hasn't renounced it. With his fluent French and his early endorsement of Quebec's distinct society, his constitutional bona fides are unquestioned in that province. And he is ready to resume his efforts. "Let's pick it up and run with it again, let's do it again." But can he get everyone on board?

The Atlantic provinces have long depended on federal equalization payments or unemployment insurance benefits to compensate for regional economic disparities. Consequently they have long defended the need for a strong central government with the fiscal capacity to keep the cash coming in. But the region's financial needs and geographic imperatives can't be viewed in isolation. Unlike tough-talking westerners who can reflect on the Quebec question from a comfortable distance, people in the Atlantic provinces view their imposing neighbour as a lifeline to the rest of Canada. If it helps keep the country together — and their own links intact — the committed centralists of the East Coast would be willing to decentralize Canada.

New Brunswick premier Frank McKenna, who led the charge against the Meech Lake Accord, is now leading the crusade for decentralization. "One thing that has become obvious to me in three years in government that was never obvious to me before is that the closer a service is to the recipients, the more effective and the least expensive it is," he says. "Provincial governments should have more responsibility over service delivery. The government of Canada would have to have a different role, perhaps a role involved in defining standards or the objectives of programs."

His views are shared by Nova Scotia premier Don Cameron. Even Newfoundland's Clyde Wells, the arch-centralist of the Meech Lake negotiations, has softened his hard-line views: "There may well be some decentralization that's acceptable or appropriate, or some concession that we can make." Wells would concede to Quebec the right to run its own employment programs, which he views as a provincial responsibility under the Constitution. Indeed, he has some demands of his own, such as a greater say for Newfoundland in fisheries management. "It may well be that some decentralization of legislative power is desirable, and I don't fight against it on principle. What I argue against on principle is, don't go so far as to make it impossible for the national government to discharge its responsibilities." Are Clyde Wells and Robert Bourassa really that far apart?

For all their differences, there are some common themes among the provinces. The trouble is that not all provinces are agreed on all points. B.C. and Quebec are united in wanting to take over more powers from Ottawa, which they believe has no business meddling in provincial programs. The three Prairie provinces have had enough of decentralization and are determined to stand up to Quebec. The East Coast fears being cut off by Quebec and so is willing to reconsider its traditional allegiance to strong central governments. Ontario is staking out the middle ground.

Most premiers want to reduce duplication and waste by taking over the delivery of government services in areas of shared or overlapping jurisdiction. A classic example is workforce retraining, where both federal and provincial governments offer a confusing welter of competing programs. The Atlantic and Prairie provinces, along with Ontario, want the federal government to bow out of the delivery of most programs. But they don't want it to butt out entirely: Ottawa should maintain and even expand its national standards to ensure reasonably comparable services across Canada. According to this view, federal oversight provides essential checks and balances to protect citizens' rights, while avoiding duplication in delivery of services. Ideally, it leads to fair and efficient federalism.

But critics in Quebec and B.C. argue that national standards are intrusive and unwieldy and reduce provincial flexibility to cut costs at a time of declining funding. They argue that national standards are also patronizing, because they presume that helpless voters need the Ottawa bureaucracy, not the provincial ballot box, to redress inequities. If the provinces could raise and spend their own money without Ottawa acting as a middleman, they reason, democratic accountability could be improved.

Even among strong federalists, there is little agreement on what programs or powers should be subject to national standards:

• New Brunswick's Frank McKenna, for example, believes medicare is a model for national standards in workforce retraining, the environment and interprovincial trade. He also wants "a national vision on education."

• Ontario's Bob Rae claims "a degree of sovereignty over education" and is sceptical about new national standards. "Adding another layer of government to something like education — I don't really think that's going to help very much."

• Manitoba's Gary Filmon supports national education

standards, saying, "I don't think you can have a patchwork quilt of standards for delivery of public school education."

• Newfoundland's Clyde Wells says education would be "too sensitive" to come under the ambit of national standards set by Ottawa. He is similarly sceptical of federal authority over employment training.

• Alberta's deputy premier, Jim Horsman, believes Ottawa should oversee workforce retraining. "If you're going to have manpower mobility, your standards have to be similar."

For all their differences, the premiers are united on one key principle: no single province can claim special powers unavailable to the others, with the possible exception of Quebec's language and culture needs. For economic powers, the Charter of Rights or anything else, there can be no special status, no "asymmetrical federalism."

To get around these apparent constitutional contradictions, many regional politicians now advocate a flexible federalism that would allow individual provinces to tailor programs or powers to their differing needs and abilities. But instead of entrenching provincial inequality in the Constitution, the practical solution would be unofficial "asymmetrical arrangements."

In practice, provinces would work out separate administrative deals directly with Ottawa, rather than entrenching any transfer of powers in the Constitution. The differences would be *de facto*, not *de jure*. If the agreements weren't carved in constitutional stone, both sides might be more willing to experiment, making arriving at a deal that much easier. It would also preclude "special status" for any one province. Instead, all provinces would remain equal in status and entitlement, but different in the powers they chose to exercise.

For example, Quebec and B.C. might opt for sole control of their own immigration and medicare programs, while the Atlantic provinces could choose to let Ottawa retain control. In this way, weaker provinces could continue to rely on the federal government for basic services, while more financially secure provinces — such as B.C., Quebec, Alberta and possibly Ontario — could do their own thing. The danger, however, is that an emasculated Ottawa would lose much of its fiscal clout, eroding its ability to disburse equalization payments to needy "have-not" provinces.

New Brunswick's McKenna is a big believer in assymetry. "We shouldn't be talking about special powers, we should be talking about different powers," he says. He uses the example of a student's high school curriculum to illustrate his point. Provinces, like students, would have to participate in certain core programs, such as health care or basic rights. Everything else — from employment to immigration — would be offered as optional electives.

There is an alternative formula for bridging the differences: it would reconfigure not just the traditional division of powers, but the way those powers are divvied up. Instead of the traditional "watertight compartments" that divided federal and provincial jurisdictions at the time of Confederation, governments could work out "complementary jurisdictions." Overlap would be no longer treated as a scourge to be stamped out, but recognized as an inevitable by-product of a complex world where co-existence and co-operation are facts of life. The environment, for example, would be subdivided into local waste management, under provincial control, and transboundary water or air pollution, which could come under federal authority.

But many politicians remain sceptical about the ultimate usefulness of all these alternative approaches, formulated by the provinces over three decades of constitutional wrangling. The division of powers is an abstract subject, of interest to provincial premiers and federal bureaucrats, but remote from the daily lives of most Canadians. In the final analysis, they doubt that constitutional tinkering will achieve very much. What matters most to people is symbolism — bilingualism, medicare, the Charter of Rights, nationalism and regional alienation. Those are the real passions Canadians have in common, even when they strongly disagree. The provinces, too, are as divided on symbolism as they are on substance.

On a more speculative note, the conflicting provincial demands may yet make Canadians nostalgic for strong central leadership to restore some semblance of constitutional coherence. Indeed, as the myth of regional solidarity continues to crumble, national unity may slowly take root.

"What do the regions want of Canada?" The question yields a constitutional cacophony, but some harmony may yet emerge if Canadians come to terms with the next question: "What does Canada want?" Or, more precisely, "What does Canada want of its regions?" The country may ultimately decide that, above all, it wants to stay together — with its national standards, and national fabric, essentially intact. But that is at best, an intuitive — and perhaps recklessly optimistic — guess.

Aboriginal Issues and the New Political Map of Canada

Tony Hall

Tony Hall teaches in the department of Native American Studies at the University of Lethbridge and is president of the Canadian Association in Support of Native Peoples.

Masked Mohawk warrior locked in steely gaze with iron-faced Canadian soldier. The shocking TV images out of Oka and Kahnawake blazed nightly into the bewildered eyes of a disbelieving audience. We had clearly passed the point of departure into a dangerous future of uncertain nationhood. Incredibly, the aroused passions were by and large contained. Discipline and restraint overcame frustration and rage during the bizarre Indian summer of 1990.

The reaction of native people throughout Canada to the confrontation was primarily characterized by the peacefulness of protest demonstrations. Although isolated acts of destruction did take place, the prevailing thrust of the activism across Canada had more in common with the tactics of Gandhi or Martin Luther King than with those of Che Guevara. For the time being at least, the Canadian preference for moderation withstood even the stupendous failures of leadership at the highest level, which daily compounded the danger of confrontation.

Perhaps the most marked exceptions to the prevailing restraint turned up in the non-Indian population. As Mohawk elders, women and children left their besieged reserve of Kahnawake, dozens of residents of Chateauguay and Lasalle savagely threw stones at the escaping vehicles in full view of passive provincial police officers.

Another chilling spectacle unfolded a few days later in Provost, Alberta. Hooded Klansmen and swastika-bearing white supremacists openly celebrated their racist creed. They burned crosses, gleefully fired their weapons and shouted their bigoted slogans in full view of the TV cameras.

Although the rock throwing in Quebec and the white supremacist demonstrations in Alberta mark political extremes, it is difficult to see these incidents as totally unconnected to more broadly based political movements. Alberta and Quebec, the two bastions of the Mulroney mandate, have more and more become political mirror images. Both are home to the forces of militant unilingualism. Both are host to powerful political constituencies who fervently believe that the federal authority in Ottawa is heavily oppressive.

The Reform Party and the Bloc Québécois have become primary beneficiaries of this growing wave of anti-Ottawa zeal. While stressing the need for greater regional autonomy, the adherents of both movements often show corresponding impatience with the special needs of racial and linguistic minorities. Both movements are providing a political home for the bigotry and xenophobia that have never been absent from the spectrum of political belief in this country.

It was especially interesting, therefore, to watch the reaction of the leadership of the Reform Party and the Bloc Québécois to the most provocative displays of race hatred that marked the dangerous summer of 1990. Rather than distancing themselves from the lunatic fringes of the movements they represent, the leading proponents of western alienation and Quebec sovereignty avoided clear condemnation of the ugly spectacles. Unfortunately, they were not alone in their timid response. The affirmations of aboriginal people stand in stark contrast to many of the political options advocated by the Reform Party, the Bloc Québécois and the host of other interests that have associated themselves with the drive for greater regional self-determination.

Registered Indians and Inuit have historically been placed outside the legal structures of Canadian citizenship. They have never been invited to join in the exercise of Canadian self-determination as constituent members of the federation.

Their reserves have been governed by an Indian Act not of their own making and by successive ministers of Indian affairs not of their own choosing. Today's politics of aboriginality are therefore the politics of inclusion. Will the governments of aboriginal people be acknowledged as having their own distinct basis of jurisdiction within the framework of Canadian federalism? If so, what will be the meeting points between the structures of aboriginal democracy and the major forums of Canadian self-government? In meeting questions such as these, non-natives in Canada will be facing the invigorating challenge of bringing their own political institutions more in line with structures of decision making whose deepest origins lie not in Europe but uniquely here.

The politics of aboriginality stand to enhance the politics of federalism just as these politics stand opposed to the excesses of provincialism. Since the earliest days of North American colonization, the interests of aboriginal people have been more aligned with the interests of the central government than with those of the state or provinces. In the United States in the nineteenth century, for instance, Georgia's assertion of states' rights forced Cherokee relocation as the land was opened for cotton. The controversy surrounding this most renowned instance of Indian dispossession resulted in the judicial finding that Indian tribes constitute domestic dependent nations whose relationship with the United States runs exclusively through the federal government.

Similarly in Canada the provincial governments, jealous of their claim to exclusive jurisdiction over natural resources, have historically been at the cutting edge of Indian dispossession. With this pattern in mind, the British imperial authorities specifically charged the federal government with the constitutional duty to protect the aboriginal interest in Canada. The record of federal authorities as protectors of aboriginal people has been far from satisfactory. The defence of aboriginal interests has lacked the political advantage that federal politicians can sometimes acquire by pandering to provincial authorities. The patriation deal first proposed in November of 1981, when Pierre Trudeau initially agreed to the provincial demand that aboriginal and treaty rights be cut from the text of the new Constitution, neatly exemplifies the problem. The pattern was repeated in 1987 with the formulation of the Meech Lake Accord. With sublime indifference to his special fiduciary obligations to aboriginal people, Brian Mulroney happily swapped away aboriginal interests to the ten premiers in the hopes of gaining a huge constitutional score.

By now assuming its responsibility to defend the land, resources and other interests of aboriginal people against provincial encroachment, the federal government would be acting consistently with a broader duty to safeguard the rights of various minorities against the electoral force of dominant groups in Canada's regions. From the legalized oppression of Canadians of Oriental background in British Columbia to the effort of the government of Quebec to quash the Jehovah's Witnesses, this country's history shows ample evidence that there is sometimes a need for the federal government to intervene in provincial affairs as a champion of human rights.

If the federal authority continues to fail to fulfil its obligations to uphold the constitutionally entrenched provision of aboriginal and treaty rights, chaos will almost certainly result. Inevitably, native groups will do what they must to defend their dwindling resources. And just as inevitably they will meet the resistance of police. A dangerous cycle of violence will be set in motion.

The events of the summer of 1990 should have sent warning signals that this destructive process, which serves nobody's interests, is already well developed. The largest part of the responsibility for the break-down of Canada's civil order lies with the leaders of the federal government because it contains the major levers of authority to establish a basis for more harmonious relations between native people and non-natives.

By moving to affirm the federal power more assertively on behalf of the human rights of aboriginal people — by affirming the federal prerogative even to the point of directly countering provincial claims to aboriginal lands and resources — the federal leadership would introduce rejuvenating energies of pluralism and tolerance into the tired blood of Canadian federalism. The government would be sending an important signal of strengthened federal will to act across a wider front against the local oppression of various kinds of minorities.

Although the federal government has a special role to play as a defender of aboriginal lands, this approach alone is obviously insufficient to meet many of the most pressing needs of aboriginal communities. Obviously, aboriginal problems and aspirations must be met increasingly on aboriginal terms. Significant structural changes are required to reorient a complex of laws and institutions that have deprived aboriginal people of primary jurisdiction over their own lives.

With increased elasticity, Canadian federalism could become an instrument well suited to the expanded exercise of aboriginal jurisdiction. The historic burden of this system of government has been to smooth relations between federal and provincial authorities who each claim sovereignty within their respective fields of legislative responsibility. Inevitably clashes occur between the two levels of government. The integrity of the Canadian state has depended largely on the ability of the judiciary to act as an arbitrator in jurisdictional disputes or on the ability of federal and provincial officials to compromise in the sharing of power. This tradition of compromise in the allocation of power need only be expanded now to include an enhanced role for aboriginal governments.

Hence, it is no longer sufficient to envisage federal-provincial relations as the sole axis of governmental authority in Canadian federalism. Aboriginal-federal relations constitute the hidden axis of our federal system. Aboriginal-federal relations in Canada have deep roots in the organic development of this country's constitution. The most honourable strand of development in this constitutional growth finds expression in the Royal Proclamation of 1763 and in the stream of Indian treaties that flow from the Crown's historic recognition of the human rights of aboriginal people. When existing aboriginal and treaty rights were affirmed in the Constitution Act of 1982, a link of continuity was theoretically declared, connecting the new Canada to the long tradition of Crown–Indian relations that have been so important in establishing this country's geopolitical foundations.

By embracing Indian treaties as living agreements, Canadians will reclaim an important dimension of this country's constitutional heritage. They will be embracing the single phase of national development that stands opposed to the notion that this country was built on the theft and pillage of other people's resources. The key is to move beyond a view of treaties as quaint artifacts gathering dust in the archives. Treaties are solemn agreements that establish a basis of relations between self-determining peoples for as long as the grass grows, as long as the sun shines and as long as the water flows.

The comprehensive land claims process in Canada marks the modern-day continuation of the constitutional tradition of making treaties with aboriginal groups. That process is under way in those parts of the country where treaties have never been executed, that is, in most of British Columbia, the Northwest Territories, Yukon, Quebec and Labrador. While aboriginal groups by and large see the process as an opportunity to confirm their right to the enjoyment of various attributes of their ancestral territories, the federal government's objective in the bargaining is to obtain aboriginal sanction for the outright extinguishment of aboriginal rights to land and resources.

The federal government's insistence on extinguishment was one of the major factors in the break-down of the Dene–Métis land claims negotiations in the western Arctic. Indeed, the very idea of extinguishment speaks of the underlying assumptions that still inform many facets of Canadian aboriginal policy. Official expectation has long been that aboriginal groups will eventually disappear; that their existence will terminate. The extinguishment of the rights of any group carries ghastly connotations as we enter the final years of a century that has been no stranger to genocide.

Only by abandoning the legal and philosophical arguments associated with the extinguishment of aboriginal rights can Canada gain the stature of mature nationhood. By renouncing these genocidal principles once and for all, Canada stands to draw renewed meaning from an essential element of this land's history — a history that once held out the promise to aboriginal communities that their place here was to be secure in perpetuity.

Appreciation of this land's true character will be elusive as long as the blinders of ethnocentrism continue to block out understanding of this country's ancient aboriginal history. Similarly, an emphasis on more recent aboriginal history would help attune Canadians to the devastation wrought by the oppressive regime of the federal Indian Act, the church-run Indian boarding schools, the provincially controlled child welfare agencies and the jails where hugely disproportionate numbers of aboriginal people languish. What are the destructive forces driving high rates of aboriginal suicide, the drug and alcohol abuse, the family violence? Without the insights that can come only from a better understanding of history, the deep social malaise in aboriginal societies is inexplicable and its cure remote.

Increasing our awareness of aboriginal history would advance our understanding of the ecological patterns of life that have long connected humanity to this land's diverse geography. From the buffalo-hunting peoples of the prairies to the Iroquoian agriculturalists of the Great Lakes area south of the Laurentian Shield, the aboriginal map of Canada reveals a vast mosaic of distinct societies, each intimately related to the unique character of specific regions. Superimposed on this age-old map are the political jurisdictions surveyed onto the land by European newcomers. These political outlines have changed dramatically since Confederation, as new territories have been annexed, as colonies have become new provinces, as new provinces have been carved from the Northwest Territories and as existing provinces have been expanded. By and large, the new lines have been drawn on the map with little regard for the deeper natural contours of human and physical geography.

Today the political map of the Northwest Territories, the federally controlled part of the country situated at the farthest horizon of many Canadians' sense of national destiny, is beginning to reflect aboriginal outlines. The Dene Indians in the western Arctic are working towards the creation of Denendeh, while the Inuit in the treeless eastern Arctic are seeking recognition of Nunavut. Denendeh and Nunavut would each be subject to the authority of strong local governments with firm control over land and resources. Although both these governments would be democratic, the form of democracy practised would be more reflective of aboriginal traditions of decision making. Similarly, the Dene languages would have official status in Denendeh, and Inuktitut would have comparable status in Nunavut.

But the drive to elaborate the constitutional outlines of Denendeh and Nunavut remains mired in the profound inadequacies of the federal government's aboriginal policies. In particular, the federal government's unwillingness to attach consideration of aboriginal self-government to the negotiation of comprehensive land claims creates significant obstacles to the elaboration of political institutions genuinely indigenous to the North.

Native people living in the northern portions of Canada's provinces face the real predicament of political and economic marginalization. Although they often constitute a large percentage or even a majority of the permanent settlers in their own regions, the political power of these aboriginal constituencies is dwarfed by the electoral and economic clout of the south. The resulting disenfranchisement of so many northern native people adds weight to the arguments in favour of further modification of the political map of Canada.

The apparent disarray and sense of powerlessness that permeate so many northern native communities constitute a particularly severe indictment of this northern country. The difficulties faced by aboriginal groups in the North are often compounded by the frequent desecration of their natural food supplies by industry and ecologically disastrous mega-projects. It is a ruinous proposition to advance northern development without the adjustment of political institutions to enable those indigenous people with the deepest understanding of northern environments to play a major role in deciding how to use their ancestral lands.

To embrace the aboriginal dimension of Canada's identity, then, would be to move towards reaffirmation of the country's northern destiny. The Inuit have played an especially significant role in helping to orient the government of Canada towards its northern responsibilities. Not only have the Inuit carried the flag of Canadian sovereignty in the high Arctic, but they have been instrumental in opening channels of communication with other polar nations. The primary vehicle of this Arctic collaboration is the Inuit Circumpolar Conference, an organization that draws together Inuit people from Canada, Alaska, Greenland and the Soviet Union. The benefits brought to Canada by the ICC in enhanced relations with our northern neighbours represent but a mere sample of the international advantages that could be achieved by making this country the site of more innovative and more outward-looking aboriginal policies.

The centrality of aboriginal issues in questions concerning the destiny of Canada's North, however, should not be allowed to obscure the broader dimensions of the picture. Many of the largest concentrations of aboriginal people live in southern regions of the provinces. Among the most heavily populated aboriginal communities in the country, for instance, are the Blood Reserve of Southern Alberta, the Walpole Island Reserve near Windsor, the Six Nations Reserve near Hamilton and Akwesasne and Kahnawake on the St. Lawrence River. In spite of the numerical strength of aboriginal groups in the south, they nevertheless tend to be vastly outnumbered by the larger non-native populations around them. As with their northern brethren, their political influence in their home regions tends to be negligible. Native people in the south also face a more pressing crush of outside influences in their effort to maintain their cultural identity.

A reflection of the federal government's failure to address the specific needs of aboriginal people in the south is the lack of any coherent broadcasting policy for this important constituency. In the North, aboriginal people face less severe obstacles. Even as the Canadian Broadcasting Corporation absorbs massive cut-backs, a narrow band of CBC's Northern Services remains the domain of aboriginal broadcasters and their audiences. As the airwaves increasingly become a lifeline for the survival of distinct languages and for the survival of distinct political communities, this broadcasting vacuum in the south mutes important voices that should be provided a forum.

The development of a well-conceived system of aboriginal broadcasting could be a major tool in the elaboration of aboriginal self-government. Like aboriginal self-government, such a system requires local, regional and cross-Canada capabilities. The development of a cross-Canada capacity for First Nations broadcasting holds especially important promise. Without such a capacity, it is difficult for aboriginal groups in different parts of the country to become acquainted with one another's culture. Without such a capacity, it is difficult for democratic discourse on the major issues confronting aboriginal societies to move beyond the local level. If aboriginal societies are to be treated as constituencies who have political personalities that are regional and in some instances even cross-Canadian in scope, it is vital that they have access to the broadcasting tools they need. Furthermore, the broadening and strengthening of aboriginal broadcasting would open new channels of understanding for non-aboriginal Canadians who want to learn more about native societies.

So far, thinking about aboriginal government and aboriginal jurisdiction has been too closely linked to thinking about the legal status of Indian reserves. It was not many years ago that the freedom of registered Indians to travel away from their reserves was often severely restricted by a strict system of passes given or withheld by local Indian agents. Today there are a host of other cultural, economic or purely personal factors that hold the largest part of the Indian population to their homes on reserves. These reserves will always be of key strategic importance as primary centres of Indian life — as primary locales where the links of continuity are maintained between the past and present of distinct aboriginal societies.

Larger numbers of Indians, however, are now spending extended periods in towns or cities. Consequently many centres including Regina, Winnipeg,

Toronto, Edmonton and Vancouver have aboriginal populations far bigger than the populations of the largest reserves. The lure of universities and colleges is becoming especially powerful in pulling native people to urban centres. In the aboriginal student protest of 1989, this important new constituency flexed its new-found political muscle. A thirty-day fast started by native students in Thunder Bay to protest federal capping of funds for Indian post-secondary education mushroomed into a nationwide movement.

The tendency to associate Indian identity too closely with the limited sphere of Indian reserves is nicely illustrated by the present approach to Indian taxation. While the federal and provincial governments in Canada still begrudgingly acknowledge the principle that registered Indians are exempt from many forms of taxation, the effort is to limit application of the principle to Indian reserves. For instance, registered Indians in Ontario are charged sales tax on items they purchase unless these items are to be consumed on Indian reserves. The intent of the federal government is that Indians must pay the GST like everyone else except when purchasing goods and services on Indian reserves. Similarly, Indians pay income tax on income earned outside the reserve.

This approach clearly expresses a view on the part of both levels of government that aboriginal and treaty rights can be geographically limited within the narrow domain of Indian reserves. If the aboriginal dimension of this country's identity is to find forthright expression in the new political map of Canada, there will have to be some form of mobility rights related to the responsibilities of aboriginal citizenship.

Designating seats in the federal parliament for representatives of distinct aboriginal constituencies would be one of the ways of addressing the issue. The reform would involve the superimposition of large aboriginal ridings on top of the regular electoral map of Canada. In federal elections, every native voter would have the option of using his or her franchise to choose a parliamentarian who represents some sort of regionally based aboriginal constituency. The number of aboriginal ridings would be calculated according to the regular Canadian formula of representation by population. Native people would not be voting twice, nor would they be getting a mathematically larger say than any other voter in the selection of parliamentarians. But they would henceforth be acknowledged not only as individuals but also as members of larger aboriginal collectivities with distinct political personalities.

Entrenchment of permanent aboriginal seats in Parliament would signify acknowledgement of aboriginality as a feature of Canada's identity. Furthermore, this reform would symbolically acknowledge that there is a distinct layer of aboriginal jurisdiction covering the whole country. No longer would Indian reserves be treated as almost the exclusive preserve of Indian identity and Indian decision making.

Parliamentarians representing aboriginal constituencies would not be leaders of aboriginal governments. The task of choosing those leaders must take place within an institutional framework of aboriginal people's own making. But parliamentarians representing federal aboriginal ridings would be well placed to act as intermediaries who could help smooth the relationship between aboriginal governments and the federal government. Certainly they would be in a better position to perform that function than the individual who presently holds that responsibility, the minister of Indian affairs.

The choice, then, is clear. Old patterns can be perpetuated that relegate aboriginality to a marginal and diminishing feature of Canada's emerging identity. Or we can embrace aboriginality as a fundamental characteristic of Canada.

There can be no question that the future status of Quebec is an issue of underlying importance in determining how the new political map of Canada will be drawn. Major portions of Quebec remain uncovered by Indian treaties. Many aboriginal groups, who remain the majority population in huge areas of the province, have never entered into any formal land agreements with a non-aboriginal sovereign. Moreover, the northern sections of the province are not historically well connected to New France or the colony of Quebec as shaped by the Quebec Act of 1774. Rather the northern portions of the province draw more heavily on the legal and cultural heritage of the Hudson's Bay Company, a trading monopoly that sold its interest in Indian lands to the Dominion of Canada in 1870. The Dominion government, in turn, transferred part of these lands with conditions to the province of Quebec in two transactions that took place in 1898 and 1912. A concrete legacy of this history is that native people in northern Quebec more frequently speak English than French as their primary non-aboriginal language. The same is true of the Mohawks in the south.

Aboriginal issues will have a significant bearing on the geopolitical future of Quebec. Premier Robert Bourassa can hardly be unaware of this reality. He began his massive James Bay installation in the early 1970s with the assumption that he could bulldoze aside any aboriginal resistance to the project. Instead, a lower court affirmed the aboriginal rights of the indigenous people of eastern James Bay, a decision that forced the Bourassa government into negotiations with the Cree and Inuit holders of unceded aboriginal title. An agreement was first reached in 1975. Bourassa received an even more intense lesson in native studies fifteen years later, when Elijah Harper was instrumental in killing the Meech Lake Accord.

It is difficult to avoid the suspicion that the original attack of the Sûreté du Québec against the Oka Mohawks was in some way connected to the Meech Lake débâcle. While the municipality's right to expand a golf course was the immediate issue, the right of the province to push ahead with the immense waterworks of James Bay II was hanging in the balance. The Sûréte's attack may have contained a warning to all native people throughout the province that they would not be permitted henceforth to stand in the way of the drive by the Québécois for greater autonomy and independence. The resulting friction between the movement for aboriginal self-determination and the movement for greater Québécois self-determination has important strategic implications for the shape of the new political map of Canada.

There has been very little formal acknowledgement in Quebec of the aboriginal role in the demise of the Meech Lake Accord. The depth and substance of the aboriginal critique of the first ministers' constitutional initiative tends simply to be overlooked or dismissed out of hand as misguided. And there has been even less inclination to ponder the connections between the aboriginal protests of 1990 and the constitutional flaws that contributed to the social and political context for aboriginal discontent. The oversight is not surprising. Such contemplation might well diminish the force and utility of a simpler argument that advances the cause of an independent Quebec. As repeated again and again before the Bélanger–Campeau commission, the death of the accord was said to represent the rejection by English Canada of the province's most moderate constitutional demands.

Quebec nationalists would be well advised to heed the lessons Premier Robert Bourassa should by now have learned. No matter how concerted the conspiracy to keep them submerged, aboriginal issues have a way of bobbing to the surface, sometimes at the most awkward moments. Therefore the effort to relegate aboriginal issues to the margins of the debate about the constitutional future of Quebec is as danger-prone as the earlier decision to exclude any aboriginal representation from the closed circle of negotiations at Meech Lake. Similarly, the tacit agreement among most Québécois nationalists to ignore the significance of the aboriginal role in the demise of Meech Lake is to perpetrate a misrepresentation that damages the credibility of the movement for an independent Quebec.

If the government of the province of Quebec is to justify a move towards independence on the basis of the results of a referendum, surely aboriginal societies within the province of Quebec cannot be denied access to the same tool of self-determination. Among the choices aboriginal groups may wish to consider are greater autonomy with primary links to the government of Quebec, greater autonomy with primary links to the federal government or sovereignty-association within a rearranged Canadian federation. Aboriginal groups in those parts of the province that were attached to Quebec in 1898 and 1912 may have an especially difficult series of decisions to make. Because their lands were once claimed by the Dominion government, these territories may well become the focus of heated jurisdictional contention between the governments of Quebec and Canada.

If the political map of Canada is to be readjusted to conform more adequately to the wishes of the people of Quebec, it is vital that aboriginal groups in the province not be treated as mere pawns to be passed back and forth in the negotiations. Not only do aboriginal people have the basic human right to represent their own interests with their own voices in any change to Confederation, they also can assert a fundamental right to assert political will from their own unique basis of inherent aboriginal jurisdiction. Only thus will aboriginal representatives be in a position to bring the full power of their insights to an enlightened redrawing of the political map of Canada.

Nevertheless, in Quebec as elsewhere in Canada, Section 91 of the British North America Act remains as a major shield for the protection of aboriginal interests against the acquisitive grasp of provincial interests. The section states that "Indians and Lands reserved for the Indians" lie within the legislative domain of the federal parliament. Given that aboriginal title remains uncompromised over most of Quebec, Section 91 affords the federal authority considerable latitude to affirm the continuing force of Canada's territorial jurisdiction throughout the province. What is lacking, however, is the political will to assert this federal jurisdiction in a constructive fashion. The consolidation of a new federal regime dedicated to a more flexible and humane federalism would have to fill this vacuum.

Unprecedented tensions are developing in this country as many interests and peoples compete to control the agenda of government decision making. Although aboriginal people have a major stake in this struggle, they have few means to defend their rapidly dwindling interests. When peoples have for so long been denied access to the tools of power, self-dignity demands that they somehow find a means to break the cycle of their op-pression. The events of the summer of 1990 suggest an important threshold of this process has already been reached.

Rather than perceiving aboriginal assertiveness as a threat to Canadian federalism, we can see the aboriginal will to survive as informing and illuminating the struggle for Canadian self-determination. Wider appreciation of the continuing dynamic force of aboriginality could be an essential element in awakening our imaginations to the range of creative options before us in drawing the new political map of Canada.

The Northern Boundary of Quebec: The James Bay Crees As Self-Governing Canadians

Bruce W. Hodgins

Bruce Hodgins teaches history at Trent University and has written extensively on land claims and other native issues.

The people and the lands of far northern Quebec, of the watersheds of James, Hudson and Ungava bays, must not be abandoned to the will of a narrow majority dominated by Quebec's southern heartland. What is sauce for the goose is sauce for the gander. The predominantly Cree and Inuit peoples of what is now far northern Quebec, people with clearly identifiable "distinct societies," have more right to opt effectively to stay in Canada — with significant self-determination — than a francophone majority has the right in southern Quebec to secede unilaterally from the Canadian federation against the wishes of a large provincial minority made up of anglophones, francophones, Mohawks, Italian Canadians and others.

For Canada to adopt any other position would be to betray our heritage and our growing recommitment towards aboriginal self-determination. It would also condone the world ecological disaster implicit in the hydro project called James Bay II.

Within the bounds of present-day Canada, the French settlement colony of the 1750s, that is, just before the Conquest, was very small, restricted primarily to the seigneurial lands of the St. Lawrence and the lower Ottawa. The French-dominated commercial empire was huge, but it existed primarily on North American Indian lands stretching in a great arch from Gaspé to Louisiana. Later, the Lower Canada of 1791, though larger, did not extend north of the Arctic–St. Lawrence divide. In 1867, the province of Quebec, like that of Ontario, was large but similarly constrained. At least since 1713, the Hudson Bay–Ungava tracts were, according to British and international law, part of Rupert's Land. Until 1870 they were Indian (and Inuit) lands with Hudson's Bay Company economic and political ascendancy under ultimate British sovereignty. They clearly were not part of Canada. In that year, they came under Canadian federal jurisdiction as part of the very large Northwest Territories.

In 1898 the Dominion Parliament unilaterally (and unwisely, I would argue) transferred to Quebec the jurisdiction over those lands between the divide and the Eastmain River. In 1912 the Conservative government of Robert Borden foolishly transferred to Quebec the lands from the Eastmain north to Hudson Straits (extending well above the sixtieth parallel). But the actual lands themselves remained largely "Indian lands" under the Royal Proclamation of 1763. When Crees converted to Christianity, they joined the anglophone Anglicans. Communications remained sea-borne and English. In 1939, with Quebec approval, the courts declared the local Inuit to be like Indians under the BNA Act; they and their aboriginal lands were declared to be federal responsibilities. Indeed, Quebec showed very little interest in James Bay and its people until the Quiet Revolution of the 1960s. Certainly Quebec has no right to take these northern lands out of Canada, against the wishes of the local people.

The current crisis of Confederation is said to involve many issues. They include an inefficient and confusing federalism with overlapping jurisdictions argument about the authority to oversee economic policy; the unsatisfactory position of aboriginal people; the relative de-industrialization of Ontario; the financial crisis in our still incomplete universal social, medical and educational programs; the regional imbalance of power and benefit within our federalism; and the way to reconcile Quebec nationalism with the continued viable existence of the country. There is also, undoubtedly, the serious problem related to popular disillusionment with federal political leadership.

In my judgement, the most serious intrinsic ethical problem relates to the recalcitrance of our political leadership, federal and provincial (except very recently in Ontario), to deal self-governing aboriginal people into the federation as identifiable group members and as a separate order (or level) within our federalism. The deepest and most genuine biculturalism in Canada is not English and French, but Euro-Canadian and aboriginal-Canadian. Despite the determined survival of organic aboriginal forms of self-government, the weaker but resilient culture is still treated with condescension by the stronger one.

Oka and the events of the summer of 1990 brought the intrinsic issue of too long delayed aboriginal self-government face to face with the crisis related to the demand to transfer much more power to Quebec.

Premier Bourassa's Liberals, including the much-revered Claude Ryan, dreadfully mismanaged the Mohawk dispute, and a compliant Mulroney allowed the Canadian army to become entangled in an awful fiasco.

Today Hydro-Québec and Bourassa's fanatical determination to proceed with James Bay II in far northern Quebec–Ungava are a much graver threat to native survival than the planned golf course extension at Oka. The overwhelming majority of the Crees, and their sophisticated and brilliant leader, do not want that project. Most Inuit do not either, but they seem more prepared to accept a major cash and service settlement. Virtually all broad environmental groups in eastern Canada (including Quebec) and in New York and New England oppose the project.

James Bay II, by far the largest project of its kind in the world, could be both an ecological disaster and a severe social calamity. Proceeding with the project would violate the slow painful progress of recent years in environmental issues and in native affairs. The federal authorities, till perhaps very recently, seemed prepared to endorse the severing of environmental assessment of roads and services from that of dams and diversions. In light of evidence concerning sweetheart deals with energy-hungry aluminum companies, James Bay II might also be an economic mistake.

Nevertheless the project seems to be the foundation stone for Bourassa's grand plan for Quebec's massive development. This is hinterland politics with a vengeance. Within a Canada that has a clearly recognized external sovereign personality in the world community, it should be the local Crees and Inuit who decide on the project and presumably reject it.

Euro-Canadians have little reason to be proud of our governments' Indian policy, certainly not of that between

1885 and 1973, with its disturbing commitments to paternalistic assimilation verging on cultural genocide. But we have to agree with some historians that the pre-1755 French imperial policy towards First Nations, with its recognition of full aboriginal title to land and to extensive domestic sovereignty, was much better and more generous than the contemporary English and Anglo-American policies. Even Britain's Royal Proclamation of 1763 at least partially adopted the French position.

It is thus a pity that Quebec's recent policy towards its aboriginal people has been so increasingly negative. The Quebec thrust for something approaching separation from Canada endangers or should endanger its hold over James Bay and Ungava.

Although the debate on the boundary extension of 1898, which gave Quebec jurisdiction over lands between the St. Lawrence–Arctic divide and the Eastmain River, was extremely brief, in keeping with the short two-paragraph nature of the statute, the intent was very clear. It related to political equity between Quebec and Ontario, whose growth was aided by a Judicial Committee decision in 1884 and imperial legislation in 1889, which extended Ontario's boundaries north to the Albany River. Ontario clearly recognized, however begrudgingly and reluctantly, aboriginal title in the area acquired. Ontario officials participated with federal Crown officials in negotiations leading to Treaty 9 in 1905–06. Later, in "New Quebec," a lot of francophones settled in the southern portions of the Quebec extension, that is, in the Great Abitibi Clay Belt. Certainly in any future plebiscite, this Clay Belt area, now by usage clearly Québécois, would have to be calculated separately from the areas to the north, which are overwhelmingly dominated by the Crees. The Cree aboriginal title to their homeland was clearly recognized in 1973 during the controversies surrounding the early phases of James Bay I.

In 1912, with the huge extension northward to Ungava, about half a million square miles, the language and the nature of the debate were much clearer. This extension paralleled similar though smaller ones that year for Ontario and Manitoba. The federal statute clearly stated that Quebec had to "recognize the rights of the Indian inhabitants in the territory" and obtain land cessions in the same manner as Canada did and only with the approval of Canada. It also provided "that the trusteeship of the Indians in the said territory and the management of any lands now or heretofore reserved for their use, shall remain in the Government of Canada subject to the control of Parliament." In the debate over the bill, Maritime representatives showed grave concern that a very large part of the common patrimony was being transferred to Quebec. The prime minister noted, as Eugene Forsey reminded us just before his death, that the population of the "added territory, according to the census, was 1,262, including 663 Indians, and 543 Inuit, 46 'Half-breeds,' eight English and two Scots." Apparently there were no French-speaking Canadians in the entire land.

The federal government, with the participation of Ontario and Manitoba, dealt shortly thereafter with aboriginal land title, however inadequately. Quebec did not, on the spurious ground that treaties of land cession had not normally been the practice in old seigneurial southern Quebec. Ottawa acquiesced. Now, historian W.J. Eccles has given the tradition of the *ancien régime* a different and very powerful interpretation, one that emphasizes imperial France's general recognition of something close to First Nations autonomous sovereignty and full land rights, while noting the relative emptiness in the early seventeenth century of the former Iroquoian lands of most of the St. Lawrence lowlands. We know what problems have ensued from extending the seigneuries up the lower Ottawa Valley, by giving lands in 1717 to the Sulpicians that probably were Mohawk lands and perhaps Algonquin territory as well. Oka was the result.

Notwithstanding the failings of the tripartite James Bay Agreement of 1975–76 and Quebec and Canada's relatively stingy and bureaucratic way of trying to avoid several of its more ample and autonomous aspects, the agreement was built on the recognition of aboriginal land rights, modest self-government and support for maintaining the distinct society of the Crees. That agreement is now entrenched as a modern treaty under the 1982 Constitution.

The Crees argue that the agreement does not give Quebec the right to develop the Great Whale and other northern watersheds for James Bay II. Furthermore they argue that it does not give Quebec the right to proceed with the separate plan to harness thereafter the "NBR," that is, the Nottaway–Broadback–Rupert valleys south of James Bay I. But the Grand Council of the Crees, led by Grand Chief Matthew Coon-Come and Executive Director Bill Namagoose, have decided to focus their political action on the ecological damage that the huge dams and diversions would cause.

The Crees are not separatists. The Crees are unfulfilled Canadians. Recent Supreme Court decisions, especially *Sparrow* and *Sioui*, have emphasized the deep fiduciary responsibility of the Crown in the right of Canada to support aboriginal people. I trust that Canada will be equal to the challenge.

Events could take an even more ironic twist. Because of the bizarre and ineffectual response of the Mulroney government to aboriginal initiatives in James Bay and other instances, the Crees are recently appearing somewhat less than sanguine about their future in Canada. The PQ, in contrast to the Bourassa forces, is at least verbally showing more sympathy towards an internal federalist place for First Nations in an independent Quebec and appears almost ready to reconsider James Bay II. The constitutional views of the James Bay Crees, like those of the Mohawks, have not yet been absolutely fixed.

The fundamental issue remains. Quebec does not have the right — historic, legal, moral or "Canadian"— to take the James Bay–Ungava lands and people out of Canada, certainly not without the support of its people. Such action could happen only with English Canada's cowardly connivance.

The purpose of this collection of essays is presumably, however, to help save the country and to preserve a strong, federal Canada able to stress its east-west links and maintain the positive features of its genuine regionalism. It certainly would be best to do this with a vibrant Quebec society existing inside the union. If not, then we must have the will to survive with strength without Quebec. We must not acquiesce in the abandonment of those things that made the Canadian experiment, with its adaptable federalism, workable at home and envied abroad.

A strong unequivocal Canadian response to this northern and aboriginal issue would show clearly that Canada has a will to live and to flourish as a country with a vision. Canada outside Quebec must be strong and confident. The many French-speaking Canadians in Quebec who are not yet resolutely separatist must be able to see our strength, to see that we exist.

We will have to go over and around Bourassa. Quebec must not be ignored. Some modest asymmetrical federalism involving substantively and pragmatically defined items covering much of the Quebec thrust in Meech are clearly possible. But Quebec cannot have radical special status if coupled with continued "rep by pop" in the House of Commons and a major say in the operation of the potentially still strong Canadian central government. Quebec (and Ontario) will also have to accept an elected and effective Senate, one that gives much greater representation to the Prairies, to B.C., to the Atlantic provinces and to the complex North.

One way to achieve these goals is to emphasize the non-dualistic nature of the Canadian union, the fragility of Quebec's claims over the far North if it chooses to separate and the positive benefits of a Canada that is legally at least bilingual (with Ontario and Quebec as formally bilingual as New Brunswick now is). We must urge a Canada that shows deep concern over regional disparities and east-west trade and is committed to a social charter, as urged by Ontario premier Bob Rae, based on universal social programs.

If we believe in ourselves, as we have in the past, we can win. If we are rejected by Quebec, we should have a generous divorce, with continuing trade and contacts. We must not, however, accept such a divorce with the current boundaries of the province of Quebec. The Cree, Inuit and other people of the far North must have the right to remain Canadians in their own land.

Northern Identity: Barometer or Convector for National Unity?

Shelagh D. Grant

Shelagh Grant is the author of Sovereignty or Security: Government Policy in the Canadian North, 1936–1950. *She teaches history and Canadian studies at Trent University.*

During the first century of Confederation, many Canadians looked upon their North as a symbol of identity and destiny. Claiming to have originated from a notion that the nation's distinctiveness derived from its northern location, rigorous climate and settlement by northern races, the so-called "myth of the North" acquired a number of interpretations and adaptations to fit changing times. One variant involved a shared spiritual reverence for the northern landscape. Another conjured visions of great future wealth. Overall, the northern ethos offered a sense of national purpose and pride and became a recurrent theme in Canadian nationalist rhetoric.

Some sceptics considered the myth to be little more than a romantic illusion, a jingoist by-product of nation-building euphoria. Most Canadians, however, believed it had a unifying influence. Few seemed aware of its declining significance in recent years, and fewer, if any, expressed concern. Yet when considered in conjunction with the rise of regionalism and political discord, the declining significance of a northern identity appears linked with the downward spiral of national unity.

The impact of the northern myth on the Canadian psyche is intangible, yet it reflects common aspirations that once inspired loyalty, trust and optimism. When related to visions of a permanent or open frontier, it provided Canadians a promise of greater freedom and opportunity than the old world of their ancestors. In addition, the vast wilderness reaches of the Arctic were perceived as both virile and virginal, symbolizing vague, amorphous dreams, yet centring on a physical entity that exclusively belonged to Canada. As a consequence, concern for any potential threat to northern sovereignty was often obsessive and over-reactive.

The image of North was enhanced by our history, especially that of the fur trade, which tended to romanticize the *voyageurs* and the Hudson's Bay Company. Arctic history played a role as well. English Canadians were inspired by tales of the British Admiralty's search for the Northwest Passage; French Canadians likely identified more with Captain Bernier's expedition to claim sovereignty over the Arctic islands. Pre-contact history of the indigenous peoples who lived in harmony with their environment now gives even deeper meaning to our northern heritage. Although unquestionably derived from quite separate ethnocentric interpretations, the unifying bond of Canada's northern heritage stemmed more from a shared vision of landscape than from similar experience.

At the same time a quite different image of North evolved that promised tangible wealth through extraction of natural resources. This theme was expounded by developers, businessmen and politicians to justify public and private investment in hinterland development. The focus was on challenge and the future. This northern vision was unifying in the abstract, but disunifying when one region was perceived to benefit at the expense of others. Until the emergence of the environmental movement, little thought was given to the inherent contradictions in the two primary perceptions that combined in Canadians' interpretation of their northern identity: permanent wilderness versus resource development. As long as the North appeared limitless and unsuitable for large-scale settlement, the two perceptions could co-exist and even meld.

From a global perspective, Canada's northernness or *nordicité* created a unique identity in North America, a positive image of what Canadians were, as opposed to what they were not, when measured against their southern neighbour. Canada was the "North" of North America, as distinct from the "American" identity adopted by the United States.

Over the years, the North gradually receded and acquired relative distinctions such as near, mid and far. The lakes, rivers and mountains of the near North became much revered vacation lands, a respite from urban ills, shared and often envied by American visitors. The mid-North contained pocket frontiers of mining and lumbering towns. The high Arctic was the *ultima Thule* — a symbol of mystery and adventure. Overall, the expanse and beauty of the wilderness gave Canadians a feeling of intense pride in their country's landscape, a pride that was celebrated in art, music and literature.

Canada's northern identity also developed distinctive regional perspectives. Atlantic ports witnessed the arrival and departure of Arctic supply ships, patrol vessels, icebreakers and scientific expeditions, whereas on the Pacific coast, there was the added excitement of the big-game hunters and gold seekers heading to the Yukon. Some provinces attempted to create direct access to the

Arctic: Manitoba successfully with the construction of the Hudson Bay Railway, Ontario unsuccessfully with the Temiskaming and Northern Ontario Railway. Physical links encouraged images of mystery and adventure and gave even greater importance to the myth of promised wealth and destiny.

The Québécois, meanwhile, looked inward for identity, centred more on province, culture and agrarian settlement. Significantly, there was no attempt to create a land bridge to the Arctic, despite the projection of the Ungava peninsula thrusting towards the Archipelago. Roads and rails were only important to bring provincial resources south. For the most part, the Canadian Shield was looked upon as an obstacle, depriving the agriculturally minded Québécois of fertile lands.

Not until the 1970s and events surrounding the James Bay Project was it apparent that Premier Bourassa's interpretation of Quebec nationalism had acquired a distinct northern vision, one that emphasized conquest and exploitation, with little concern for the indigenous peoples, the protection of their lands or the rest of Canada. Similar attitudes emerged in the resource-rich provinces of British Columbia and Alberta, accompanied by a rise of western nationalism. Such "northern visions" were inspired more directly by provincial economic ambitions than by culture-based nationalism.

In English-speaking Canada the nation-building component of the northern ethos was still in its ascendancy during World War II, as evidenced by public reaction to the Alaska Highway. The initial optimism made headlines such as "War Unlocks Our Last Frontier ... Canada's Northern Opportunity" which appeared in *The Financial Post*. Other newspapers described "a new North" and the "birth of a new Empire." Lester B. Pearson wrote of "the unexplored frontier, luring the pathfinder into the unknown." Charles Camsell, as deputy minister of mines and resources, described "the lure of the North as something inherent in the human heart and soul." Significantly, there were no comparable headlines or oratory in Quebec.

Accompanying the euphoria was an outcry against a perceived threat to Canadian sovereignty. In response, the King government paid more than $123 million to gain clear title to American-built facilities in the North, thus forestalling any claim to post-war use or benefit. The dilemma of balancing sovereignty with security requirements arose again in 1946 during negotiations with the United States for a post-war joint defence agreement. Without a workforce or funds to participate fully in the proposed security arrangements, Ottawa compromised by agreeing in principle to American proposals, but with the proviso that each step be negotiated to include tacit recognition of Canadian sovereignty. Where possible, preparations were carried out under "civilian cover" to avoid public criticism, strict censorship was applied because of "political sensitivities," and provision for "Canadianization" was to take place as soon as possible. The precedent was thus set for all major joint defence agreements. Meanwhile, the federal government publicized its new northern development programs, thus diverting attention away from increasing military activities.

In the 1953 DEW Line negotiations, strict censorship was again requested to "avoid any embarrassment to the government." At the same time, the department responsible for northern affairs was renamed, expanded and given new leadership and a significantly larger budget. And while it was appropriate for John Diefenbaker as leader of the opposition to criticize alleged abuses of Arctic sovereignty, in 1957 he too followed the set pattern when elected to office. When the NORAD agreement was signed that year, the public was assured that sovereignty was intact, and the election campaign the next spring would promote a national development plan based on a "northern vision" and Canadianization.

To his credit, Diefenbaker attempted to accelerate Canadian take-over of American and joint-controlled operations but was faced with the same difficulties as his predecessors: lack of funds, trained workforce and technical equipment. Meanwhile a *de facto* loss of sovereignty was now more visible as tens of thousands of Americans took part in northern defence construction, air reconnaissance and military exercises. As reports gradually filtered south, the lustre of a truly Canadian North began to tarnish.

Once the "cover-up" policy had been introduced, it became politically impossible to expose the situation without incurring public criticism and embarrassment on the world scene. The extent of concealment was not required for reasons of national security; it was simple political expediency. The guise was inherited by succeeding governments. Eventually, however, the degree of American military presence and loss of Canadian control began to surface. A situation that would have been unconscionable in the 1940s was accepted reluctantly, but not without a sense of betrayal. Faced with the embarrassing reality that Canada could not defend its own territory, the northern vision began to lose its virility, the federal government its credibility.

Other problems clouded the romanticized image of the North as militarization began to affect the lives of the Inuit. Destitution, disease and social disorientation not only increased but became more visible. In spite of genuine efforts to provide adequate education and health services, the government could not keep pace. Isolation and censorship restrictions helped slow media exposure, but only in the short term. The once-virginal image of the North began to fade, almost without notice.

Conservative gains in Quebec in the 1958 election were attributed to Union Nationale support, but Diefenbaker's "northern vision" captured the imagination of English-speaking Canada. The vision was dramatized to promise "future wealth and national sovereignty" and "a new sense of national purpose and national identity." According to Alvin Hamilton, minister of northern affairs, "the North represents a new world to conquer... a great vault, holding in its recesses treasures to maintain and increase material living standards." Although coupled with Canadianization measures to control foreign investment and protect cultural interests, the major emphasis was clearly on resource development and material gain.

The Conservatives made a genuine effort to fulfil their promises. In the process, and perhaps unwittingly, the northern development program would benefit the resource-rich provincial economies to the disadvantage of the others. In addition to expanding transportation and communications within the Yukon and Northwest Territories, the government offered up to $7.5 million to each province under the Roads to Resources Project to develop air, land and sea transportation links to the resource-rich hinterlands. For British Columbia and Alberta, this meant reinforcing and extending ties to the Yukon and Mackenzie Valley. Elsewhere, other north-south connections were established and linked to vertically aligned provincial metropolitan centres. The notable exception was Quebec, whose premier did not welcome the cost-sharing arrangements attached to the grants. Once competition for American markets increased, so did the inter-provincial and federal-provincial turf wars and weakening of east-west bonds.

The loss of a northern identity was not clearly discernible until recently. The northern ethos was still strong during the "*Manhattan* crisis" in 1969 and 1970, when an American oil tanker entered Canadian Arctic waters without first requesting permission, and it was reflected further in public support for the combined environmental/sovereignty solution offered by the Arctic Waters Pollution Prevention Act. On the other hand, there was decidedly less reaction when another American vessel, the *Polar Sea*, made a similar incursion in 1985 and even less concern when part of the solution — the proposed Polar Class 8 ice-breaker — was cancelled. The protest against purchase of nuclear submarines appeared to be driven more by anti-military and anti-nuclear sentiments.

Canadian nationalism experienced a resurgence during the centennial celebrations, but in spite of attempts to promote Canada's bilingual and binational heritage, a more aggressive Quebec nationalism was on the rise. Other issues began to surface in the 1970s, namely environmental concerns and aboriginal rights. Neither was limited to the North, although related incidents were often northern-based. Strong public support for the Berger Commission's recommendation to defer the Mackenzie Valley Pipeline Project seemed to indicate there were still remnants of a northern vision, but for the first time this issue clearly defined the contradiction between the wilderness preservation and development goals inherent in the myth of the North.

The northern ethos was now irreparably fragmented, dividing its adherents into three distinct streams. The grand-design visionaries, who believed that mega-projects were the key to tapping the treasure trove of Arctic resources, absorbed the believers in progress and economic growth. The anti-nuclear, anti-war and environmental movements acquired the more avid northern wilderness devotees. War was declared with the one side branded as "capitalist pigs" or "big business" and the other labelled as tree huggers, environmental terrorists, aged hippies or anti-nukes. Caught in between were the largest group, the moderates, who sat home or at their cottages, gazing at their Lawren Harris and Tom Thomson prints, in mourning over the end of a golden era and frightened for the future. Inevitably, the split in the northern identity drastically weakened its unifying influence on Canadian nationalism.

Further weakening of east-west ties took place in the late 1980s with the Free Trade Agreement, with privatization of Crown corporations such as Air Canada and Petro-Canada and with budget cuts to VIA Rail, the CBC and the Canada Council. These policies would combine to have a devastating effect on the credibility of the federal government. As American goods poured north and Canadian jobs went south to the United States, disillusionment intensified. Once decline of the manufacturing sector set in, the provinces competed even more feverishly for new export markets to bolster sagging economies. Visions shifted south in search of prosperity, with the provinces claiming sole rights to benefits from the resource exports.

Other images of the North were threatened. Wilderness areas were decreasing in size, threatened by increasing population, urban sprawl, industrialization and pollution from resource extraction. The Americanization of oil and gas development and cruise missile testing in the North had a further psychological impact. There seemed less and less reason to be proud of the North, and for many the anger dissolved into helpless despair. The decline of the northern ethos paralleled the rise of national disunity, the two forces seemingly feeding upon each other. In this respect, Canadians' belief in a northern identity was not merely reflective, or a barometer, of unity, but a critical unifying bond and convector.

Without a common purpose — the bonding fabric of federalism — provincial leaders continued fighting among themselves over economic benefits and with Ottawa over rights. The struggle for political power was largely played out in the constitutional debate. In the end, the failure of the Meech Lake Accord was merely symptomatic and perhaps inevitable. As described by Mordecai Richler, the outcome was "a wasting tribal quarrel that diminishes everyone." Out of the ashes emerges a much clearer picture of the drastic surgery necessary to restore health to a failing federation.

In the past, national policies designed to encourage unity, such as bilingualism, multiculturalism and the "just society," have lacked staying power, perhaps because they were politically created and force-fed rather than inherent in the Canadian psyche. By contrast, images of North still linger, though they may be fragmented by regional outlook. Perhaps it might be possible to rejuvenate our northern identity and reorient the focus on the twenty-first century, while emphasizing environmental protection, responsible stewardship, respect for human liberties and aboriginal rights to self-government.

Environmental protection would have been debatable as a unifying cause even three years ago. Recent public opinion polls now suggest otherwise. According to the Angus Reid Poll released in April 1991, 76 per cent of all Canadians agreed that "government should keep environmental protection as a priority during a recession, even if it means a slower economic recovery." Only 20 per cent disagreed. More surprising was the fact that results in Ontario and Quebec were almost identical, reporting 78 per cent and 77 per cent respectively. Yet in May, the federal throne speech virtually ignored environmental concerns and instead promised economic prosperity as a panacea if Canadians would embrace national unity. Whether by ignorance, incompetence or self-denial, the government proved itself to be totally out of touch with more than three-quarters of the population.

We must not overlook other means of rebuilding a northern identity and national unity. Instead of isolating the territorial North as an inferior entity, a firm timetable should be set for the imminent creation of three new northern provinces in Yukon and Northwest Territories, with full control over their natural resources. A renewed northern focus would stress closer ties with other circumpolar nations at all levels of government, with special emphasis on environmental protection, concerns of the indigenous peoples, new economic ties, co-ordinated development and exchange of scientific expertise.

Our present military policy, in particular, requires revision. Canadian NATO forces should be returned home and retrained to assume full responsibility for "defence" of the North. Emphasis would be on peacekeeping, surveillance, search and rescue, and communications. Naval forces could be strengthened, but with vessels designed for Arctic use, and closely co-ordinated with Coast Guard efforts. Similarly, the Canadian Rangers, who are now active in sparsely settled northern regions, could be upgraded as armed forces reserves to assume various functions of the RCMP and to act as environmental ombudsmen.

The Free Trade Agreement should be carefully reconsidered and perhaps renegotiated to fit our northern-specific interests. We are not an important industrialized nation, nor will we be, until we can bring our manufacturing sector into proper balance with our exports of raw resources. If the present trend continues, we are in serious danger of becoming akin to a Third World nation.

Canada, as a sovereign nation, has inherent responsibilities to all its citizens. If the Québécois choose to secede, then northern Indians and Inuit should decide if their lands — transferred in 1912 to Quebec *as a province of Canada* — should remain part of a revitalized Canada or be absorbed into a new Quebec sovereign state. If they were to choose the former, negotiations would follow to arrange a rental agreement for the lands covered by the James Bay Project. Presumably, there would have to be similar arrangements to cover use of the St. Lawrence Seaway and disposition of federal property within Quebec. In the event of secession, the unravelling of existing ties will be onerous and painful, but regardless sovereignty is the will of a Quebec majority, Canada must focus its energies towards the creation of a truly democratic and happily united country.

A successful renewal of Canadian federalism can be achieved only if all existing provinces and territories, including representatives of the original peoples, contribute to its design, and if all Canadians have the opportunity to vote its approval. The rebirth of a new northern identity — combining the ethics of sustainable development with the vision of prosperity, environmental protection with the image of wilderness, settlement of aboriginal rights with social justice, and self-defence with peaceableness — would add further inspiration and motive. Perhaps then, Canadian nationalism could regain its true *raison d'être* of unifying the country.

The Atlantic Provinces
and the Territorial
Question

Ian Ross Robertson

Ian Ross Robertson, born in Prince Edward Island, teaches at Scarborough College, University of Toronto. He writes on his native province and on Canadian intellectual history.

The crisis in national unity that has emerged in the wake of the failure of the Meech Lake Accord may lead to sovereignty for the province of Quebec. The knife-at-the-throat approach of the Bourassa government has already provoked pessimism about the future of the country among many Canadians outside Quebec and has led to a hardening of attitude towards any proposal for accommodating Quebec further within Confederation.

Pessimism should not be allowed to turn to fatalism, resignation, passivity and acquiescence. While desiring as a first choice that Quebec remain part of Canada, it is nonetheless necessary to address realistically the issues that may arise between Quebec and the rest of Canada.

As a Maritimer, I reject absolutely any notion that the eastern provinces are so many ripe apples that will fall into the hands of the United States should Quebec secede. Maritimers are Canadian through the common experience of more than a century. They do not want annexation, regardless of the ruminations of then-premier, now-senator John Buchanan in the spring of 1990. Although those words fit well with the Bourassa–Mulroney strategy of raising the stakes as they rolled the dice over Meech, they do not reflect popular sentiment in the region. Yet there are real dangers for the Atlantic region in the event of Quebec sovereignty. No friend of Atlantic Canada wishes it to become Bangladesh North, partitioned from Canada and wretchedly impoverished compared with its neighbours.

From a Maritime point of view, the most important single question to be addressed in the event of Quebec's withdrawal from Confederation is territorial. This interpretation is predicated upon the assumption that there is no such option as sovereignty-association. Either Quebec remains within Canada or it does not. It is unrealistic of Quebec separatists to expect the rest of Canada to surrender its fiscal and monetary self-determination while accepting the political break-up of the country. Sovereignty-association is, in the words of Eugene Forsey on February 7, 1991, "a horse that can't run."

"Special status" is also a non-starter. Asymmetrical federalism means a unique degree of authority for the politicians and bureaucracy in the province of Quebec — while Quebec voters retain their strong influence within the federal government, a weight increased by a tradition of bloc voting. This practice has ensured federal politicians from Quebec disproportionate leverage within federal institutions. "Special status" would, in addition, make Quebec as a province more than equal to each of the other provinces. The growth of a quasi-independent state-within-a-state is intolerable to majority opinion in the rest of Canada.

The remaining options may be summarized as radical overall decentralization without special powers for Quebec and separation. The former will almost certainly be unacceptable to most provinces and the vast majority of Canadian citizens outside Quebec. Atlantic Canadians in particular have accepted strong central institutions as a necessary precondition of equalization. The prime source of dissatisfaction with federalism has been the inability of the region to influence decisions made by the central authority. But concern with the way federal powers are exercised does not translate into desire for decentralization. Moreover, it is doubtful that Quebec's political élite would be satisfied with a status within Confederation equal to that of Manitoba and Newfoundland, their current *bêtes noires*, even if equality were accompanied by new powers.

If sovereignty-association, "special status" and radical decentralization *without* special powers for Quebec can be ruled out, and if basic constitutional change is still regarded as necessary, separation may be the likeliest outcome. Some will draw solace from the fact that support within Quebec for sovereignty began to decline by the spring of 1991. Yet separatism in Quebec has been declared dead before. The argument for Quebec's place within Canada, and whether Quebec should be part of Canada at all, will never entirely disappear in a world that witnesses the resuscitation of Armenian, Croatian, Estonian, Latvian, Lithuanian, Scottish, Slovak and other separatist movements decades after these issues had seemed sealed.

The prospect of an independent Quebec raises particularly fundamental questions for the Atlantic region. Most obvious is the splitting of Canada into two geographical sections separated by the land mass of a semi-hostile Quebec. In the event of separation, negotiations will have to proceed on the assumption that since the vital interests of both Quebec and the rest of Canada are affected, the future boundaries of Quebec are negotiable. The present borders are the product of a history that includes enormous grants of territory from the Dominion of Canada to the province of Quebec. In order to ensure the internal cohesion and therefore the survival of Canada, a land corridor through the southern portion of an independent Quebec would be essential.

Some will point to the United States, with Alaska separated from the lower forty-eight continental states by British Columbia, as an example of a country enduring and even thriving despite geographical separation. Such a comparison is possible only for those who are blind to the role of power in world politics. Shorn of Quebec, we would be in a much different situation than that of the United States. We would be a country of perhaps 20 million, with a population of 6.5 million Quebeckers dividing 18 million from some 2.3 million, and with the world's one remaining superpower to our south. National unity, and how to maintain it, would seem more pressing than ever before. A strong central government, with a vigorous commitment to unifying pan-Canadian institutions, would be an absolute necessity; without it, Canada would be ground between the millstones of continental north-south pulls and centrifugal regional forces.

One of the constant and most vexing problems would be relations with the "new neighbour," Quebec. Without a change in the present boundaries, the territorial situation would continually tempt Quebec to use threats to extract favourable terms from Canada. The costs of maintaining secure links between the centre and the East would constantly increase.

If Quebec separates, then the rest of Canada should negotiate hard and tough. The most obvious demands for Canada to make with respect to territory are: the future of southwestern Quebec, including the western (English) part of Montreal, to be decided by a free vote; resumption of federal title to northern Quebec; and establishment of a corridor through Quebec to the Atlantic region.

First, let us examine the process and then some matters of substance. Who would negotiate? What would be taken for granted? What would happen first, negotiations or independence for the province of Quebec?

Setting separation negotiations in motion would be a delicate task. From a Quebec perspective, the ideal solution might seem to be a unilateral declaration of independence (UDI), followed by negotiations with the federal government. The remainder of Canada would be presented with a *fait accompli* and would have to strike the best deal it could with Quebec. Far-fetched? On May 16, 1991, the Quebec intergovernmental affairs minister, Gil Rémillard, stated that such would be Quebec's procedure in the event that it failed to obtain a suitably "renewed" federalism: declare independence first, arrange terms later.

There are several reasons this should be unacceptable to the rest of Canada. In the first place, such a pre-emption of negotiations by a UDI — presumably followed by Canadian recognition of the *fait accompli* — would have the effect of creating a new Quebec nation-state with its *present* boundaries. Yet boundaries have to be one of the prime subjects for negotiation. There are historical and prudential reasons why Quebec must not be allowed to use a UDI to gain an irreversible advantage. If Quebec should resort to a UDI, that illegal act should be followed by such sanctions as suspension of transfer payments, with the economic pressure escalating until such time as Quebec representatives sit down to negotiate what has to be settled between them and the federal government.

But wait, which federal government? The one today, with a large Quebec caucus, Quebec ministers and a prime minister from Quebec? If Quebec were to secede, it would be as unthinkable for Canadians to entrust their interests to negotiators accountable to a Quebecker as it would be for Quebec to invite Canadians from Saskatchewan or Newfoundland to negotiate on its behalf. Before negotiations could take place, the Canadian government would have to be reconstituted.

For such a new Canadian government to have legitimacy in the eyes of Canadians, a general election would be necessary. A new election would put much pressure on all parties to adopt a hard-headed approach in negotiations. Once a new government had been formed, then negotiations could ensue. But an opening Canadian demand would have to be that, in terms of territory, nothing except the separation of *some entity* known as Quebec would be taken as a "given" — *some entity* because the boundaries would be negotiable. Minorities in the present Quebec would have to be granted the same right of self-determination as the majority. The most important minorities in this context are the English-speaking population and the aboriginal peoples living on ancestral lands.

Matters become extraordinarily complex as soon as discussion of self-determination for minorities and alteration of boundaries begins. The prospect of Canadian enclaves within an independent Quebec raises the spectre of Nagorno-Karabakh, an Armenian area within Azerbaijan. In order to avoid that pitfall, it would be wise to accept as a fundamental principle that only minority areas within Quebec that are geographically cohesive and either contiguous with the land mass of Canada or facing open water could vote for continued membership in Canada. They would enter Confederation as a new province (possibly as more than one new province), so as not to increase the dominance of Ontario within the new Canada.

Some would say that partition of Quebec is inherently wrong and would lead only to strife. But those persons should have the question put to them. Why is it inherently wrong to partition the province of Quebec if it is inherently right to partition the Dominion of Canada?

The second objection concerns the practical consequences of partition: the possibility of ethnic or communal strife. It might be argued that even if Canada has, in principle, the right to insist on redefinition of boundaries, it should refrain from doing so because of the likely results. The answer to this is that separation of Quebec with maintenance of present boundaries would probably cause more human suffering and dislocation of population than partition. Ultimately, people are more important than boundaries, and partition would be in the interest of all but the political and bureaucratic élite of Quebec.

If Quebec separates, one can predict that many people will leave, because of either disquiet over the economic prospects or fear of intolerance by *pure laine* Quebeckers. Such an exodus happened after the election of the first Parti Québécois government in 1976.

Those in favour of separation with maintenance of present boundaries are unlikely to conceive of a mass departure of English-speaking Canadians from an independent Quebec as a reason to rearrange boundaries. But the migration that has already occurred has probably had a more negative impact on attitudes within English Canada towards Quebec, and a more destabilizing effect on French-English relations, than Canadians as a whole realize. Disaffected former Quebeckers were key figures in the notorious Quebec flag-trampling and flag-burning incident in Brockville, Ontario, in 1989.

If Quebec separates with its present boundaries, there will certainly be additional exchanges of population and further destabilization of relations. It would be better for both Quebeckers and non-Quebeckers if the boundaries changed and if as many people as possible were enabled to remain where they are. That means part of the border would run through Montreal.

The decisions as to where separation votes for minority areas would be held would have to be the result of negotiation, on the basis of census data. There would be a temptation for each side to attempt to define the voting areas so as to maximize the number of probable supporters. That should be balanced by the realization that going too far would, in the event of losing the votes, lead to greater loss of population to the other side after separation. In other words, the winner-take-all nature of a referendum on adhesion to an independent Quebec or adhesion to Canada would work against, for example, Quebec insisting that an adjacent francophone area be included in a vote.

Northern Quebec presents a different set of issues. The old Province of Canada, 1841–67, brought into Confederation a Lower Canada much smaller than the present province of Quebec. The Dominion of Canada acquired the present northern Quebec as part of the Northwest Territories in a purchase from Great Britain in 1870. Over the ensuing forty-two years, the Dominion transferred most of this land to the province of Quebec. Whether the province that brought only the St. Lawrence Valley into Confederation should be permitted to take much more out is certainly debatable. Moreover, the descendants of the original inhabitants of northern Quebec will have their own preferences. Their wishes should be paramount over any desire of Quebec separatists to take the aboriginal lands of northern Quebec with them into an independent nation-state. In other words, the Swampy Cree, the Ungava Inuit and other "first peoples" must have a veto on any transfer of their ancestral areas to an independent Quebec. International opinion would almost certainly support them.

There remains the crucial matter of a corridor. The width and location would be subject to negotiation. The necessary width would be in the range of thirty to fifty kilometres. The location raises additional problems. It could be either along the American border, thus depriving independent Quebec of adjacency to the United States, or elsewhere through the southern portion of the present province of Quebec. The latter will probably be at least as objectionable to Quebeckers, for its effect would be the division of Quebec into two sections, one north and one south of the corridor.

Some Quebeckers will wish to say a simple no to the idea of a corridor and to dismiss it from consideration out of hand. But Canada has a duty to its citizens to inform Quebec that the choice is either, for example, a corridor to the Maritimes or no hydro corridor through Canada for Hydro-Québec. Newfoundlanders can testify that Quebec is familiar with such negotiation tactics and indeed has used them itself.

The prospect of an independent Quebec divided into sections north and south of the corridor may engender opposition from those elsewhere in Canada who are unconditional sympathizers of Quebec. But the question needs to be answered: Is a Canada divided into sections west of Quebec and east of Quebec, with no territorial link, a promising prospect for a continuing Canada? Canadians have a right to require that anyone negotiating on their behalf ensures that Canada remain a territorially contiguous entity. The only way this can be done without denying Quebec a similar territorial integrity is to place the corridor in a strip along the American border. Such a corridor, dividing Quebec from the United States, would probably be the best solution for both Quebec and the rest of Canada.

Persons living within the corridor would be required to elect allegiance to Canada or to Quebec. If the latter, they would have to move unless their presence in the corridor were deemed an asset to Canada; those required to move would be compensated, jointly by Quebec and by Canada, for their immovable assets.

It is critical that the territorial concerns of the Atlantic provinces be seen as more than regional in nature, for their successful resolution is central to the internal cohesion and survival of a post-separation Canada. Moreover, they are part of a larger complex of issues focusing on the boundaries of an independent Quebec and including the right of self-determination for the inhabitants of the southwestern and northern parts of the province. In the event of separation, such issues can be resolved only by negotiations between legitimate representatives of Quebec and the rest of Canada. These negotiations are bound to be difficult, but to fail to undertake them would be short-sighted in the extreme and would cause additional continuing friction.

To settle for anything less than major territorial adjustments in the event of separation would be unfair to the people of the Atlantic region, the aboriginal inhabitants of Quebec and the non-aboriginal minorities within Quebec. The legacies of such unfairness would include much hardship for Atlantic Canadians, increased difficulty and uncertainty in maintaining Canada as a nation-state, large-scale departures from an independent Quebec with the attendant embittering and hardening of attitudes towards Quebec in the rest of Canada and probably intensified strife within Quebec between aboriginals and non-aboriginals.

One would have to be foolhardy or dishonest to suggest that all problems will be resolved painlessly if these issues are addressed directly in negotiations. But the long-term results will be worse for both Quebec and the remainder of Canada if they are not confronted. A clear glimpse of what lies across the abyss of separation may even reduce the temptation to separate.

Goodbye Noblesse Oblige: Quebec Anglos in Crisis

Richard Smith

Richard Smith is a businessman who lives in Gatineau, Quebec. He is active in the English-rights movement.

A favourite analogy among journalists, academics and political pundits compares the widening rift between English Canada and French Quebec to a badly strained marriage on the verge of collapse. In the moments of high drama in June 1990, French Quebeckers witnessed a handful of unilingual English-Canadian politicians and one native MLA refusing to pass the Meech Lake Accord. During the hearings of the Bélanger–Campeau commission last fall, the defeat of Meech and of the "distinct society" was portrayed as a final indignity heaped upon Quebec and as a rejection of its people. As the analogy goes, Quebec is now contemplating suing for divorce.

It is tragic that the Meech Lake Accord would prove to be the first attempt made by Canadians to amend their Constitution since the amending formula was changed in 1982. The new provisions requiring unanimous provincial approval for major constitutional amendments all but guaranteed that if Quebec's initial demands were deemed unacceptable, then it would fall to an English-Canadian premier to voice the final rejection. In the upcoming round of negotiations, the issue of Quebec's distinctness will emerge again. This time the request will be to cede to Quebec full jurisdiction over language and culture. Again the rest of the country will be called upon to provide the ultimate approval or disapproval.

Of primary concern to Quebec's English-speaking community, of course, is whether these new powers would be used to further repress the English fact in Quebec. The distinct society clause was to confer on Quebec a new, unqualified role in the area of language. Now Quebec is asking for explicit control over what it couldn't obtain implicitly, namely, a blank cheque in the form of exclusive provincial jurisdiction over language and culture.

Although francophone Quebeckers got wrapped up in the symbolism of the distinct society clause, it seems unlikely that they were fully aware of the concern among provincial premiers that it could be used to repress minority language rights. During its three-year ratification period, none of the serious critics of the accord suggested that Quebec was not a distinct society. In fact, a consensus seemed to emerge among most English-speaking Canadians, both in the rest of the country and in Quebec itself, that Quebec as a distinct society was a reality. Although politicians could agree on Quebec's distinctness as a social entity, they seemed unable to agree on how best to formalize this recognition.

Quebeckers and other Canadians, most of whom are not lawyers by profession and who are, therefore, not adept at the subtleties of legal negotiation, must have found it difficult to follow the arguments over which legal vehicle would be most appropriate as a formal recognition of Quebec's distinctness. The Quebec government wanted recognition entrenched in an interpretive clause, whereas Jean Chrétien and others preferred using the preamble to the Constitution for this purpose. The Parti Québécois under Pierre-Marc Johnson preferred a new provincial constitution, while Jacques Parizeau preferred no definition of Quebec's distinctness in a Canadian context, favouring instead a totally independent Quebec.

Some may argue that the failure to agree on a proper legal vehicle during Meech simply resulted from an excessive fastidiousness among the key players involved. To dismiss the issue so lightly, however, would be to ignore the true nature of a problem that continues to dog us today. The conflict extends beyond a group of English-Canadian premiers behaving like a collective big brother looking out for the welfare of Quebec's English-speaking minority. Clyde Wells, Sharon Carstairs and others believed strongly in the principles of individual rights and bilingualism underlying Pierre Trudeau's vision.

Wells feared that a future derogation of the rights of non-French-speaking Quebeckers through use of the interpretive clause would certainly lead to a backlash against francophones outside the province. English-speaking Canadians would surely balk at the notion of continuing to shoulder the burden of promoting standardized bilingualism while Quebec absolves itself of this shared responsibility. Those who would suffer the consequences of such a turn of events include not just existing francophone minority communities but those that may develop in the future should francophones decide to settle in new areas.

The existence of a double standard and the resulting diminution of francophone rights outside the province would play right into the hands of Quebec separatists. They would argue, according to Pierre Trudeau in his book *Federalism and the French Canadians,* that francophones do not enjoy true linguistic mobility outside Quebec and that they should therefore consolidate their numbers and their powers within that province.

From the very beginning, Wells, Carstairs and other Meech Lake opponents clearly understood the instinctive reaction Canadians would have should the meaning of the distinct society clause be brought to unfavourable light in future court rulings. Their fears were clearly justified, as evidenced by the angry response that greeted passage of Quebec's Bill 178, legislation that governs the language of the province's commercial signs. Up until that point in 1988, much of the English-Canadian public seemed to know little or nothing about the accord. The Meech Lake debate to that point had been waged on largely theoretical grounds, and the public found it difficult to form any firm opinions of its own. Quebec's adoption of Bill 178, however, transformed public ambivalence into concern for the hidden dangers of the distinct society clause. Bill 178 and the distinct society clause were both creations of the Quebec Liberal government. They therefore were assumed to be instruments designed to achieve the same goals.

The efforts of Wells and Carstairs to protect the aims of the Canadian Charter reflected their sympathy for the faction of French Canadians both inside and outside Quebec who believed in the Trudeau vision. The latest battle in an ongoing ideological civil war was being waged between two factions of French Canadians who differed on how best to ensure survival of the French fact in North America. The embarrassing thing for English Quebeckers and other Canadians is that, like Wells and Carstairs, we have become embroiled in what is essentially an internal fight among French Canadians. The unity of the country and the future of Quebec anglophones within Canada hangs in the balance.

This ideological civil war is as old as the country itself and predates Confederation. Within the history of modern Canada, the conflict can be traced back to Henri Bourassa and Wilfrid Laurier. They both wanted to reinforce the French fact throughout all of North America. Bourassa often criticized Laurier, however, for favouring provincial powers over language. A century ago, just as it is today, provincial control over language was seen by many as a licence to chip away at minority language rights.

As time passed, French Canadians continued to debate how far the French fact in North America could risk extending itself before becoming too thinly spread, risking assimilation. Eventually the focus on *la survivance* turned inward to deal primarily with the French fact above the forty-ninth parallel. Laurier's belief that French-speakers should consider all of Canada their homeland found a new heir in the writings and political activism of Pierre Trudeau. Trudeau was convinced that if the French language was only narrowly based in Quebec it would perish. Unlike Laurier, Trudeau eschewed provincialism, favouring instead a strong federal government unbridled in its ability to promote French throughout the rest of the country.

The emergence of Quebec separatism and the rise of the Parti Québécois brought to the forefront a whole new theory on how best to protect the French fact. This theory holds that the French fact and *la survivance* would be in peril if spread too thinly across Canada and, therefore, francophones should focus solely on Quebec. Clearly, this theory runs diametrically opposite to Trudeau's vision. Although the belief in a part of Canada becoming the exclusive enclave of French language and culture is something new in the Canadian context, such a strategy has been used elsewhere in the world. In his book *The Patriot Game*, Peter Brimelow draws a parallel between Lévesque's strategy and that of Turkish nationalist Kemal Ataturk, who "salvaged modern Turkey from the collapse of the Ottoman Empire by coldly abandoning Turkish communities in the periphery and concentrating all efforts on the defense of the Anatolian heartland."

The vision of the two sides for the future of francophones was implicit in the respective laws that they proposed. It was these laws that would draw English-speaking Canadians inside and outside Quebec and Quebeckers into the ideological war. For Trudeau the Canadian Charter of Rights, and for Lévesque Bill 101. In any country, though, the laws of the highest level of government must prevail. Within Canada the supremacy of the Canadian Charter meant that Trudeau's vision would prevail. If Lévesque wanted his laws and vision to win out, Quebec would have to separate from Canada in order to make the Quebec government the highest authority among its citizens.

Even a cursory examination of Trudeau's public record reveals the patriation of the Constitution to be one of his principal objectives. His guiding motive in so doing was to see the principle of Canada as a bilingual and multicultural nation, recognized in earlier legislation, entrenched in the fundamental law of the land.

However, the principles of bilingualism and multiculturalism were not new. The Official Languages Act of 1969 had given English and French equal status in the domain of the federal government. From the outset, Quebec anglophones have been among the biggest supporters of Trudeau's blueprint for promoting bilingualism. They saw it as the best means of defending their interests as a minority in Quebec. It was no accident that Trudeau was elected in a primarily English-speaking Quebec riding — and he was not alone. All of the predominantly English ridings in Quebec returned Liberals during the Trudeau years.

The Quebec English-rights group Alliance Quebec, founded in 1981, has consistently demonstrated its solidarity with French-speaking minorities outside Quebec by supporting their struggle for the extension of bilingualism. Acceptance of national bilingualism had implications not just for Quebeckers but for all English Canadians. For if Trudeau's vision that all of Canada was to be recognized as the French-Canadian homeland were accepted, then it is only natural and just that all of Canada, including Quebec, be considered as the homeland of English-speaking Canadians.

Trudeau's personal belief, according to biographer Richard Gwyn in *The Northern Magus*, "was quite different from the political defining principle. . . . His chief concern was neither to save Canada nor to affirm the French Fact, but to liberate man. . . . For Trudeau, 'pluralistic federalism' was simply a logical consequence of applying rationalism to government."

English-speaking Canadians outside Quebec have largely seen bilingualism as a hard-boiled compromise needed in order to maintain Canadian unity. Provision of English-language services in Quebec was to be their pay-off for supporting their end of the bilingual bargain. However, the notion that this would make them feel more at home in Quebec held little appeal. If Quebec is also the homeland of English-speaking Canadians, they do not seem to be taking advantage of the fact; since the introduction of official bilingualism, Quebec has been consistently losing rather than gaining English-speakers. Nevertheless, the boosters of bilingualism were able to secure English Canada's support by appealing to its sense of fairness and using guilt as a tool when necessary. Bilingualism, as they saw it, was the price they had to pay to give French Canadians, and French Quebeckers in particular, enough of a sense of proprietorship in Canada to maintain the nation's unity.

At the time of the first Official Languages Act in 1969, many English-speaking Canadians had an insecure sense of nationhood. English-Canadian culture, with the advent of television and mass communications, was increasingly becoming subsumed by North America's larger English-language culture. Consequently, English Canada increasingly saw its distinct identity in terms of the territorial integrity of the country, which had to be maintained at all costs. Quebec separation was regarded as the event that could trigger the larger dissolution of Canada. This rationale begins with the premise that the separation of Quebec would precipitate a sort of domino effect. The blow to self-confidence and the disruption of national trade, communications and travel resulting from Quebec's departure would weaken the glue that binds us, leading various regions to opt for annexation, one by one, to the United States.

The support of English-speaking Quebeckers for bilingualism was motivated by other considerations than Trudeau's lofty ideals. Fearing that they would be hijacked by a separating Quebec, anglophone citizens have been grasping at ideological straws in hopes of appeasing Quebec nationalism. Their motivation for appeasement is quite apart from that of the rest of English-speaking Canada, however. Representatives of Quebec's English community such as Alliance Quebec believe in making English Canada pay the price for their continued attempts to "buy off" Quebec nationalism. They do this by convincing English Canadians to accept more French in the rest of Canada in return for more

English allowed in Quebec, from which only Quebec Anglos gain.

While Quebec nationalism hangs over English Quebec like a gathering storm cloud, it is not without its silver lining for English Quebec's political classes. The appeasement of Quebec nationalism has given Quebec anglophone politicians a disproportionate share of influence in the national government relative to the size of the community from which they originate. Quebec anglophones have always had a local advantage in becoming more bilingual than the rest of French- and English-speaking Canadians. Brian Mulroney, for instance, used his bilingual and bicultural attributes to great advantage in seeking the PC leadership in 1983. He was able to secure his first mandate, in turn, by appeasing Quebec nationalism by embracing a Quebec nationalist constitutional reform agenda. Members of these political classes claim that by appeasing Quebec nationalism they will be able to redirect its energy from a separatist agenda to the spreading of French across Canada. Meanwhile, by attempting to co-opt Quebec nationalists rather than challenging the basic tenets of their nationalism, anglophone appeasers have allowed nationalism to decimate their own community. English Quebeckers outside Quebec's political classes fear that employers in the private sector, seeing nationalism and provincial unilingualism go unchallenged, will pass over bilingual anglophones in favour of bona fide French Quebeckers.

When the Quebec government overrode the individual rights provisions of the Canadian Charter to enact Bill 178, the revulsion was felt right across English Canada. The appreciation of English-speaking Canadians for individual rights is much more than a product of the traditional cultural preferences of Canadians of Anglo-Saxon descent. An influx of non-Anglo immigrants from all corners of the globe has not weakened but rather has been the primary factor strengthening support for individual rights. Defining the individual as the basic unit of society allows Canada's new citizens to feel secure in the knowledge that they must be treated equally no matter what their race, language, culture or country of origin.

A belief in individual rights, language rights and multiculturalism forms the cornerstone of the Canadian identity as envisioned by the Canadian Charter. As a document, it represents an attempt to compromise and balance the country's many competing interests. Representing a faction in French Canada's ideological civil war, Pierre Trudeau did make strategic alliances and include the agendas of other groups in the country, to build national support for patriation. However, Trudeau's vision of the interrelationship between individual rights and linguistic and collective rights was always exposed for the public record. Quebec nationalists have not been so forthcoming.

Two major pieces of legislation, the Quebec Charter of Rights and Bill 101, the Charter of the French Language, best illustrate the interrelationship between individual and collective rights as envisioned by nationalist forces. The Quebec Charter of Rights was quite generous in terms of individual rights. Bill 101, on the other hand, leaned much more towards the notion of collective rights. In the 1977 Quebec white paper that preceded Bill 101, collective rights were considered as an appropriate means to re-mould the character of the province into an "essentially French" entity "support[ing] a reconquest by the French-speaking majority in Quebec of that control over the economy which it ought to have.... There [would] no longer be any question of a bilingual Quebec."

Ironically, after supporting both the Quebec Charter and the Charter of the French Language, the PQ government failed to establish which would take precedence over the other. The two charters collided in 1988 when the Supreme Court of Canada struck down the French-signs provision of Bill 101, ruling that it contravened sections of the Quebec Charter. Since that ruling, the Quebec Liberal government has failed to take the initiative and establish that its charter has supremacy. The same Quebec Liberal government that finds itself unable to make this fundamental choice now seeks in its new internal constitutional program, the Allaire report, to exempt Quebec from the Canadian Charter of Rights.

The indecisiveness among politicians seems to be mirrored among the francophone population at large. Francophones have given little indication that they are fully committed to the notion of French unilingualism and collective rights as envisioned in Bill 101. Public opinion polls have consistently shown that an overwhelming majority of French Quebeckers support the provision of bilingual services throughout the country. Paradoxically, a majority of Quebec francophones responded favourably to the "Touche pas loi 101" (Don't touch Bill 101) campaign leading up to the 1988 court judgement. When asked if languages other than French should be allowed on commercial signs, a clear majority respond positively. The catch-22 in this scenario stems from the fact that Bill 101 would have to be amended to allow languages other than French to be displayed on commercial signs. Such contradictions not only confuse Canadians outside Quebec but confound and anger local Anglos as well.

Viewing Quebec through the eyes of the various news organizations outside the province is equally deceiving, for the language conflict is actually a surreal battle between language activists. The intensity projected at media-covered demonstrations by such activists is likely to mislead observers into believing that such ill will is widespread among ordinary francophones and anglophones. English-speaking Quebeckers can attest to the fact that the reality is quite different. Individual francophones and anglophones actually go out of their way to be courteous to one another in everyday life. If francophone Quebeckers as individuals were as aggressive in promoting French unilingualism as Bill 101 suggests, Quebec would not be such a nice place to live. Perhaps the discrepancy between the Quebec envisioned by Bill 101 and the everyday reality of Quebec society is rooted in francophones' preference to use Bill 101's unilingual vision as a means, not as an end.

I would submit that one of the reasons Quebec francophones appear so reluctant to tamper with Bill 101 is that they perceive it as a sort of linguistic moral code. Just as the church is unlikely to condone premarital sex — in spite of the general acceptance and practice of such behaviour — for fear that it would encourage greater participation in such "sinful acts," so too is there a reluctance to loosen the "moral tenets" of Bill 101. The drafters of Bill 101, according to Graham Fraser, in his book *PQ: René Lévesque & the Parti Québécois in Power*, were inclined to "assumptions shaped by Catholicism" when considering language legislation. They realized the tough vision of the law would be compromised by individual bilingualism (i.e., francophones and non-francophones reverting occasionally to English in daily conversation), but concluded that any net increase in French usage would be beneficial nonetheless. To amend Bill 101 to recognize bilingualism would be to risk encouraging further "indiscretions among parishioners." However, if Bill 101 was intended to encourage non-francophones to speak French and integrate more fully into French society, it clearly backfired: unilingual as well as bilingual non-francophones perceive Bill 101 as a testament to the intolerance of the French-speaking majority and are simply opting to leave the province.

Given the legislative and social contradictions surrounding the definition of Quebec either as a bilingual or as a unilingual society, it is easy to understand why the prospect of recognizing Quebec as a distinct society posed such a vexing problem. Perhaps if Quebec had asked to be recognized as a "confused" or "contradictory" society, everyone might have been able to reach agreement. Instead, national politicians, Quebec's Anglos among them, continue to keep alive the diametrically opposed concepts of national bilingualism and Quebec unilingualism while neglecting to establish which will prevail. In the spirit of bigamy, the distinct society clause tried to satisfy both sides while committing to neither. It was reasoned by Meech supporters that if the rest of the country did not acquiesce in this constitutional double standard, then Quebec would have no choice but to secede.

The Meech Lake episode clearly revealed that English Canadians are not as insecure as they were in 1969 when official bilingualism was first introduced. They no longer fear that Quebec secession will precipitate the dissolution of Canada. Indeed, there seems to be a growing belief among Canadians outside Quebec that the province's departure would enhance, not diminish, the spirit of Canadian unity. With the possibility now unlikely that Quebec can cow the rest of the country into ceding to it a new linguistic and cultural blank cheque, the Quebec government might be better advised to spell out the true meaning and implications of the distinct society. Preston Manning, leader of the Reform Party of Canada, suggested that the Quebec government should draft a sample constitution before asking Quebeckers whether they wanted to separate so that they can see whether such drastic action would actually afford them any greater protection or benefits than they already have.

The youth association of Quebec's Equality Party has proposed one way around the current impasse, citing the American system of state constitutions. According to the association, Quebec's distinctness could be implicitly defined in a new provincial constitution subordinate to the Canadian Constitution and Charter of Rights. Within this new provincial constitution, the relationship between individual and collective rights could finally be established. It would also establish once and for all what Quebec sees as its commitment to bilingualism. Recently, the Parti Québécois and the Quebec Liberals have similarly toyed with the idea of a Quebec constitution. Of course these parties will define Quebec's distinctness in their own sweet time through a constitution that is not so much provincial as national.

Pierre Trudeau's faction of the French-Canadian ideological civil war made its views on individual and language rights perfectly clear before adopting the Canadian Charter. The Quebec nationalist faction should be forced to do the same. English Canada should not have to choose between the visions of the warring factions until both sides have, as Manning suggested, at least explained the consequences of their proposals to the Quebec population at large so that it can make a fully informed decision with no potential for misunderstanding.

Moreover, English Canadians have indigenous interests to protect in constitutional reform. Extending to Quebec new means of opting out of the Canadian Charter for reasons that are not clearly defined and delimited in advance could have severe repercussions for the future of Canadian pluralism. If, as a province of Canada, Quebec is allowed to curtail individual rights, then other provinces could curtail the rights of their linguistic and cultural communities. This creates a very dangerous precedent, for adherence to individual rights is the only glue that holds English-Canadian pluralism and peaceful co-existence together.

Quebec Anglos must keep in mind the concerns English Canada has over the protection of the country's pluralist nature and Quebec's responsibility to uphold its end of the Charter aims of bilingualism and individual rights. Perhaps because they fear knowing what French Quebeckers mean by "distinct," Quebec Anglos seem least likely to push for a clarification of Quebec's distinctness. Groups such as Alliance Quebec are likely to ignore this issue and try to redirect Quebec nationalism towards the spreading of French outside Quebec, but they will not confront it. Quebec's demand for recognition of its distinctness, either explicitly through an interpretive clause or implicitly via linguistic dualism, will not go away. The best contribution English Quebeckers can make to national unity and to their own plight is, as a minority, to have themselves recognized as a distinct community within Quebec's distinctness, perhaps in a Quebec provincial constitution or by some other means.

English Canadians will likely support Quebec's English minority in the risky undertaking of developing a provincial constitution through consensus. English Quebeckers will lose credibility, however, and test the good will of English Canadians, if in the process they continue to ask the rest of the country to accept more French in an unproven effort to thwart Quebec nationalism. It would clearly be embarrassing if the rest of the country is forced, in order to safeguard its own interests, to go over the heads of Quebec Anglos in an effort to smoke out the real intentions of Quebec francophones. Durable constitutional solutions will require all Canadians, including English Quebeckers, to stop humouring and accommodating the Quebec government in its deliberate attempts to obfuscate the true meaning of Quebec's distinctness. Only when all Canadians negotiate constitutional change on the basis of common values that they believe to be fair and just, in an atmosphere free of threats and intimidation, will we be able to discover the genuine spirit of unity that has eluded us for so long.

Out, Damned Spot:
English Rights in Quebec

Robert Bothwell

Robert Bothwell, a historian at the University of Toronto, is the co-author of Canada Since 1945 *and many other books.*

Civil rights are an old and vexed question in Canadian history. Initially our civil rights were those of Britain, a small and homogeneous island, which had experienced difficulties in extending those rights to populations different in character. When it annexed New France in 1763 England created what was, effectively, a new right: the right to the officially recognized use of two languages. But what might from one point of view be construed as an act of liberalism and generosity also carried with it the intrusion of the state into the question of language. Rights, language and politics would thereafter be inextricably mixed in the history of Canada.

Subsequent decades frequently gave both English and French reason to question the linguistic arrangement of the 1760s and 1770s. In the 1830s, accommodations were reached between English and French. Despite some backsliding after the rebellions of 1837–38, the politicians easily found a way to finesse the problem and recognize the use of both languages in a process of mutual concessions. They practised a politics of accommodation and the accommodation itself was a significant bulwark of rights. The result was a careful saw-off, which resulted in trading of concessions over schools in 1863, which led to the establishment of protected, taxpayer-supported Protestant schools in Lower Canada in return for taxpayer-supported Catholic schools in Upper Canada.

When the politicians of the 1860s drafted the Confederation Bill, they acted in recognition of the dual nature of the new nation they were creating. Although Lower Canadian A.T. Galt resigned on the question of minority rights in the future province of Quebec, believing that the protections embodied in the British North America Act were insufficient, politically Galt's gesture was quixotic. The minority might have had some forebodings, but it was well entrenched, economically powerful and numerically significant. Guarantees of bilingualism in the national Parliament, provincial legislature and the courts were considered adequate for Confederation, and the establishment of a bilingual province of Quebec with a French majority became one of the major achievements of the constitutional settlement of 1867.

The Constitution dealt only indirectly with rights. Historically certain rights have been protected because they were in the federal sphere rather than the provincial: such was the case in Alberta during Albert's regime in the 1930s. Sometimes rights have been protected by imperial or federal courts when local majorities acted to infringe on them: such was the case with inter-faith marriages in Quebec in the 1920s, or the Jehovah's Witnesses in the 1950s. Such infringements on the local majority's right to legislate or administer its own affairs were accepted as part of the larger Confederation deal; but the impression rankled, especially among French-Canadian nationalists, that the superior English were imposing their values from on high. Even today, the idea that Canadian individuals have certain rights in common seems to awaken a fear of condescension among Quebec nationalists: their watchword has always been "We have nothing to learn from the English" on civil rights.

The language question did not cease with Confederation; it simply took on a continent-wide dimension, frequently centring on the control of schooling. Except in Quebec, French-language minorities had to contend with English-language majorities, and victories for the French language outside Quebec were few. Only in Quebec did the French language enjoy official standing, and there French flourished and spread, despite a tide of immigrants who passed almost exclusively to the English side of society. English power, particularly in Montreal, was obvious; that City remained the financial centre of Canada. English Montrealers condescended to Canadians not fortunate enough to live in the Square Mile or on the slopes of Westmount. Their arrogance fixed English Montrealers in a historical quartz, their reputation for haughty impregnability an imperishable artifact that affected how succeeding generations of English Quebeckers were viewed.

By the 1950s, however, English Montreal's position was not as absolute as it had been. Toronto was no longer a distant rival; it was the political and economic centre of a larger and richer province. Montreal also lost ground in its English-language cultural institutions. When Toronto began to surpass Montreal, the position of the English in Quebec became precarious, their function as business leaders for Canada undermined. Teetering, the English community gradually toppled before the demands of a new generation of Quebec nationalists to be *maîtres chez nous.*

In the sixties the English institutions of Quebec became the targets of the new nationalism. In 1963, bombs exploded in Westmount's mailboxes, placed there on the assumption that anyone who might be harmed would not be French Canadian. When a watchman with an Irish name was murdered by terrorists, his death was excused, if not justified, in some quarters on the grounds that he was an Anglo.

English Canada was increasingly willing to give ear to Quebec's complaints. No longer as sure of itself or its values, English-speaking society understood its French counterpart to be demanding its *rights*, and *rights* was a word to conjure with in the 1960s. The *rights* demanded were supposed to place French-speakers on an equal basis with English-speakers, and *equal rights* had even more resonance than *rights* pure and simple.

Conceding language rights, for example, would help obviate unhappy episodes such as the language riots in Saint-Léonard in 1968. The conservative Union Nationale government in Quebec thought it was recognizing, and doing, the obvious, when it embodied the linguistic status quo, as far as education was concerned, in law in 1969 via Bill 63. What is usually forgotten is that the government of Jean-Jacques Bertrand withdrew a more far-reaching set of linguistic guarantees, Bill 85, under threat of mob violence. The vehemence of anti-English feelings profoundly shocked Quebec's political élite, who had, until then, carried on in the Canadian political tradition of compromise and accommodation. Though Bertrand did his best to continue, others took note that the "civil peace" of the province was in danger of crumbling. The foundations of agreement between English- and French-speaking politicians began, slowly, to erode as nationalism, or panic, or intimidation took its toll.

The breadth of anti-English and anti-bilingual feeling

was indeed surprising. Teachers, students, nationalists, demographers all said their piece. Their message was that French was in danger of actually disappearing. Bilingualism was at best a Trojan horse. The simple existence of a large and, it went without saying, rich body of English in Quebec was in itself a threat. Action, and if necessary firm action, was required — action that would necessarily be outside politics and possibly outside the law. Hence the "McGill français" demonstration with its armies of the night marching and singing before the bastion of English power. Hence, too, the troops secretly deployed, and the battalions of police nervously standing by. On one occasion feelings ran so high that all English-speaking schools in Quebec City were closed for fear that their pupils would come to harm. Evidently, the right to study in English, to live in English, was proving a strain on a society that was beginning to look on bilingualism as a zero-sum game. To the nationalists, what existed on the English side of the line was something subtracted from the French side, politically, economically and even psychically. For, according to no less an authority than French president Charles de Gaulle, bilingual societies were profoundly artificial and federal structures a sham. Some Quebec savants were quick to follow the reasoning and to proclaim a bilingual society — in all its aspects — to be psychologically damaging.

This news was rather slow to sink in to other sections of the country, and even in Quebec it was valiantly denied by those who had an interest in making the old system of accommodation function. English-speakers voted massively Liberal in the provincial election of 1970, as they had in every provincial election since 1939. They had little choice. Had not Daniel Johnson, the Union Nationale premier, in analysing his victory in the 1966 election, although his party got fewer votes than the

Liberals, explained away the results by noting that most "real Quebeckers," the French ones, had supported his party?

Drowning in unfamiliar waters, English-speakers grasped at the comforting reed of the Liberal Party. English-speaking support was a powerful electoral tool for the new Liberal leader in Quebec, Robert Bourassa, both in 1970 and 1973, when he won an extraordinary huge majority in the Quebec legislature. The latter election also confirmed the separatist Parti Québécois as the only serious alternative party in the province.

Meanwhile, outside Quebec, voters attempting to shore up the old ways of compromise and accommodation had more of a choice: all national parties supported the implementation of bilingualism and multiculturalism by the federal government in the late 1960s and early 1970s. The Liberal government of Pierre Trudeau took the lead in these matters and also the blame, as resentment rolled in from Canadians who felt left out in a society that required fluency in French for success in the service, political or administrative, of their national government. Because the élites of the media, politics and the bureaucracy agreed that bilingualism was a civilized and civilizing trait, it was easy to dismiss the opposition to bilingualism in English Canada as reactionary, obscurantist and even bigoted.

A new generation of English Canadians, raised on the values of tolerance and liberalism in successful baby-boom families, sent their children to immersion classes in French. Little Mark and Samantha (this was the seventies, after all) followed the adventures of Pierre and Huguette and gazed respectfully at bilingual beavers on the Canadian version of "Sesame Street." This enthusiasm occurred even in areas where, to judge from the electoral map, Trudeau and his government were deeply unpopular. Although provincial governments were more timid, there were advances in Ontario and in New Brunswick, which passed legislation declaring itself bilingual.

These developments were largely ignored inside Quebec. There attention concentrated on data demonstrating that French-speaking Quebeckers were at the bottom of the ladder economically in their own province and on alarming demographic projections that showed that French was doomed to disappear inside Quebec. The equation of the interests of French-speaking Quebec and the French minorities outside Quebec, never strong, weakened considerably; as a result it became increasingly difficult to persuade French-speaking Quebeckers that the survival and tolerable treatment of the French minorities outside the province depended on preserving the status and language rights of English Quebeckers. *Les anglais*, a privileged minority, were well on their way to becoming *les anglos*, a minority pure and simple. Their situation was not, in the long term, helped even by the measures that were taken to protect them.

The October Crisis of 1970 did not improve matters. The use of drastic wartime powers for the first time since 1945 indicated the measures that might be necessary to preserve order in case of a serious nationalist challenge. Recourse to force, or the threat of force, to preserve liberties such as freedom of speech (for opponents of nationalism) or freedom of language (for the English) posed a nice dilemma for Quebec's political élite. Not surprisingly, once the crisis subsided, they once again sought the familiar way of compromise — not, this time, with the English, but with the nationalists.

And so the Bourassa government moved to restrict the rights of the English through Bill 22 in 1974. The demographic problem was to be dealt with by abrogating freedom of choice in schooling by restricting admission to

English schools to children who already knew English. The English were reminded that they lived under the jurisdiction of a French-speaking majority by forfeiting the official status of English in the province: henceforth Quebec would have but one official language, French. Other symbolic changes were demanded: applicants to the civil service, for example, had to be competent in French — a bizarre stipulation, given the almost entirely French character (in origin and language) of the Quebec civil service, in which the English were traditionally unrepresented. (As of 1990, less than 1 per cent of the whole provincial civil service was of English-speaking origin, and only 1.8 per cent of its most senior ranks, although the proportion of native English-speakers in the population is rather more than 10 per cent, to which a fair number of the immigrant community can be added.)

In the private sector *francisation* made its appearance. Businesses were commanded to transform themselves into entities proficient in French, and they were provided with positive and negative incentives to speed the accomplishment of this task. They were compelled to replace unilingual signs with bilingual ones, even in areas where French-speaking customers were few and far between. It became more difficult for young English Quebeckers to find jobs and increasingly they left the province.

The reaction of the immigrant community in Montreal was incredulity and then defiance. The act compelled four-year-olds to undergo tests of linguistic competence. Not all of those who failed automatically passed to the French side: some started to attend underground classes in English, recalling the great American experiment with Prohibition. Anglophone parents dared Bourassa's minions to raid their linguistic speakeasies. The situation was gloriously photogenic, and the media revelled in it.

Bourassa had created a classic confrontation between the state and a population that considered its basic rights to have been violated.

The premier appeared to imagine that the English would understand that he was seeking a middle way between the extreme demands of the radical nationalists and the English community's supposedly indefensible privileges. It was not the last time that he would be impervious to the concerns of English-speakers. Then and in the 1980s, he sought refuge in cant, interpreting English-speakers' reluctance to part with their rights, or to accommodate the collective rights of French Quebeckers, as mere bigotry. He was shocked when, in the provincial election of 1976, many of the English fled the Liberal fold and helped to defeat his government — even though the alternative was the nationalist and separatist Parti Québécois, and René Lévesque.

The PQ government had a language program of its own. Through its Bill 101, passed in 1977, it regulated the school question by restricting admission to English-language schools to the children of those who had already been educated in English, in Quebec. It made what had been optional under Bourassa compulsory: *francisation* would now proceed at a faster pace and by fiat. The language of government and the courts would be French only. And, in its most striking symbolic enactment, the PQ government called even the appearance of English in public "difficult and embarrassing," and forthwith banned all commercial (and many other) displays that were not in French only. Minor exceptions were made for tourism only. The Office de la langue française was established, and materials violating the language laws were seized and burned. Sometimes the enforcement took on the character of a scene from *Alice in Wonderland*. In Westmount and elsewhere, painters obliterated offending words such as "Street" or "Avenue" from signposts. All this gave rise to speculation. What was now permitted? If one wrote "Street" on a letter to Quebec, would it even get delivered by a nationalist postal worker?

In the years after Bill 101, more and more English-speaking firms left the province, and with them more and more English-speakers: 167,000 between 1976 and 1986 (about 90,000 allophones and francophones left too). Though the emigrants tended to be the youngest, most active and most enterprising part of the English-language population, the nationalists were not greatly distressed: they would replace the English, in their desirable jobs, with French-speakers. Politically, the English naturally opposed the separation of the province from Canada, and in the referendum of 1980 they indicated their discontent by voting massively on the *non* side. That rather more than half of French-speakers voted on the same side seemed to indicate that the traditional politics of accommodation still held: there was still hope that English-speakers could survive in Quebec with something like equal rights.

Bill 101 was ultimately contested politically and in the courts. Prime Minister Trudeau in his 1982 Charter of Rights and Freedoms limited some of Bill 101's more sweeping enactments. But to get his package past the provinces, Trudeau had to agree that as far as Charter rights were concerned, Parliament or the provincial legislatures should possess a power to override the so-called "notwithstanding clause." René Lévesque objected to the deal, but his power to do mischief was limited. The nationalist tide in Quebec had peaked and was now ebbing.

The English ambled back to the Liberal corral in the 1981 election under Bourassa's successor, Claude Ryan (who had opposed Bill 101), and they stayed there when

Bourassa rose from the political dead and once again became Liberal leader in 1983. In the aftermath of the referendum, linguistic controversies cooled down somewhat and Bourassa promised to ease the restrictions of Bill 101 on signs and the public display of English. Once again, in the provincial election of 1985, the English voted for the Liberals, and Bourassa became premier.

But Bourassa did not carry out his promises. Acting out of either intimidation or conviction, he was reluctant to tamper with Bill 101's language provisions. In a notable lapse of political judgement, he preferred to leave the problem to the courts, affording time to the nationalist defenders of French-language exclusivity to rally to the defence of official, enforceable unilingualism. The political climate worsened as a result, since it appeared quite likely that the Supreme Court of Canada would indeed overturn Quebec's law requiring exclusively French signs.

For a time, the Meech Lake Accord of 1987 suggested a way out. Possibly that was Premier Bourassa's intention: by securing new rights, however vague, for Quebec, he could better handle his province's minority in the legislature, and in the courts. Bourassa procured a "distinct society" clause for Quebec in the accord, a change that suggested that the courts could interpret Bill 101 in a broader manner, more respectful of the rights of the majority and with less consideration for those of the minority. So at least Quebec's minister of justice thought, when he explained the Meech proposal to the Quebec assembly. And there were many in English Canada who thought he was right.

The doubters briefly included Ian Scott, then Ontario's attorney general, who attempted to argue to Prime Minister Brian Mulroney and the assembled premiers that the phrase "distinct society" was dangerously vague. When Scott cited the example of Quebec's language legislation, Bourassa was offended: "And what is the interest of an elected Ontario politician in the language dispute in Quebec?" None, in the view of the other elected politicians in the room: "It's none of our business," Richard Hatfield, the premier of New Brunswick, declared. Astonished and disquieted, Scott subsided, and Meech Lake was signed.

But Scott's was the sounder instinct. The notion that civil rights were divisible was, at best, politically questionable, especially if the division occurred within the same country. It was also morally unsound and as such would eventually produce considerable discontent. A "distinct society" would surely find ways to preserve its distinctiveness. Those ways would logically include the preservation and even the extension of French unilingualism — for example, painting out "bridge" on federal bridges across the St. Lawrence, as one of Bourassa's ministers suggested at the time. Bourassa promptly passed Meech Lake through his legislature, starting the constitutional clock ticking towards June 23, 1990.

Meech had a timetable, but in retrospect it was not the three-year deadline that was most critical. The accord had precisely eighteen months to run before the Canadian Supreme Court handed down its decision on Bill 101. The court did two things: it showed that it had jurisdiction on the subject. And it sought to render Bill 101's provisions less embarrassing and irritating to the English-speaking population of Quebec. Within days the Bourassa government used the notwithstanding clause to re-enact the controverted provisions of Bill 101, replacing it with Bill 178. It was the expression, in direct, political terms, of the Quebec government's forecast the previous summer that Meech Lake and its "distinct society" would indeed make a difference, and Bill 178 served as a most useful guide to the probable consequences of the 1987 agreement.

The first point, obviously, was the symbolic assertion that no institution with an English-language majority could be trusted to rule on the question of language in Quebec. The notwithstanding clause became the bulwark of Quebec's language jurisdiction over and against the "rights" of its English-speaking citizens. Now French Quebeckers truly had no reason to learn about rights from English Canadians: the notwithstanding clause gave them a fine set of constitutional ear-muffs.

The passage of Bill 178 scuttled the chances, already poor, of Meech Lake passing in the Manitoba legislature, and that was merely the beginning. Newfoundland's new premier Clyde Wells, elected after Meech, turned out to care for rights too: he demanded universal rights applied uniformly across the country. The possibility or probability that Meech was unbalanced, that it restricted the rights of the English minority in Quebec, proved to be an irritant outside the province as well as inside. As polls showed, English Canadians opposed Meech. And when, to secure its passage, Mulroney and Bourassa resorted to the threat that Quebec would otherwise separate, the public's response was if anything more negative. The politics of accommodation had reached the end of its tether, over precisely the issue that had given it birth in the nineteenth century. As if to mark that fact, the English minority massively deserted the Liberal Party in the 1989 provincial election, electing its own ethnic representatives in the forlornly named "Equality Party." It was a sign that the English felt as unrepresented by the political system as they were already disadvantaged by the constitutional structure.

Today English Quebeckers' future in Quebec appears

to be anything but secure. Despite promises of improvements from Quebec politicians, the English minority seems poised for an even larger emigration than that of the late 1970s. If federal powers over the economy are diminished in a solution to the Quebec crisis, the minority's ability to withstand Quebec's regulation of the language of work will be further eroded. And if independence is chosen, most of the English minority will effectively become internal exiles in the land of their birth. Small wonder, then, that so many contemplate departure.

Constitutional architects in many countries have over the years contrived many wonderful governmental edifices. Most have some form of external walls and central heating, fuelled by tax money. Some, like Canada's, seem to defy the laws of gravity as one after another of their central pillars are removed. Some, along the same road, have already collapsed. Those that remain standing do so because their inhabitants are convinced that they have something in common: common interests or at least common rights. Those common rights have recently come under threat in Canada as the pressures of Quebec nationalism have driven the governments of that province, willingly or unwillingly, to disregard the interests of its English-language minority in favour of the collective rights of its French majority.

This unhappy situation will not suddenly disappear, whether or not Quebec separates from Canada. External minorities are just as potent a force in public opinion as those inside a country, and perhaps more so. For as events in South Africa or eastern Europe and even Iraq have shown, the power of civil rights and their appeal to the imagination exceed the ability of a repressive government, even one supported by a tide of fervent nationalism, to suppress them.

Ontario and the
Deconfederation of Canada

Donald Swainson

Donald Swainson, born in Manitoba, teaches history at Queen's University and researches and writes about the city of Kingston and the province of Ontario.

Since the eighteenth century, Ontario has existed in a variety of sizes and constitutional configurations. Prior to 1791 it was part of the old Province of Quebec. The Constitutional Act of 1791 established the southerly portion of present-day Ontario as Upper Canada, a province of the British Empire. Upper Canada came into jurisdictional existence in 1792 when John Graves Simcoe was sworn into office as the province's first lieutenant-governor. Upper Canada ceased to exist in 1841 when, under the terms of the Act of Union, it was merged with Lower Canada into a legislative union. That experiment lasted until 1867 when our present federal state was born and Ontario regained its status as a separate constitutional entity.

The United Province of Canada, the legislative union that lasted from 1841 until 1867, was a profoundly troubled entity. Those troubles were similar to some of Canada's contemporary problems. During the period of the Union, the anglophone and francophone blocs could never arrive at a mutually acceptable balance of political power. They could not find a political/constitutional formula that satisfied the interests of both blocs. They did not share a common vision of economic development and were never in agreement concerning the allocation of public funds between the two sections of the Union. The issue of westward expansion into the prairies and beyond became divisive: Ontario felt that its expansionary ambitions were constrained by Quebec's indifference and a constitutional system that made expansion impracticable. These basic differences were reflected in a variety of ways. Electoral politics became increasingly polarized on a regional basis. Differences concerning cultural policy — in this instance revolving around language and denominational versus public education — became central concerns and produced nasty and brutal debates. Attempts were made to provide solutions through electoral and parliamentary reform, attempts that led to further acrimony.

By the 1860s it was clear that the Union system had failed: there were no solutions within its framework that were satisfactory to both the anglophone and francophone communities. Politics had become hopelessly deadlocked; the Union was ungovernable.

To find a solution, the Union had to go. It was replaced by the confederation of 1867, which united Nova Scotia, New Brunswick, Quebec and Ontario in the federal union that in an expanded format is the Canada that we know. Confederation, certainly in anglophone Canada, is usually viewed positively as a nation-building measure. At the same time it should be remembered that it also represented the breakdown of the Ontario/Quebec legislative union. It is legitimate to view Confederation, for Ontario and Quebec, as a process of de-integration — as the admission of failure to integrate into one structure the anglophone and francophone societies of central Canada. When considering the possibility of imminent deconfederation, it is useful for Ontarians at least to remember that they have done something similar before and that the reasons for our present crisis are broadly understandable within the framework of the 1860s.

Of course the players then did not act as they do now. In the 1860s Ontario was the unit aggressively pushing for change, and the province obtained that change along with a number of valuable concessions. Fundamentally Ontario had won a major victory, a fact well illustrated by its place in the new federation. According to the census of 1871, Ontario had 1.6 million persons or 46 per cent of a total Canadian population of 3.5 million. It was easily the wealthiest and most dynamic of the provinces. Its share of seats in the House of Commons in 1867 was proportional to its population, namely 82 of 181 members, or 45 per cent. The prime minister, Sir John A. Macdonald, was an Ontarian, as was George Brown, the key opposition figure from his resignation from the Confederation Coalition in 1865 until his personal defeat in the general election of 1867. Brown's position was then taken by Alexander Mackenzie, who in turn was succeeded in 1880 by Edward Blake.

Both Mackenzie and Blake were Ontarians: it was assumed by most public figures that a potential prime minister should be an Ontarian, not a Quebecker. In addition to Sir John A. Macdonald, Ontario had four federal ministers, for a total of five out of thirteen federal cabinet places. The capital was in Ontario. When a provisional government was established for the North-West in 1869, William McDougall, a long-time Ontario Grit expansionist, was named lieutenant-governor. This appointment symbolized the understanding that the opening of the West would be an Ontario enterprise. At the same time, Ontario retained its access routes to the Atlantic.

What did Ontario pay for this great place in the new dominion? In reality, amazingly little. The Senate was to have equal representation on a regional basis — twenty-four members each from the Maritimes, Quebec and Ontario. This meant that Ontario was substantially under-represented compared with the other regions. On the other hand, representation in the House of Commons was to be based on population: representation by population was a major victory for Ontario, which had agitated for such a system for some time. The federal Parliament and federal courts were to be bilingual. That concession to francophone Canadians was very limited. Francophone Ontarians, unlike anglophone Quebeckers, received no linguistic guarantees whatever.

Ontario's only major concession related to education. That concession is located in a sub-section of Section 93 of the British North America Act (1867): "Nothing in any such [provincial] Law shall prejudicially affect any Right or Privilege with respect to Denominational Schools which any Class of Persons have by Law in the Province at the Union." This sub-section guaranteed in perpetuity the existence (with public funding) of Ontario's Roman Catholic separate school system. It was a major concession because the separate school system had been imposed on Ontario by Quebec votes in the Union's legislative assembly. A majority of Ontario's members consistently voted against establishing and later expanding the system, which was and has remained bitterly unpopular with many sections of Ontario opinion.

Ontario maximized the powerful position that it had obtained at such little cost. Much of this work was accomplished by Sir Oliver Mowat, Liberal premier from 1872 to 1896. Three important processes occurred during these years. First, Ontario evolved into a mature and definable unit economically, socially and politically. Second, the nature of the Canadian federal state, which Ontario had been so instrumental in founding, was in many ways defined. Third, Ontario's primacy within that federal state was definitively established. Dr. Margaret Evans, Mowat's biographer, was perfectly correct when she commented: "Under [Mowat's] careful but forward-looking guidance, the province left behind its pioneer youth and moved steadily and prosperously toward maturity in the twentieth century, when his type of leadership with the same success, would pass over to the Conservative party of Ontario."

Hence twentieth-century Ontario has been a politically stable and mature society possessed of Canada's most sophisticated economy. It is the federation's most important province and exercises enormous clout in federal politics. Toronto is now Canada's largest and most important city financially and culturally. In short, twentieth-century Ontario has been for the most part a highly successful society. Thus it has a substantial interest in the maintenance of the status quo. After all, the province has achieved its high degree of success within the institutional and economic frameworks established in 1867. From time to time, those frameworks have been modified, but the Confederation mould, while regularly challenged, has never been shattered.

That is now changing. Quebec seems intent on revolutionizing Confederation in its own interest or leaving Canada to become a sovereign state. This situation presents Ontario with a complicated problem and that problem is made even more difficult by the current Canadian political situation. In response to the Meech Lake fiasco, Premier Robert Bourassa and his associates have staked out a reasonably clear political position. They want that position dealt with by Canada within the framework of a timetable dictated by Quebec. In essence, the government of Quebec wants a radically decentralized Canada with so many powers transferred to the province that, for all intents and purposes, Quebec would become *de facto* a sovereign state. Further, Quebec wants this new constitutional arrangement finalized over a very short period of time and has made it clear that it will entertain proposals from the rest of Canada but has little interest in any real negotiations. Mr. Bourassa's position is widely approved by francophone Quebeckers.

The rest of Canada is in disarray. The national government is led by a prime minister who is a Quebecker closely tied to francophone nationalists who sympathize with Mr. Bourassa's position. The Conservative government's support nationally has plummeted so dramatically that it is now probably the most unpopular federal regime since that of Alexander Mackenzie (1873–78). In any event, Mr. Mulroney and his colleagues have offered nothing of constitutional utility since the failure of the Meech Lake Accord. The Mulroney government cannot negotiate a "deal" between Canada and Quebec: it lacks credibility, policy, will and a viable amending mechanism.

The provinces are not much better off. It is difficult to envision the provincial premiers working out arrangements that could satisfy both Quebec and their own electorates. Several of them are likely to be out of office shortly. Others, like Don Getty of Alberta, possess no national stature whatever. Premiers Frank McKenna of New Brunswick and Joe Ghiz of Prince Edward Island preside over stable political situations, but neither has the national prestige or political power base to lead the country. Clyde Wells is regarded as a Trudeau partisan while Gary Filmon of Manitoba leads a government that is not distinguished and that has only a tenuous claim to the support of Manitobans. In Ontario, Premier Bob Rae has a run at power of four or so years with a strong legislative majority, although he came to power with a very small popular vote of roughly 37.5 per cent. It is hardly likely that Premier Rae can provide the necessary leadership to resolve the constitutional problems that confront us.

This lack of useful leadership from Ottawa or from the anglophone premiers has led a variety of experts and commentators to argue that we should circumvent normal channels and procedures. It has been suggested that we have a national referendum or plebiscite on the issue. Presumably some package of concessions would be submitted to the people in this manner. The last national plebiscite was held in 1942, regarding conscription; a better recipe for disunity and disaster can scarcely be imagined.

Others recommend the formation of a constituent assembly. In many respects this notion is droll. If the objective of such an assembly was to amend the constitution in ways satisfactory to the national government, Quebec and most of the other provinces, it would have to be staffed with constitutional experts and lawyers — the exact groups that have placed us in our present position. If the objective was to draft a new Constitution from scratch, the assembly would have to be prepared to replace the existing constitution, which protects a massive number of important and entrenched interests.

A basic problem with the referendum/plebiscite and constituent assembly options is that it is difficult to understand how they could bypass the existing amending formulas unless we enter a revolutionary phase and are willing to dispense with the law of the land. It would seem that the national government and the provinces that must confront the Quebec issue have painted themselves into a most unfortunate political/constitutional corner. The existing situation made it easy for Quebec to seize the initiative and renders it extremely difficult, if not impossible, for the rest of us to respond adequately. It is within this grim context that Ontario must respond to the unity crisis as it continues to unfold.

The province's response will come in two major stages. First, during the months ahead the process of trying to patch things together will continue. Various proposals will be added to those already suggested. Second, if the patch-things-together process fails, we will have to face the crisis of deconfederation. Ontario will have to make some important decisions about its relationship with those parts of Canada that remain within Confederation as well as about some aspects of its own structure.

Numerous proposals for patching things together will be made and will continue to be made until the last minute. If sufficient desperation is generated, some of these proposals could become highly dangerous. Writing in the *Kingston Whig-Standard* on May 8, 1991, Peter Trueman said: "I no longer oppose giving Quebec more or less what it wants. I have finally come to the edge of the cliff, and now that I have seen the abyss, I think we've got to placate Quebec any way we can, and maintain a formal relationship at all costs. Formal separation would be ruinous, both for Quebeckers and the rest of us." Using a signed blank cheque as a patch could (and almost certainly would) produce a Canada with a central government that was nothing more than a powerless shell. The anglophone component of Quebec would live in perpetual humiliation. Most Canadians of ethnic origins other than English or French would be enraged. Quebec would enjoy *both* sovereignty and the benefits of provincehood. The resultant country would be a sham, capable of enjoying neither national interests nor national standards.

The primary mandate of the government of Ontario, which also takes a proper interest in the welfare of the country as a whole, is to protect and further the interests of the province it governs. Any patching proposal must be viewed through the prism of those interests. It is in Ontario's interest to assure that Canada's central government — whatever form Canada takes — remains strong. For example, Ottawa could not share control of fiscal and monetary policy with a sovereign or quasi-sovereign Quebec. Control over international trade must remain a federal jurisdiction and Ottawa requires sufficient taxing authority to maintain (and increase) its system of transfer payments. The national debt must be shared equitably by those who incurred it, whether they are within or without the federation. Completely free access to Atlantic Canada and the ocean is a vital Ontario interest. The various social programs that are central to the quality of life of Ontarians cannot be Balkanized, because that process would lead to the erosion of their quality. National institutions must remain viable. It would not be acceptable, for example, for MPs from provinces that have opted out of a program that affected Ontarians to participate in the design or modification of that program. There are, of course, many additional vital Ontario interests. They must not be sacrificed in rushed and desperate attempts to appease the nationalist movement in Quebec.

If Quebec does separate and we face the reality of deconfederation, Ontario will have to consider the second stage of its response. It will have to consider its relationship with what remains of Canada. The assumption here is that the federation will continue without Quebec.

Under the conditions of deconfederation, Ontario will want to reflect on the agreements it made when it entered Confederation. For example, the province's system of separate schools exists because of one of those agreements, and this arrangement was very much an Ontario/Quebec agreement. The separate school system is heavily entrenched and Ontario's Roman Catholic community is substantial and influential. Nonetheless, it would be naive not to assume that this agreement would come under heavy attack. Separate schools might well survive, but the issue would be hotly and bitterly debated.

Language rights are similar. It is true that the original Confederation agreement bound Ontario to do nothing concerning language rights for Franco-Ontarians. However, as part of the process of accommodating Quebec during the post-1960 period, extensive privileges were arranged for Franco-Ontarians. Under deconfederation those privileges would be vulnerable. Ontario would likely become a unilingual anglophone society.

Regional equality in the Senate was another of Ontario's Confederation concessions. The absence of

Quebec need not change the logic of the Senate, such as that logic is. We could continue to have regional equality with three rather than the four current regions. However, regionalism will become a most pressing problem in a Canada without Quebec — even more pressing than is currently the case. Ontario will be so large in relation to the rest of the country that its very size will engender great fear. There will be a campaign to limit Ontario's power through a triple-E Senate. Another proposal to limit Ontario's authority would be the dismemberment of Ontario, the division of the province into several smaller provinces that would be more in balance with western and Atlantic provinces. It is doubtful that Ontarians, except possibly for some in the north, would accept dismemberment, and the provincial leadership could not accept any such proposal within its mandate of defending the interests of the unit it governs.

Regional polarization within a deconfederated Canada would be a significant problem and should, in the interests of a properly functioning federal state, be minimized. The best way to do this might well be to introduce a system of proportional representation for the House of Commons. That kind of arrangement would ensure that major political parties would have significant representation from all regions. Representation of that sort would be a major unifying influence.

For the last decade lawyers, business leaders, public servants, politicians, academics, constitutional experts and journalists have been heavily engaged in the debate over the state and future of the Canadian federation. Many grass-roots Canadians have been involved as well, but to date outside Quebec the discussion has tended to be heavily élitist. We do not really know what emotions will be unleashed if, as a society, we actually go to Peter Trueman's "cliff" and look over at the "abyss." By accommodating Quebec at any cost, we might well let loose forces in Ontario and elsewhere that we did not anticipate, do not understand and will not be able to control. Ordinary Canadians might then revolt against the political leadership that has brought the country to this point and demand a change in direction. We can only hope that happens. Certainly the traditional élites have led us nowhere but into a hole so deep that there seems no way out. It is difficult to understand how Ontario or any other region will benefit from the trauma of deconfederation. What Ontario and Canada desperately need is a very strong dose of old-fashioned good luck.

Cardinal Points
on a Prairie Compass

Gerald Friesen

Gerald Friesen teaches Canadian history at the University of Manitoba and is author of The Canadian Prairies: A History.

Canadian political journalism is rife with directional metaphors — the West, the North, the East and so on. From my own point of view, Canadians hear too much about that monolithic entity the West, and not enough about the crucial division within the Prairies, that between conservatives and social democrats. Left and right are the truly important points on the Prairie compass.

That Prairie folk debate the merits of Devine and Romanow, Getty and Martin, Filmon and Doer in just that way — as a duel between opposites — might not seem surprising. And when talk turns to national politics, the pattern remains left-right. If the debaters are conservatives, their subjects are recession, the high dollar, interest rates and grain subsidies. If they are social democrats, they add Mulroney, the GST and free trade to the list. This pattern will sound familiar: it is the dominant pattern in Canadian politics.

A casualty in the growing influence of left versus right, or social democracy versus conservatism, is the old assumption about a homogeneous Prairie society. The idea of "West" belongs to another age. It had resonance in the days of the *Pays d'en haut,* the fabulous fur country beyond the Great Lakes. It meant a great deal to "easterners" when their children headed "out there" or "up there" to farm and every Canadian family had, as Stephen Leacock wrote, its western odyssey. It even mattered in politics when Ottawa governed the land and resource policy for the entire western interior (1870–1930) and when aboriginal people resisted Canada's race-based imperialist presumptions (the Indian Act, the suppression of religious ceremonies, the introduction of residential schools). And it had some economic meaning when agriculture dominated the economies of the Prairie provinces (though grain farms and mixed farms and ranches were very different, they could be seen in the same light). But today? We live in a new era.

The Prairie provinces are urban. Very few Prairie people farm. About two-thirds of all jobs are in the service or tertiary sector. Though national journalists, when they turn to the Prairies, talk about farm-income programs called GRIP and NISA, they would be justified in devoting equal space to health care and education and media workers who, by virtue of their numbers, if not their historic wealth-creation roles, are just as important in the local economy.

A key question in this modern Prairie world, as in other developed economies, is one's employer. Are you paid out of tax dollars and thus sustained by the entire community? Or do you depend on a buyer, a consumer who pays you directly for your wares? And does the distinction influence your political perceptions?

The market dominates Prairie political debates. If you choose to concentrate on the collapse of the centrally run command economies of Eastern Europe, the apparent abundance of material goods and the greater economic efficiency of Japan, the alleged feather-bedding in government bureaucracies and the "lean, aggressive" approach to production and sales in private enterprise corporations, you are of the right. If you prefer to discuss health and social issues in terms of safety nets, goods production in terms of use values and environmental impact, marketing in terms of consumer education and personal control, you are of the left. Of course, the possibilities of overlaps and cross-overs are infinite. But the pattern is clear in the Prairies as it is in many other parts of the world.

Prairie people choose one side or the other of the great left-right divide in national politics, too. Free trade and Meech Lake are, of course, the recent code words for our grand national political discussions. Most Prairie New Democrats opposed both measures, at least until the climactic week in June 1990 when hope of constitutional compromise was exhausted. Most Prairie Conservatives, at least those prepared to follow the official line on Meech handed down from Edmonton and Regina (Manitoba Tories eventually had to perform a balancing act), supported both. The difference of opinion was left-right: social democrats preferred some regulation of the market, some Crown corporations, some nationally established standards in health care and day care, and so on. The Tories preferred a more decentralized, privatized, deregulated, open trading environment.

There are issues on which Prairie perspectives reflect a distinctive Prairie political and cultural experience. The Senate leaps to mind. So do multicultural, bilingual and aboriginal policies. But they do not add up to a "western" vision for the nation.

Talk of the triple-E Senate has been passed off as a universal western demand in the current constitutional discussions. Behind the catch-phrase lies an assumption that western interests are not taken into account in national policy making. A Maritimer might well reply that westerners are running the present federal Conservative government and, for the moment, branches of the same party hold power in the three Prairie provinces. If they can't get their way now, what difference would a Senate make?

Surely the answer is none. The problem is not the Senate. It is politics and policy choices. CF-18 is the code word that best illustrates the problem. Or, ten years ago, NEP (National Energy Policy). Or, a decade before that, LIFT (Lower Inventory For Tomorrow, a wheat-acreage reduction scheme). The details of these ill-fated programs matter to the leaders of Manitoba's aerospace industry, Alberta's petroleum industry, and Saskatchewan's grain industry, respectively, but need not be rehearsed again. From today's perspective, instead, these policy choices are important because, though simply that — policy choices — they were interpreted in the Prairies as regional affronts. The explanation of that leap in logic, from necessary policy choice to regional crisis, lies first in the history of Prairie protest (the "regional bias" of Prairie politics from Riel to Lougheed) and, second, in the structure of a national electoral system that reinforces territory-based dissent.

Senate reform would not end the need for difficult policy choices nor would it ensure that mistakes never occurred. On the other hand, a reformed and respected Senate (should we launch a double-R campaign?) would offer a forum in which to air grievances and present alternatives. Other societies, among which the aboriginal and Asian come immediately to mind, find important roles for elders in their social, family and political deliberations. Our task is to create a better vehicle for the voices of experienced statespersons and for province-based perspectives on national issues. The campaign led by the Canada West Foundation to create a triple-E Senate is not a "western" demand in constitutional talks. But it is one western contribution to a debate that requires much more attention before the nation chooses a path.

Another western perspective on the Constitution, or so it is often treated, concerns language and cultures in Canada. Indeed, popular disturbances about bilingualism and multiculturalism are often given a western colouring in the so-called national media. French-language services in Manitoba, the use of French as an "official" language in Saskatchewan and Alberta, petitions concerning the integration of Sikh turbans and Indian braids into RCMP uniform and dress codes, distribution of racist pamphlets and the teachings of an anti-Semite who wishes to rewrite the history of the European Holocaust have all received media attention. They offer easy and spectacular targets. Treated in isolation, they can blacken unfairly the reputation of entire communities.

The creation and maintenance of a plural society is a difficult task. But, if any community has grappled seriously with the assignment and achieved a modest degree of success, it is the Canadian West. Look for a moment at the past century: suppression of aboriginal religion and culture; exclusion policies and riots over Asian immigration; Mennonite exodus; Doukhobor marches; Ukrainian internments; "enemy alien" disfranchisement; anti-English and anti-German hiring policies; quotas in universities; Japanese eviction and resettlement; and the unsubtle daily racism of majoritarian public schools. The list is long and painful and yet it represents, in retrospect, a small victory. The persecuted groups remain in this community, having adapted and yet still able and determined to remember.

Multiculturalism is today's term for our attempts to continue and improve upon the inherited pluralism. It reflects a desire to seek a less uniform, less fervent identity than that created in another great model of multinational readjustment, the United States. The concept finds its political expression in the wish of long-established ethnic groups such as the Ukrainians and Italians and Germans to see the plural ideal enshrined in the Constitution as one of Canada's fundamental characteristics. This may or may not be wise — like the Senate, it requires careful review — but it is worthy of serious discussion. Having left our "British century" behind, we may be embarking upon a "Canadian century." In an ideal world, this new age would be plural without being plagued by racism, on the one hand, or insistently majoritarian and conformist, on the other. Whether there will ever be a Canadian century, let alone one founded upon pluralism, remains to be seen.

Bilingualism has run into a rough patch in recent months. Prairie Canadians are not alone in challenging its efficacy. But after twenty years of remarkable achievement, the strife need not be the source of despair. Rather, we might recall that parts of Canada, not least the grain economy, have been under stress and that in tough times the stranger is often made the scapegoat. The response of more-favoured citizens should be patience, not condemnation.

Aboriginal issues occupy a special place in western constitutional discussions. The recent hearings of the Manitoba legislature's Constitutional Task Force encountered strong popular support for immediate action on the concerns of Canada's aboriginal people. Left-right or East-West politics played little part in this interest. The citizens who presented briefs were urging the completion of the unfinished business of the 1982 Constitution.

In the aftermath of the crisis at Oka, the British Columbia court decision in the Gitksan and Wet'suwet'en lands case, the Ontario court ruling in the Temagami land case and the Nova Scotia hunting rights trials, Prairie Canadians cannot claim a unique interest in aboriginal issues. However, they can claim to be acutely aware of these matters and to be in daily contact with aboriginal people. This contact is unequalled in eastern Canadian cities. Moreover, aboriginal representatives have won public respect in the Prairies. To use the Manitoba example, Elijah Harper, Phil Fontaine, Ovide Mercredi and Murray Sinclair are celebrities not only in the facile sense that they are media stars, but also because they have earned the confidence of Manitobans by their words and behaviour in difficult situations. For these reasons, a constitutional settlement on aboriginal issues has become, in the Prairie approach to the national debate, a priority.

We face important decisions. The economic restructuring that confronts the entire globe requires continuing Canadian responses. The Pacific Rim nations at once command the attention of British Columbians and dispatch immigrants who have changed the character of that province. The American north-west, as rich and diverse as the two adjoining Canadian provinces, raises the prospect of a transnational entity of a different kind. Already a committee of civil servants has met to discuss the potential of this federation. Confronted by economic decline, Saskatchewan turns increasingly towards Alberta for support. Manitoba looks to Ottawa and Toronto. The pressures on Confederation, in short, are as real in this part of the country as elsewhere.

There is no natural law that decrees the continuing necessity of a transcontinental nation on the northern half of North America. Rather, political will has sustained Canada, and it can be rallied once more. The flexibility of our constitution will be crucial as we grapple with these issues. One can only trust that our cultural institutions will be equal to the task of facilitating a national debate. One might also express the pious wish that the eventual choice will represent genuinely democratic decision making. And one can only hope that our compatriots in Quebec will see, as we in the Prairies do, convincing reasons to renew the homeland that has endured for so long.

As they reflect on these matters, let these Québécois be assured by the Prairie residents who rejected Meech Lake: we did so, in many cases, because we are motivated by social democracy and national self-preservation. Thus, on the political map, we are concerned about "left" and "North." We saw the Meech Lake amendments as an attempt to entrench a more right-facing and more southerly aspect in Canada's constitution. We see no need to fight again over old East-West or French-English quarrels. Not all Quebeckers will accept our views, we know, because some among them will prefer a more rightist vision, too. They are free to choose. We said no to Meech Lake because we, too, have a vision of a homeland.

Reconciling Our Origins,
Facing Our Future

Johanna den Hertog

Johanna den Hertog lives in Vancouver. She has been president of the federal New Democratic Party and ran for the party in the 1984 and 1988 federal elections.

The overwhelming majority of Canadians agree that we will all be the losers if the outcome of the current constitutional crisis is dissolution of our federation. Substantial numbers of Quebeckers — including those who think independence is a very real option — still wish and hope for a national reconciliation that will permit a united Canada.

Others who have deep grievances over matters left unresolved by our current constitution, such as aboriginal people and northerners, argue strongly for maintaining a united Canada. Voices for increased decentralization, both among those who have partisan and self-interested provincial agendas, and among others who are responding to public disillusionment with some aspects of federalism, still argue for a united Canada. And those who want a stronger national government, in order to respond to regional disparity, child poverty or unemployment, passionately assert their belief in the importance of "one Canada."

But even a genuine will towards unity will likely not be enough to satisfactorily resolve the constitutional dilemma. Three main issues have contributed most to the current impasse. First, we have a profound disagreement within Canada about the importance of the constitutional impasse. There is a great deal of difference between the views of anglophone Canada and Quebec over the centrality of the current crisis. In anglophone Canada, doubt persists that the debate is as serious as some claim it to be. There is also a view that even if the crisis is serious, its outcome will make little difference to anglophone Canada. This scepticism leads to a profound lack of urgency. This is not the situation in Quebec, nor is it so among aboriginal people.

Secondly, the impasse is assisted by our overwhelming collective ignorance of our country's history. The understood bargains upon which Canada is based are not common knowledge, especially outside of Quebec. We are not familiar with the political, legal and economic contracts Canadians have lived under for almost 130 years. This ignorance has fuelled misunderstanding and prevented agreement about the specifics of what is in debate among the public, including many provincial politicians. The vacuum of historical knowledge has been filled with various myths about Canada, about how it works and how we got to where we are today, myths that severely limit the options for accommodation.

Third, a fundamental impasse has evolved over the purpose of constitutional change. This has contributed greatly to the frustration felt by all Canadians with the current constitutional crisis. Some see the current agenda as merely codifying in words the current realities. Others see constitutional reform as prescriptive, a process that will determine "what Canada should look like in the future." Their anxiety can be summed up as: "If we don't get it in the Constitution, we won't get it at all, in any way, in the future." This lack of agreement over the basic objectives of constitutional reform is debilitating and severely hampers the likelihood of getting majority agreement on even what issues can be tackled. We are in danger of losing Canada partly because we (especially those of us in anglophone Canada) are starting to demand results from a constitution that are far beyond what can be delivered by any constitutional document, let alone by limited changes to an existing and highly complex compact.

Let us now look at these three factors of the constitutional debate in more detail.

Canadians are on a course of almost accidentally losing our country, because we are not able to come to grips with how crucial the constitutional issue is to our future. While Quebeckers may have developed unrealistically high expectations of how significant their demands for additional constitutional powers are to their goal of protecting and enhancing a unique francophone culture, in the rest of Canada we have sadly downplayed the importance *for ourselves* of success in resolving this constitutional impasse.

Some say the debate is not important, because they believe that in the end Quebec may stay anyway. Others say that the "real" debate is on how we achieve economic, environmental or social changes. Some assert that we should not be blackmailed into having to come to a resolution "according to Quebec's timeline," and that we should let the process take "as long as it takes." Others, again overwhelmingly in anglophone Canada, are not convinced of the importance of the outcome: whether Quebec stays or not is of little concern to them. Some take the tack that what the rest of us do will be irrelevant to Quebec's decision anyway, so why debate or confront their specific demands. Some assert the view that Quebec's separation is inevitable, so why bother to consider changes in the meantime. There are even some who take the view that we may be better off if Quebec is no longer part of Canada — from the political right (we can get rid of the Official Languages Policy) and from the political left (without Quebec we may not have had free trade — or Brian Mulroney, for that matter).

These are all seductive and powerful arguments, because they contain some important kernels of truth. Nevertheless they are frightening and inaccurate and may be helping to make a constitutional resolution less achievable.

Economically, the road ahead is challenging whether Quebec remains part of Canada or not. But without Quebec, the road to achieving greater prosperity and greater equity will be many orders of magnitude more difficult. A separate Canada and Quebec would make us both smaller players within the continent, within the OECD, with Europe or with Japan and other East Asian economies. We will face far more unpleasant tensions over export markets when we are no longer part of the same economic unit: imagine the effects of competition over logging, mining, hydro-electric contracts if Quebec's success means a loss to Canada, or if Alberta's success means a reduction of Quebec's market. The lack of national co-ordination of economic strategies is already a major weakness in Canada's international approach to trade. The fracturing of this country will be a boon to our competitors and customers, but will weaken our economic clout.

Surely we know in our bones that as Canadians we have been able to create the existing levels of affluence and equity only in spite of our enormous geographic size and small population base. We have succeeded precisely because through our railways and canals in the 1800s and early 1900s we made a large economy out of some very small regional economies. We are still doing the same today — in telecommunications, in energy, in publishing, in education and in health care.

A separation between Quebec and the rest of Canada would be a wrenching and diminishing experience for both economies and would reduce our ability to use efficiently our sparse human resources for future economic development. In economic terms, Quebec is not merely one of ten provinces. The separation of Quebec would mean the loss of fully one-quarter of our population.

For those most at risk within a pure market environment, the economic consequences of a split in the Canadian nation will be most severe and most immediate. Head offices, managers, investment capital are all more mobile than workers. Corporations may not like the short-term costs of instability and change, but in the long run less public or government involvement in cross-Canada standards or programs is only going to be looked on favourably by business. Conversely, trade unionists who will face competing labour markets in Quebec and Ontario, for example, whether in automobiles or in telecommunications, are not going to find it easier to negotiate fair settlements. Parents are going to find it harder to insist on national day-care strategies. The perennial balancing act between a densely populated Ontario and Quebec, and the resource-oriented and less populated other regions of Canada, will be more fraught with tension and harder to sustain politically without Quebec.

The economic impact of separation on equity and national economic strategy is only one reason why we must be concerned about the outcome of this constitutional crisis. We must succeed for political reasons. To fashion the kind of country that we identify as distinctly Canadian requires governments that are sufficiently strong domestically to be a countervailing force to corporate concerns, whether they be Canadian or foreign. As well, we Canadians pride ourselves, perhaps sometimes too quickly, on our unique abilities and roles internationally. Our importance as a country in the international arena — in peace, in development, in minority and equality issues, in the environment — can only be diminished if we become two countries. If we are seen as incapable of accommodating within our own borders the legitimate aspirations of a large Quebec minority, or a smaller but arguably even more legitimate aboriginal minority, how much claim will we have on ideas for peacemaking in other parts of the world? And as two countries how much less clout will we all have in asserting an independent Canadian way within the overpowering context of North America, with our large superpower neighbour to the south with ten times our population?

What we do in the next twelve months is not irrelevant to what Quebec sees as its options. This is not a time for more suggestions of what should be changed. This is a time for more listening to the suggestions that have already been made — primarily by Quebec — for resolving the constitutional impasse.

Most Quebeckers want to find an accommodation *within* Canada. This means they want to be fully part of our federal system, of our national economy, of our Parliament. But it also means they want to retain a unique culture in Quebec. The rest of Canada *must fully accept this uniqueness within Canada*. The results of our approach in the rest of Canada will be key to whether an accommodation or a "renewed" contract with Quebec is possible. If we fail, it is hard to imagine that it then will be easier to find a new accommodation in some sort of "superstructure" that embraces both Quebec and the rest of Canada.

The "superstructure" approach threatens to limit the jurisdiction of the federal government even further. Monetary policy (bank rates), exchange rates, international positions, national security, trade — are these to become the purview of this limited but powerful "super-house"? Are we in fact proposing equal status for Canada and Quebec within one national structure? This is surely a recipe for total paralysis. A superstructure that gives Canada one vote and a sovereign Quebec one vote on so-called common concerns is unrealistic and a non-starter.

The second major impasse is the fundamental disagreement we have come to about whether Canada's federal structure requires equality among the provinces. This issue has become an enormous hurdle not so much because of clear differences expressed about what Canada should look like, as because of different assumptions about how the present federation works.

We do not have a symmetrical federal system now, nor have we ever had. Provinces have varying powers, and this applies not only to Quebec. This variety is the product of a country that was formed not at one moment, but over many decades, as pieces — distinct cultural and economic pieces — were added over the years. For example, Prince Edward Island has unique parliamentary protection in seats in the Commons, in recognition of its unique size. The Prairie telephone systems were in provincial jurisdiction, while the federal government chartered the British Columbia system. British Columbia has unique constitutional protection for the railroad, reflecting the federal commitment in the early 1870s to this province. Other provinces have unique language and school guarantees.

The territories have changed in size and in degree of autonomy many times over the last one hundred years, and this process continues. The territories may become two or three provinces, and many in these regions hope the day of provincial status is not far off. There is no reason to think that these "new" provinces will be any different than the "new" provinces of Newfoundland, Alberta and Manitoba were in their times. Each of these provinces came into Confederation on slightly "unique" or "distinct" terms, and few Canadians argue that this has seriously weakened our federation.

Aboriginal land title and self-government are two more areas where a belief that we will somehow create one standard model for the whole country flies in the face of reality. As we resolve these issues, aboriginal nations, the provinces and the federal government will likely wish to entrench slightly different political options across the country.

We are rewriting Canadian history if we demand symmetry either in our existing constitutional arrangement or in every future change. If we were to go back to the 1860s, and to "do" Canada over again, we would soon discover that we could never forge a nation if we insisted that no province could be distinct in any way or receive any powers or protections not afforded to others.

This constitutional round is truly a "Canada Round" in that it is a hard test of how well we can come to terms with our evolutionary history as a nation. The recognition of distinctness and difference, not only through legislative means but also in constitutional arrangements, is in many ways the essence of Canada's unique history and political system. Every country's constitution reflects its history, and ours is no exception.

The third important impasse is our complete lack of agreement on the purpose of this or any round of constitutional change. Perhaps because we are new to the problem of amending a constitution; perhaps because the current impasse has begun to approach its tenth anniversary; perhaps because the failure of the Meech process has led to tremendously high expectations — for whatever reasons, Canadians nourish dangerously high hopes and wishes from this "Canada Round" of negotiations. The risk is that we could fail even if a constitutional resolution is possible.

The first factor contributing to this risk of failure is the tendency to treat these constitutional discussions as efforts to create a new Canada, rather than to improve the existing Canada. The failure of the Meech proposal was partly due to this same disease. Too many issues were hastily added to the agenda: Senate reform, unclear changes to the national role in provincial jurisdictions and changes in unanimity requirements, to cite three examples. Now some are proposing to revamp the whole Constitution. Expanding or changing the Charter (multicultural recognition, collective rights, economic rights), changing federal institutions such as the Supreme Court or Parliament, Senate reform, changing amending formulas and processes, institutionalizing new forums of constitutional development (constituent assemblies and the like): our expectations have become impossible to fulfil. Impossible at least in one constitutional round.

Let us by all means work at creating as much agreement or even consensus on as many outstanding questions as we can. The more issues that can be identified as issues that will unite Canadians, the more likely a constitutional resolution is. But those items will be very few. And that is only normal; constitutions are by nature extremely sensitive. We must not create a potential tragedy by succumbing to the illusion that somehow with Quebec out of the federation other issues will be easier to solve, and more likely to find pan-Canadian agreement. On issues of Senate reform, federal spending powers, settlement of native land claims, enshrining additional individual or new collective rights in the Charter, there is no evidence of agreement, or even unity of interest, in the majority of other provinces.

Our need to address outstanding and urgent constitutional questions should encourage us to look for ways to get results in relatively manageable and distinct "rounds." This means returning to the objective of amending the existing constitution, not rewriting it. We should make some issues the centre of our concern and focus on what we really want on those issues. We should accept that we may have to wait to see change on other matters.

The first essential issue of this round is to describe in constitutional language the "bottom line" for Quebec. The second is to recognize aboriginal aspirations for self-government. Including other issues as essential to success at this time will do only one thing: make resolution less likely, thereby ensuring Quebec's separation.

It is absolutely true that the most important daily issues for most Canadians are not constitutional, but economic, and social. Unemployment, cut-backs to higher education and health care, environmental problems, poverty, free trade and globalization — these are the issues that should get Parliament's top priority.

Should we link these issues with the Constitution? Should we elevate these matters and attempt to address them as "rights" in the Constitution itself? The answer is no; we may paradoxically help to set progress on these issues back, instead of forward, if we do. Under any amending formula or any constitutional change process, the test for adopting any position is always much greater unanimity than the standard of agreement required for regular policy or legislative matters. So the possibility of success in resolving social and economic concerns by linking them to the Constitution is even more remote than usual.

We cannot realistically hope current constitutional forums are going to respond seriously to these many and varied issues. By creating expectations that the constitutional arena is where these questions should or can be handled, we will contribute to public frustration and cynicism. We will also be letting the federal and provincial governments off the hook. We should insist that our governments work, discuss and build consensus on the outstanding constitutional issues that threaten to tear apart our federation. At the same time, we should insist that these same federal and provincial governments act now — without waiting for constitutional reform — on poverty, social inequity, unemployment, environmental crises and the like. These issues do not require a constitutional solution. It is politically indefensible to suggest they cannot be tackled on their own.

In spite of all the obstacles enumerated here, constitutional resolution is within our grasp, because the will still exists, in every part of Canada, to have one country. But clearly failure too is within our grasp. We cannot just "muddle through." If we do not achieve a new historical accommodation with Quebec, we will be doomed to be even more preoccupied with constitutional crises than we have been in the last three or four years.

Success and failure will be very much assisted — although not of course solely determined — by what we in the rest of Canada do. If we want to create the opportunity for constitutional resolution to take place, we need to do all we can to break down the causes of the current impasse. We need to encourage a deliberate focus on the specifics of the constitutional disagreement with

Quebec. We need to find specific options to establish a constitutional recognition of self-government for First Nations. We need to be consistent with our history. We need to accept our asymmetrical country, and its asymmetrical current constitution. We need to keep the agenda simple and manageable. We need to be realistic with ourselves and with the public and desist in raising expectations over what it will take to get resolution. We need to accept that the capacity to let this constitutional round take more time is limited. Resolution will require a specific proposal, with sufficient time to give Canadians a real say, a real choice in this "round for Canada."

Part III:

Citizenship and Rights

Multiculturalism in the New Canada

Al Meghji

Al Meghji is a recent graduate of Harvard Law School who practises law and teaches part-time at Dalhousie Law School.

Instead of seeing my Indianness as a fragile identity to be preserved against obliteration (or worse, a "visible" disfigurement to be hidden), I see it now as a set of fluid identities to be celebrated.... Indianness is now a metaphor, a particular way of partially comprehending the world.

Bharati Mukherjee, Darkness *(Penguin Books, 1985)*

As we grope to define a new Canada, with reformed institutions and perhaps even a new social and political identity, there will inevitably be a scramble on the part of different groups to ensure that their "place" and status in the new Canada is recognized. It is also inevitable that in the midst of the debate defining the nature and character of the emerging Canadian polity, there will be those self-appointed leaders of the various "ethnic communities" who will argue that the aspirations of Canadians, particularly ethnic Canadians — and indeed the success of the Canadian state — can be assured only in a "multicultural Canada." Unfortunately, politicians, preoccupied with reaching an accommodation between "the two founding peoples" and addressing the compelling concerns of aboriginal Canadians, are likely to embrace the multiculturalism agenda as a means of placating that other group — the "ethnic Canadians." They will adopt the view of the ethnic leaders that it is in the national interest to have a Canada where one's ethnicity is accentuated, recognized and "celebrated" as a matter of high public policy. They will argue that for ethnic Canadians to belong, the Canadian state must continue — and indeed enhance — its ideology of multiculturalism and diversity. From this view, I dissent.

The first thing to note about the policy of multiculturalism is that it has never been truly "multi." French Canadians have never considered multiculturalism particularly useful or relevant in the protection of their cultural identity. They have fought not for cultural diversity but for power: linguistic rights; greater autonomy for Quebec; representation in the central social, economic and political institutions of the nation. In fact, Quebec has always viewed multiculturalism as a threat to French culture. Canadians with British roots, on the other hand, have never needed any explicit state action to protect their culture. Indeed, it is not an exaggeration to say that multiculturalism is synonymous with policy and attitudes towards ethnic Canadians.

In contemporary Canadian usage, the term "ethnic Canadians" means Canadians whose origins are neither French nor British. Further, the tendency to perceive someone as "ethnic" increases with how "different" that person is from the social, cultural and racial norms of the dominant groups. The more assimilated one becomes, the less likely one is to attract the ethnic label. Recent immigrants to Canada, who have tended to be people of colour and who are the least assimilated, have been the largest "beneficiaries" of the ethnic label. So when Canadian politicians speak of multiculturalism, they are speaking not of the francophone farmer in the heartland of Quebec nor the anglophone banker in Toronto, but of those who have brown or yellow faces, of those who choose to wear turbans or of those who still speak with the accents of their previous homes. If the label "ethnic Canadian" ever functioned as a benign descriptive term, it no longer does. The term has become a euphemism to distinguish ethnic Canadians from members of the "founding races."

The irrelevance of multiculturalism to the aspirations of the two dominant groups suggests the first big objection to multiculturalism policy: multiculturalism has contributed to the marginalization of ethnic Canadians in the central arenas of political discourse. It has been the standard diversionary reply given when, in the midst of a spat between English and French Canadians, ethnic Canadians anxiously ask how they fit into the debate. At that point, ethnic Canadians are told, typically by English or French politicians, "We are a multicultural country and you should feel part of it."

This marginalization of ethnic Canadians from serious political discourse is illustrated by the fact that politicians in multicultural Canada have come to believe that they need not appeal to ethnic voters on the same basis on which they appeal to others. In all too many instances, when they talk to audiences composed primarily of ethnic Canadians, they mouth banalities about tolerance and diversity while avoiding serious discussion of other issues. Often these speeches are remarkably patronizing. Politicians, usually being members of the dominant cultural groups, praise particular ethnic groups for their contributions to Canada, figuratively patting them on the head as though their self-worth as good citizens depended on such confirmation.

As an "ethnic Canadian," I find the philosophical underpinnings of state-sponsored multiculturalism problematic in another way as well. Multiculturalism is insulting because it tends to denigrate the individuality of ethnic Canadians and instead defines them as members of "different" groups — different, that is, from the mainstream. It treats ethnic Canadians as a homogeneous, single-issue interest group. It ignores the fact that, like Canadians in the dominant groups, ethnic Canadians are individuals with different experiences, values and aspirations. The policy encourages the valuation of ethnic Canadians not by the content of their characters nor by their abilities but by reference to their ethnic origin. Multiculturalism is, in effect, a form of stereotyping that perpetuates the social hierarchy of the status quo.

The damage done by multiculturalism to the sense of belonging that many new Canadians seek is poignantly expressed by Bharati Mukherjee. In *The Middleman and Other Stories*, a collection of short stories about the immigrant experience in North America, she says of Canada, "[It] has chosen to be a mosaic, but by preserving differences, it also preserves biases." Blaming Canada's obsession with multiculturalism for making her a "psychological expatriate," Mukherjee moved to the United States fifteen years after she arrived in Canada from her native India.

The alienation felt by Mukherjee, myself and other so-called ethnics opposed to Canada's policy of multiculturalism is rooted in limitations imposed by this policy. Multiculturalism prescribes the nature and extent of tolerable involvement by ethnic Canadians in the intellectual and cultural life of the nation. It has created in the national psyche a belief that ethnic Canadians can speak legitimately only to parochial "multicultural issues." Accordingly, their views on other, more universal concerns are accorded less weight than those of other Canadians; in the current debate over the fate of the nation, ethnic Canadians are encouraged to stand quietly by while their interests are "looked after" for them. Moreover, multiculturalism's insistent emphasis on differences creates barriers for all Canadians that cannot easily be transcended. Its message to "real" Canadians is that ethnic Canadians are merely guests, albeit welcome guests, and should be treated accordingly.

The subtle but pernicious consequences of multiculturalism are illustrated by the government of Canada's decision to compensate Canadians of Japanese extraction for having been wrongfully moved off the West Coast during World War II. Their mass evacuation and the confiscation of their property certainly rank among the worst violations of human rights in Canadian history. Yet when the government sought to redress this injustice, responsibility was given to the minister of state responsible for multiculturalism. As MP John Nunziata, an ardent critic of multiculturalism, noted, "The confiscation of private property and the suspension of civil rights during World War II had nothing to do with multiculturalism" but "everything to do with justice." He rightly concluded that the matter should have been handled by the minister of justice. However, acknowledgement of the serious injury caused by racism was deemed to be an "ethnic issue," not one that ought to concern the collective conscience of the country.

The so-called leaders of the ethnic communities who vociferously argue for "more multiculturalism"— through policies such as increased funding and a separate (but presumably equal) ministry of multiculturalism outside the mainstream ministry of culture and communications — misunderstand or choose to ignore the effects of their demands on the place and status of ethnic Canadians. They fail to appreciate that ultimately multiculturalism is not about culture but about politics and power. This truth is eloquently expressed by Himani Bannerji, a writer and professor of sociology, who says of multiculturalism (in an interview appearing in *Other Solitudes — Canadian Multicultural Fictions*): "[It is] a way of 'managing' and subsuming us.... It is a way of containing that part of our subjectivity that is not assimilated. Peoples' memories of the places that they come from persist with them. So this spill of memory must be contained, and the dominant group contains this spill through various means so it does not take over politics and become anti-racist but remains at the level of song and dance." The consequence of "more multiculturalism" is that the ability of the individual ethnic Canadian to participate in the mainstream national agenda is proportionately diminished.

One of the supposed virtues of multiculturalism is that it engenders respect for the cultures of ethnic Canadians. In fact, multiculturalism actually trivializes and misrepresents their cultures. It trivializes by reducing culture from a complex concept representing shared experiences, values and ideas to an exhibition of its most obvious artifacts. It refines and packages complex cultures, and in the process strips them of their intellectual and spiritual content. It misrepresents ethnic cultures because it fails to acknowledge their fluid and changing natures; in the words of Himani Bannerji, multiculturalism leads to "fossilization and reification of the cultural forms that we brought [to Canada] twenty years ago." Multiculturalism ignores what Salman Rushdie describes and celebrates as the "cross-pollination of cultures" from which have emerged new "synthetic" cultures. The "true nature" of ethnic cultures has proved to be too sophisticated for Canada's multiculturalism policy to portray accurately.

Proponents of Canada's multiculturalism policy have often responded to criticism of the policy by enumerating several worthy programs that the policy has yielded: for example, programs dealing with literacy and race relations. Certainly these types of programs are necessary. However, offering them under the rubric of multiculturalism will inevitably lead to their being regarded as "ethnic programs." Literacy and race relations are not, *per se*, ethnic issues. The right not to be discriminated against on the basis of one's race or ethnicity is a fundamental human right. Racism and other forms of discrimination are serious problems in Canada. Combatting them under the head of multiculturalism, with its "folk dance" image, fails to convey the seriousness of the problem — or the gravity of the injury suffered by its victims. It is hardly effective strategy to offer a race-relations program under the auspices of a policy in which the dominant groups of Canadians (including many individuals who exhibit racism) have shown a complete lack of interest.

In the end, multiculturalism undermines the efforts of those who are seeking to forge a national identity and to prevent the disintegration of an already fragile nation. Whatever the purpose of multicultural policy, the net result is that it highlights and accentuates differences among Canadians. The linguistic and cultural battles that have plagued Canada suggest that what is needed is not a policy that emphasizes differences but one that promotes common goals and nationally shared values while at the same time allowing the expression of individual identity.

This is, of course, a critical time in the evolution of the

Canadian state, and many of the fundamental features of Canadian identity — including multiculturalism — are under scrutiny. The fate of multiculturalism policy will not be decided in isolation. Regardless of the outcome of the current constitutional negotiations, and regardless of whether we end up with a much decentralized federation or even a federation without Quebec, ethnic Canadians should be wary of settling for a "new and improved" multiculturalism policy. Their objective should be to secure a Canada with a strong and unequivocal anti-racist agenda. The new Canada should be built on a foundation of individual needs and rights, but it should also seek to facilitate the enrichment of the *common* culture by all citizens. It should emphatically reject the tribalism that has thus far disguised itself with the rhetoric of multiculturalism.

My Grandparents' Vision of Canada

Donna Greschner

A former member of the Canadian Human Rights Commission, Donna Greschner is a law professor at the University of Saskatchewan. She teaches and writes in the areas of constitutional law, human rights and feminist legal theory.

My grandparents had a vision of Canada that I believe remains instructive in shaping the future of the country. Its central idea seems more just and compelling as Quebec moves closer again to separation and the First Nations assert self-determination with new political clout. Their vision was grounded in cultural pluralism and economic prosperity for everyone. For pragmatic reasons, they believed in a big and diverse country, with federalism as its necessary political form. Federalism promoted the pluralism they believed in and lived daily, while acting as a foil to the grandiose nationalism and territorial acquisitiveness of dominant ethnic groups. It could also temper the disruptions and economic impoverishment of smaller ethnic groups wrought by ethnic and linguistic nationalism.

In the past year, I have often reflected upon my grandparents and their sense of Canada, not only because of resurgent Quebec separatism but also because of conversations with aboriginal friends. I now realize more acutely the profound harm caused to the First Nations by the non-aboriginal presence in Canada and the urgency of creating a future in which all peoples will truly share in the country's opulence. I want to elucidate my grandparents' vision by telling a chapter of their stories. Perhaps the core of their vision could promote aboriginal self-determination and the aspirations of francophone Quebeckers within the federation.

My narrative is not a repetition of my grandparents' words, for their vision is not completely known to me. My maternal grandmother died before my birth, my grandfathers died when I was in my teens, and my paternal grandmother died seven years ago. My siblings and cousins spend time, now that most of us are in our thirties and realize that our grandparents will always be part of us, reconstructing what we know about their lives and aspirations, asking our parents for their memories. We understand that our grandparents did not fully live or spin out the logic of their vision. It was incomplete in application and imperfect in detail, and it especially requires development to take account of the First Nations. We, their descendants, have the opportunity to make their vision the best that it can be. It is a chance we should not pass by.

My grandparents left the "old countries" because of political authoritarianism and its violent manifestation, war. My maternal grandparents arrived as children at the turn of the century, moving to Saskatchewan with some members of their families from a village about sixty miles from Moscow. They were not Russian and feared the political and economic oppression being inflicted upon minorities by the Czar. One specific reason for their departure was the threat of conscription by the Russian army. Although they spoke a dialect of German, my mother says they did not feel German either, nor did they identify with the German state, just as now the family speaks English but does not feel English or identify with the British state. Their ancestors had been kicked around Europe for centuries, and Canada offered the possibility of a more permanent and peaceful residence. When I asked my mother why her parents, aunts and uncles came to Canada, she said it was quite simply for personal freedom. They wanted the freedom to be who they wanted to be. My maternal grandfather became an ardent Liberal, for he was a liberal at heart, while the rest of the family flowed between the Liberals and the CCF. According to my mother, no one voted Conservative, because a Conservative government had interfered with religious instruction in schools, as the Czar's underlings had tried to do in Russia.

My paternal grandfather, Joseph Greschner, left his village, located in present-day Czechoslovakia, in 1928. He had been to town one day and had heard again the rumours of another war. An unwilling soldier in the Great War, he had sworn his family would never suffer through one. With money saved by his mother for the express purpose of giving her children passage out of the country, he left for Canada. Two years later, with his earnings from working on the prairies, he sent for my grandmother and their two children. My father was the first Greschner born in Canada.

My paternal grandmother, Klara Gross, was especially happy to emigrate. For her, Canada represented personal freedom in a different way than it did for her husband. A destitute and untrained village girl, her good looks had caught the eye of Joseph, a son of the local landowner. Her dream was to join the convent and obtain an education, but my grandfather was rich. If she married

245

him, she could provide for her dependent mother and brother. In a town with no pensions or social assistance, Klara concluded that marriage was the only plausible means of ensuring the well-being of her family. She moved into the Greschner estate outside of town and was very badly treated by several of her new relatives. One sister-in-law called her a dumb girl and treated her like a maid. Over fifty years later, she wept while telling me the stories one day in her kitchen. Canada offered freedom from personal servitude and a clean break with reminders of economic desperation.

The threat of war and political oppression drove my grandparents across continents and oceans to a strenuous life, first on a bone-dry, panting prairie and then in a howlingly harsh northern wilderness where farming still provides only a meagre and unpredictable livelihood. However, from my grandparents' perspective, Canada was a blessed land of peace and prosperity. The Greschner relatives, starving in Europe during World War II and dependent after the war upon packages sent by Klara, realized that my grandparents had been the lucky ones, achieving lasting freedom from want and war, and hence their dream of personal freedom.

Canada's expansive richness of resources offered my grandparents the capacity to be themselves, but they were not coarse individualists. The Greschners would not have survived the first winter in the north without the help of neighbours, and their children and grandchildren have joined the co-ops and credit unions of Saskatchewan. Social programs became an integral part of their vision of the country. My grandmother finally gained economic independence and security with her pension cheque, and my mother with the family allowance. My grandmother would not want interference with the economic safety net; she would not want her grandchildren to be forced to deny their dreams, as she had done, in order to fend off destitution and starvation.

So I am concerned about the current talk of decentralization of governmental powers. Usually the discussion is abstract and fails to specify the likely impact on ordinary citizens like my grandparents. History shows that a strong federal government effectively delivers social programs. The onus is on the opponents to prove that decentralization (and its consequence, varying standards across the country) can deliver the economic security necessary for cultural development, for individual and group flourishing. My grandmother understood that a decent standard of living was the *sine qua non* of other human activities and the most impervious defence against ethnic intolerance. Without a doubt, innovative provincial initiatives will always remain politically important — medicare is the shop-worn example, for unimpeachable reasons. Its introduction by the Saskatchewan government brought an instant and unqualified improvement in the lives of my family, releasing them upon serious illness from the paralysing choice of death or bankruptcy. But in an era of multi-national capital and markets, social programs will not be quickly forthcoming from small provincial economies without, at a minimum, extensive federal support.

For my grandparents, federalism was also a mechanism to give space to cultural and linguistic groups while inhibiting or managing any bellicose tendencies. My grandmother Klara often said that Europe's problems, when she was young, stemmed in part from its division into many small and big countries. A large country often could not resist the temptation to conquer a smaller one, claiming the land as its own and imposing its national identity, language and army. The size of Canada appealed to her. The country's immensity reduced the threat of invasion to a remote risk. The only country more gigantic, the Soviet Union, remained the sole source of my grandfather's fear of living through another war. He knew that the Russian army had marched into his home town during World War II and never left, convincing proof of my grandmother's hypothesis. For decades, my grandparents lived in the log cabin built in the 1930s because Joseph was irrationally convinced that the day they built a spacious, comfortable home, the Russians would seize it, as they had seized his family's stone mansion in Czechoslovakia. A big house was an invitation for invasion. A month after his death, my more realistic grandmother modernized and enlarged the house.

I think today of Klara's fear about small and big countries. The departure of Quebec would be an immeasurable impoverishment of Canada — culturally, spiritually and economically. It may also produce a number of lopsided, unequal countries rather than two large nations, for the forces of division in the rest of Canada would be great. Violence among the heterogeneous units may be an exceedingly tiny possibility but one that will not be completely discounted by my family nor by First Nations, with their history of violent suppression by non-aboriginal Canadians. Absorption of the remaining pieces by the United States would be unlikely in the foreseeable future. Too much energy has been spent over two centuries in avoiding absorption by the United States for Canadians to capitulate quickly after separation. But centrifugal forces in the regions would accelerate, exacerbating regional chauvinism and producing a greater risk of intolerant insularity.

My grandparents, coming from multicultural and multilingual communities, would not have equated a strong federal government with a uniform collective identity. Strong federalism is consistent with, and perhaps necessary for, a multiculturalism that is marked not by hostility between closed enclaves but rather by genuine respect, intermingling and sharing between distinct groups. My grandparents did not emigrate to preserve their cultural identities from change. They did not have a static conception of themselves, nor did they want a provincial or local bulwark for their culture against all influences. All my grandparents felt at home in northern Saskatchewan during the 1930s, amidst the immigrants from many countries. They had been enriched by the multiculturalism of the places where they had lived before, they acquired knowledge from their new neighbours, and they would not have believed in imposing a single culture on anyone.

Multilingualism in particular was not a public context but a personal reality for my grandparents. The Greschners had lived in a predominantly German village in Slovakia, spoke a low German dialect as their first language and saw their national or ethnic identity as Hungarian. They spoke many languages before they emigrated and absorbed more on arrival: Polish because of Polish neighbours and English because it was the common language. I have no doubt that if they had settled in Quebec, they would have spoken French. They were survivors, speaking the languages necessary for communication. When I was growing up with my paternal grandparents on the farm, aunts and uncles switched languages as easily as their affluent teen-age grandchildren now change clothes. Their fluency, indeed, partially prevented their children, my generation, from acquiring a second language naturally. After several of my siblings began to understand one language, my father and other adults would flip to another to prevent us from understanding their conversations.

The grandchildren all speak English now. Some of us speak the French learned at school, some retain a smattering of the German dialect and most still cuss in Hungarian or Slovak. Russian, one of my mother's languages, disappeared altogether. Languages were lost because my parents wanted their children to have the education denied to them by the hard economic times of their youth, and English was the sole language of school. When French was introduced in the 1960s, the predominantly German-speaking community was resentful that German would not be offered in every grade along with French, but few disputed the great value of knowing many languages. When French instruction was dropped ten years ago, my parents were angry that their youngest children still in high school would not have the opportunity to acquire the skill. The last conversation I had with my grandmother Klara before her death was about language. On a hot summer day, sitting outside on the farm surrounded by relatives and family friends, I told her about my French classes. She did not question my desire to learn French, although she had probably not met a French-speaking person since she had landed in Montreal in 1930 on her journey to Saskatchewan. She said that I should learn her languages after learning French, and I promised her I would.

It concerns me that official bilingualism has fallen into disfavour and that the rising political force in western Canada, the Reform Party, opposes multiculturalism. Spinning out the logic of my grandparents' vision would ensure more protection for all languages. Each language's different way of imagining the world is an extraordinarily valuable human accomplishment. Moreover, under-standing the languages of other peoples is a significant step towards empathy and identification, towards treating the speakers with respect. Only those myopically powerful or haughtily arrogant do not perceive the benefit of learning the languages of others. It is not too late for Canada to acquire the truly multilingual character that the settlers enjoyed in many regions across the West fifty years ago and that continues today in metropolitan areas. New immigrants, and older ones who preserved their languages, such as the Ukrainian population, ought to receive linguistic protection and nourishment. Most important, as my parents and grandparents understood, are the languages of education.

My grandparents may have appreciated the pluralism of the farming frontier, but they were ignorant of the long history of cultural diversity that existed before the arrival of Europeans. The First Nations have over fifty languages and distinctive cultural traditions. Saskatchewan farmers did not create a multicultural reality; they imposed a new version of multiculturalism over the aboriginal reality. They did not introduce linguistic diversity to Canada but merely added European languages to a rich linguistic mélange. We can bemoan the loss of the European linguistic diversity but it is recoverable. The precarious position of aboriginal languages is much more lamentable. As many aboriginal leaders have pointed out, when their languages are lost, they are gone forever. With only three aboriginal languages not in danger of extinction, the preservation of aboriginal languages must have a greater priority than the preservation of other languages. One telling indictment of the racism embedded within Canadian politics was the cruel effort by non-aboriginal governments over decades to destroy aboriginal languages. At the least, nurturing of aboriginal languages is now required by the principles of compensatory justice.

But governments were not the only culprits. Although my grandparents settled in places named by the First

Nations — Canada and Saskatchewan — and farmed the northern lands of the Cree nation, they made no attempt to learn from or about the first inhabitants. Indeed, they encountered their Cree neighbours infrequently, when old men from the reserves came to the door offering berries or fish for sale. My grandparents did not give a thought, as far as we can tell, to the fact that their land did not really belong to them and that they were participating in an act of power by "bigger groups," just like the acts of domination that they had fled the old countries to avoid.

The racism that has denied aboriginal peoples a just and secure place is inconsistent with my grandparents' vision and must be eliminated. Racism afflicts today not only the First Nations but also the new immigrants to Canada, the peoples who have been arriving in large numbers for the past twenty years from the Caribbean, Asia, Africa and the Indian subcontinent. They travel with the same hopes as my grandparents — personal freedom, peace and prosperity — and they are equally entitled to have their dreams fulfilled.

My grandparents would share with the First Nations, however, a lack of comprehension of the "two nations" paradigm of Canada. They landed in Montreal and travelled through Ontario, but none of their eventual neighbours were French or English people. In the southern part of Saskatchewan where they stopped their westward trip, in the north where they settled, and in Alberta and British Columbia where some descendants moved, the people were from every corner of Europe. "Two nations" may have represented European settlement at Confederation but it was not their reality, nor has it been the reality of their children, nor is it generally the history or reality of western Canada. The persistence of the idea of two nations is most offensive to the First Nations. Although the phrase calls attention to the exclusion of the First Nations from the Confederation bargain in 1867, its promulgation today is a continuing denial of the aboriginal reality. The argument sometimes used against my grandparents — that they had accepted minority status in relation to the two dominant cultures when they left their homelands — cannot be deployed against the original peoples.

In order for the Canadian constitution to articulate clearly the unique place of first peoples, aboriginal peoples must be fully incorporated within the practice of federalism. My grandparents' vision of federalism, with its grounding in peaceful protection of diversity, did not encompass the governments of the First Nations, as distinct jurisdictions equal to the federal and provincial governments. But aboriginal peoples are not, and actively resist being classified as, the same as the diverse ethnic and cultural groups that arrived after Columbus. Nothing prevents the full constitutional protection of aboriginal governments except our false posture of superiority to the First Nations, our clutching to the shreds of colonialism.

Although today is not the time of my grandparents, I still find their vision attractive. The need for economic prosperity and security is great today, with homelessness and hunger found in city schools and streets across the country. I find their vision of tolerance and cultural plurality compelling at a time when the forces of racism seem close to the surface of social life, when linguistic arrogance and ethnic superiority are fuelled by fires in Brockville and Chateauguay and by gunshots in Prince Albert. I also wonder whether we will have given up on Canada if we discard my grandparents' vision. Maybe the Canadian soul is a blend of cultural plurality and economic security, bonded by a communitarian glue that keeps us distinctive from our southern neighbours. If this is our soul, it does not fit at all with massive decentralization that would reduce the federal government to the keepers of jails and the counters of the national debt.

It may be difficult for others to share my grandparents' vision when it has never been thoroughly realized — not for them or their descendants, not for the First Nations, not for Quebec. For generations, the self-assumed master has sneered in Quebec's doorway. The francophone majority in Quebec suffered a lengthy denigration of their language and culture rather than respect from others for who they were. They had to fight aggressively for mere recognition, let alone for an end to their subordinate position in their own province. Perhaps the challenge and dream for my generation is the full realization, not the rejection, of my grandparents' vision across the land.

Reforming Citizenship

William Kaplan

William Kaplan is an associate professor at the Faculty of Law, University of Ottawa. He is the author of State and Salvation: The Jehovah's Witnesses and Their Fight for Civil Rights.

Whatever the end result of the current round of constitutional negotiations for Quebec and Canada, there is no doubt that Canada will continue to exist. For better or for worse, for good or for ill, we will be Canadians still. But what kind of Canadians will we be? Will we be multiculturalists first? Will we be *English* Canadians in the traditional sense with a unifying loyalty to the Crown? Or will we find some new symbols and myths to tie us together? Simply to ask these questions, each of which has its proponents, suggests that our sense of nationhood is lamentably weak, our ideas of citizenship more than a little confused. This we can no longer afford.

In the Confederation debates, George-Étienne Cartier set out the essential Canadian conundrum. Canadians are different from each other, Cartier observed, and it would be foolish to aspire to a melting pot. Not only was the idea "utopian — it was impossible." Only through the creation of a common political nationality could a Canadian nation emerge.

It would not be easy to establish this. Geography and language created barriers, not bridges. Canada's charter myth also stood in the way. Two "founding peoples," the story went, had created Canada, and they should be accorded a privileged place. Moreover, with "two nations warring in the bosom of a single state," in part the result of the "conquest" of the English over the French, the pursuit of national unity became the predominant national goal. There were "two solitudes." And the situation would only get worse.

At Confederation, the British in Canada, English, Irish, Scottish and Welsh, were united by allegiance to the Crown and not much else. And when newcomers arrived, little was done to integrate them. If anything, the opposite was true. While some new Canadians bought into Anglo-Canadian nationalism, particularism flourished. English-speaking Canadians increasingly identified themselves regionally and ethnically instead of nationally. In the meantime, French Canada, united by language, religion, history and culture, thrived. Quebeckers knew who they were — a nation. (The little that English- and French-speaking Canadians knew about each other tended to reinforce their isolation.)

As Canada grew and matured, a shared sense of nation began to develop; Canadian participation in World War II was a watershed in that process. Canada entered the conflict a colony and emerged a nation. Our contribution, in men and women and materials, was outstanding. We had sacrificed in a common cause and at the end of the day Canadians, both English- and French-speaking, had reason for national pride.

That Canadians had begun to consider themselves distinct was reflected in calls for a Canadian flag to replace the Red Ensign, for "O Canada" to replace "God Save the King" and for Canadian citizenship instead of

British subject status. Each of these demands would have been considered radical before the war, but afterwards they signalled the awakening of a new national identity. A Canadian Citizenship Act came first, and the anthem and flag followed.

Two years after the end of the war, Parliament passed the Citizenship Act. "Our new Canadians," the secretary of state observed, "bring to this country much that is rich and good, and in Canada they find a new way and new hope for the future. They should all be made to feel that they, like the rest of us, are Canadians, citizens of a great country, guardians of proud traditions and trustees of all that is best in life for generations of Canadians yet to be. For the national unity of Canada and for the future greatness of this country it is felt to be of the utmost importance that all of us, new Canadians and old, have a consciousness of a common purpose and common interests as Canadians and that all of us are able to say with pride and say with meaning: 'I am a Canadian citizen.'"

When the Citizenship Act came into force, every Canadian, new and old, could proudly say that he or she was "a Canadian citizen." Most did. But what did Canadian citizenship mean? As the years passed, less and less. Instead of serving as the foundation for a developing political nationality, government policies ensured that a common sense of nation never emerged. The promotion of group rights, already given constitutional force in the British North America Act, with its special provisions for French and English, Roman Catholics and Protestants, took on new life in the post-war Canadian polity.

Official bilingualism and biculturalism came first. Although official bilingualism was quite properly seen as one element of a common political nationality in a country with two large language groups, the "bi and bi" policy carried with it some unwelcome baggage. The policy entrenched one of Canada's great myths: that of French and English cultural duality.

Not surprisingly, opposition to special status for these two cultures soon emerged, and when it did, official multiculturalism followed. Canadians who were not members of either of the two so-called "charter groups" were not to be ignored; the government was there with money and eventually a minister to ensure the preservation and promotion of multicultural identities. Relations with government were increasingly dependent on membership in an identifiable group. Would citizenship serve as the common thread?

While other nations such as the countries of Western Europe restricted access and entitlement to citizenship, Canada expanded it. The Canadian Citizenship Act was among the most liberal in the world, and when it was amended in 1977 it became even more so. First, the amended act recognized the equality of Canadians by birth and Canadians by choice. The preferential treatment given to British subjects in obtaining citizenship was eliminated. These were good changes, for they established a common citizenship status for all Canadians. Second, citizenship was no longer a privilege; it was now a right and was granted after three years of residence instead of five. If a landed immigrant met the qualifications, it was available on request. This was also a good idea, for naturalization encourages participation in the community. And third, Canada explicitly accepted plural citizenship. Canadians were entitled by law to retain their former nationality, or even to acquire a new one, without jeopardizing their Canadian citizenship.

Plural citizenship was good, the government advised, for it fostered multiculturalism, which had by now become official government policy. Canadians did not need to abandon their old loyalties to acquire new ones. Indeed, for a long time, it was not even necessary for an immigrant to live in Canada to qualify for Canadian citizenship. The traditional view that citizenship involved some sort of allegiance to the state was, it seems, passé. The state-sanctioned encouragement of multiple nationalities led inevitably to the phenomenon of "hyphenated" Canadians and served to drive Canadians further apart.

It is hardly surprising that in these circumstances Canada soon had one of the highest naturalization rates in the world, higher even than that of the United States. There was everything to be gained and nothing to be lost by becoming a Canadian. The new model of Canadian citizenship fit well in a country that was no more than a community of communities: it encompassed everything and ultimately almost nothing.

Ten years after the amendments to the Citizenship Act, in 1987, with national unity again at the forefront of Canadian political life, the government announced that it was time for reform. Amendments were to be introduced before the end of the year. In a discussion paper released to the public, Canadians were called upon to think about citizenship and to consider those principles and values that might be included in a new act. The government had some ideas of its own: "The federal government regards citizenship as a cornerstone of national unity and is resolved to buttress it with new legislation. Its objective is to define Canadian citizenship in terms of today's national requirements.... The Government will seek to expand citizens' awareness of their rights and obligations, and to heighten both the practical and symbolic aspects of Canadian citizenship.... Throughout the amendment process, the Government will be bound by its commitment to the fundamental principles of equality, diversity and community as the basis for Canada's free, bilingual and multicultural society." The 1989 Speech from the Throne also promised that new citizenship legislation would be tabled soon, although it has yet to appear.

In the meantime, Section 15, the equality rights provision of the Charter of Rights and Freedoms, came into force. Soon thereafter, the Supreme Court of Canada got involved. "Is it contrary to Section 15 to require a lawyer to be a Canadian citizen?" was the question put before the court. The judges were unanimous that such a provision infringed the Section 15 equality guarantee. A majority of the court then rejected the argument that this infringement was justifiable under Section 1, which provides that the rights and freedoms set out in the Charter are subject only to such reasonable limits prescribed by law as can be demonstrably justified in a free and democratic society. Three of the judges disagreed. One dissenter observed that citizenship "requires the taking on of obligations and commitments to the community, difficult sometimes to describe but felt and understood by most citizens, as well as the rejection of past loyalties...." Another judge was "sensitive to the fact that citizenship is a very special status that not only incorporates rights and duties but serves a highly symbolic function as a badge of identifying people as members of the Canadian polity."

It is difficult to object to the result in this case. The justifications for requiring someone to be a citizen to prepare a will or to file a civil suit do not readily jump to mind, even if that person is nominally an officer of the court. But should Canadian citizenship be required for Canadian diplomats? For members of the Canadian Forces? For members of Parliament? Should citizenship require the rejection of past loyalties? Does it have any special status? Is there reason for concern about a citizenship that grants citizens few additional rights and assumes no obligations?

In the government's guide for new Canadians, called *The Canadian Citizen*, readers are advised of the legal rights and benefits Canadian citizens enjoy. Canadians alone can vote and carry a Canadian passport. One other benefit is the right to be considered first for some government jobs. The conclusion is inescapable that Canadian citizenship has come to mean not very much.

One benefit of citizenship that Canadians should but do not equally share is the protection of the Charter of Rights. As English-speaking and other non-French-speaking Canadians who live in Quebec are very aware, some of their most important rights have been taken away. In that province, the separatist government celebrated the patriation of the Constitution and the entrenchment of the Charter of Rights by exempting all of its legislation for five years from the application of some of the most fundamental Charter rights. And then, when its language legislation was held by the highest court in Quebec and the highest court in Canada to be contrary to both the Quebec and Canadian charters, the National Assembly passed another bill invoking Section 33, the notwithstanding clause, to override individual rights in order to bolster the supremacy of the linguistic majority, the very thing most bills of rights are designed to prevent.

The Charter, like the American Bill of Rights, could have served to unite the country. Instead, courtesy of the notwithstanding clause, we have created one more instrument of dissension, disunity and, for a large group of our fellow Canadians, considerable despair.

Dualism and multiculturalism emphasize group rights and in the process undermine any common sense of nation. To some considerable extent the Charter promotes individual rights, but like the British North America Act it also recognizes some rights of some groups. Section 27, moreover, requires that the Charter be interpreted in a manner consistent with the preservation and enhancement of "the multicultural heritage of Canadians," whatever that might mean. The notwithstanding clause, paradoxically, permits governments to ensure that the majority group can have its way. In either case, the promotion of group rights means taking our geography and turning it into public policy: the natural barriers are exacerbated by social, political and legal barricades separating Canadians from each other. Instead, we should be treating all citizens equally, irrespective of their membership in any group.

Separate is inherently unequal. We can empower groups only by empowering individuals, not by isolating them, whether it be to receive the largesse of the Department of Multiculturalism or to get education in the schools. No Canadian deserves special status. All Canadians must be treated the same, and Canadian institutions must reflect that fact. The existence of a Department of Communications "for us" and a Department of Multiculturalism "for them" segregates Canadians in a way that simply cannot be condoned in a liberal-democratic state. It is outrageous. The only groups who should be accorded special status are Canada's aboriginal peoples, whose prior land ownership rights (and unresolved land claims), separate and parallel history and communitarian values and institutions demand recognition and accommodation.

In our 125 years, we have built a country that is a paradise compared with virtually any other nation in the world. People from all over clamour at our doors and flock to our shores. Why? Not because Canada is perfect, but because it is a progressive, decent and liberal society. Our land aspires to tolerance, promise and hope: tolerance of each other, the promise of serving as a model of harmony for the world and the hope of a better world for our children. Canadians have attempted to make sharing a virtue; the national health care system and the generous transfer payments from the "have" provinces to the "have-nots" are just two of many examples that prove this point.

Nonetheless we have very serious problems in our country, and one reason is that we have failed to achieve a consensus about who we are and where we want to go as a society. One first step is to give our citizenship real meaning. It must continue to be inclusive, but at the same time it must actively emphasize and inculcate shared values. What are some of those values? Respect for one another. A belief in equality, social justice, freedom and democracy. Being Canadian means being committed to this country and its future. A citizenship policy that actually and actively promotes these values of Canadian citizenship would probably be a good start. But much more needs to be done.

Our symbols and ceremonies are in need of reform, beginning with the monarchy. This symbol, which represents little more than the ascendancy of what was once the majority group, is divisive and must go. In its place we must turn our attention to symbols that really do reflect our shared values. One need not advocate American hype, for it is not the flag that makes the nation, but the nation that makes the flag. There is also no reason to ape the Americans in their patriotic displays, but we could do much more to instill civic pride.

Our history and our heritage are worth preserving and promoting. It would be ridiculous to abandon our past in the mistaken belief that it is of little relevance to the present. But it is also essential to establish new bonds of solidarity. Instead of gutting our national institutions, why not reform and renew them so as to position Canada and Canadians for continued growth and prosperity in the years to come? Why not make our educational system the best in the world? Why not commit ourselves to resolving all unresolved native land claims before the end of the century? Why not establish Canada as the leader in environmental protection and preservation? Why not dedicate ourselves and our country to feeding and housing the hungry and the homeless in Canada and, to the best of our ability, around the world?

In all of this, citizenship can play an important part by binding Canadians together through allegiance to something greater than our differences. Citizenship does not preclude effective and meaningful participation in the world; rather, it should serve as the stable foundation for such participation.

Our differences will not go away — if there is anything Canadian history teaches, it is that. Nor would we want these differences to disappear. The genius of Canada is its pluralism and diversity. Accommodation of a wide variety of people and beliefs is part of what our society is all about. However, continued state celebration of our differences will ensure that Canada becomes nothing more, and quite possibly less, than the sum of its regional and parochial parts.

The New "Isms"

Rosalie Abella

*Rosalie Abella is chair of the Ontario Law Reform
Commission. Previously she was a judge of the Ontario
Family Court and chair of the Ontario Labour Relations
Board.*

Essentially, I find it extraordinary that we are all, in
Canada, standing on the edge like this. We're like a long
human chain, holding hands, waiting to be told whether
we're supposed to jump or wait for a new bridge to be
built. Why? To a large extent because of the impact of the
"new Isms."

When I studied at the University of Toronto in the
1960s, there were three Isms that generated endless
preoccupation: communism, fascism and humanism.
Mostly the talk was about how the first two had impaired
the third. There was, as I recall, a lot of labelling and
assignment of blame. In fact, there seemed to be more
labels and more blame than there were ideas.

Yet here we are in the 1990s and all of a sudden we're
hearing about Isms again, only now there are three new
ones: the new fundamentalism or puritanism, the new
federalism and the new pluralism. The labels may again
be no more than substitutes for constructive debate, but
it may also nonetheless be true that in understanding the
relationship between these three neo-Isms lie the seeds of

our ability either to encourage or to extinguish a vibrant sense of human rights in Canada.

First, the new fundamentalism. As far as I can tell, the old fundamentalism was about religious orthodoxy and the maintenance of clear distinctions between right and wrong, as ecumenically declared. In their personal firmament, fundamentalists found answers to most of life's tough calls and were spiritually content to resist moral ambiguity. As time went on, as is the case with many who feel they know categorically the difference between right and wrong, there grew a zeal to impose more universally the moral certainty that puritanism preached.

From there, it was a short jump from a morality whose tutor was religion, to religious morality whose student was secularism. Religious origins were sequestered, and by the fifties, after decades of moral pluralism, exhausted and wounded as we were by the horror and enormity of World War II, puritanism as secular morality surfaced as a majority phenomenon. It took the form of Dwight D. Eisenhower in the U.S., Louis St. Laurent in Canada, the suburbs, bungalows, 2.5 children per family, one spouse per marriage, a station wagon and a matching dog. The essence of the movement was conformity, and the majority cheerfully bought into it. The "truth" was obvious, compliance was expected and competitive truths and their adherents were squelched.

McCarthyism played itself out in the name of this moral purity, and decent people behaved unforgivably. They knew not what they did. And it went on for years. The people who started the movement were haters. Their followers were naive or worse. Anyone who resisted was labelled undemocratic, unpatriotic, Communist or Jewish — often interchangeable terms in those days. Careers were ruined, injustices blatantly encouraged or not discouraged, horrendous assumptions tacitly accepted, and all the while the continent yawned and stretched and felt proudly unified by the purity of its monolithic and homogeneous morality.

Is it any wonder we had the turbulent sixties? Or the loquacious seventies? Or the amoral eighties? A devastating world war shattered presumed civilities; the victims were humanism and humanity. The need for spiritual catharsis created a search for purifiers: the purification that started nobly at Nuremberg eventually ended ignobly at the House Un-American Activities Committee in Washington; the purified parents of the 1950s created predictably bored progeny in the 1960s; and a decade in the 1960s was spent over-reacting to the overpurification and oversimplification of the 1950s.

But the purification of the 1960s created its own new tyrannical truths — about adults over thirty and whether you could trust them, about respectability, about rules and about traditions generally. And many who resented the simplistic categorical formulations of their parents' generation created more complicated but still simplistic categorical formulations of their own. The only thing the people raised in the 1950s and those raised in the 1960s had in common was that each group thought it had a monopoly on truth.

And that's why we did so much talking in the 1970s. We had to try to figure out which value system was better, which side was right. So we discussed the environment, women, minorities, disabled persons, aboriginal people, marriage, religion, children, sex, language and education. We changed some laws and social norms and started to regroup. We sought refuge in like-minded people, battered as we were by the increasing stridency of the national and local conversations.

We also started to divide. By the time we finished

talking to or at each other in the 1970s, we had no idea who was right and who was wrong. There were no villains but there seemed to be a lot of victims, and we were utterly confused. No wonder the U.S. chose Ronald Reagan in the 1980s. He made it look like the 1950s — simple.

In the 1980s, we fervently became one of three things: conservatized, radicalized or solipsistic. And each side of the triangle mocked the other two, warned of impending doom unless its path was taken, claimed to represent a broad consensus and expressed frustration with democratically accountable institutions. We lost our compass — and our tolerance. We held each other under siege but we didn't know why we were giving ultimatums to each other.

And on top of all of this was imposed the Canadian Charter of Rights and Freedoms. I am a serious Charter fan and I always have been. But I think we have to be aware of what we coincidentally did in bringing in the Charter when we did. On top of a cynicism about whether democratically elected political institutions were properly accountable, we imposed unelected, unaccountable jurists to decide whether rights and freedoms no one understood — but in which everyone passionately believed — were being violated. On top of a debate about whether individual rights or collective rights were supreme, we imposed a Charter that was ideologically schizophrenic on the subject and offered as a tool for brokering the issue the great jurisprudential problem-solving concept found in Section 1: "It depends." On top of the public's relief that the concept of human rights was at last constitutionally entrenched and therefore supreme, we imposed a notwithstanding clause, assuring people that in their own interests and for their own benefit, governments could suspend their otherwise constitutionally protected rights and freedoms (but not, ironically, governments' own constitutionally protected division of powers). And on top of a nation increasingly divided over how to unify whatever it was that was holding it together, we imposed a unifying document that seemed to protect everyone's right to stay diverse.

Everyone now began to claim a monopoly not only on truth, but on justice as well. What could once have been labelled an individual's personal and idiosyncratic point of view was now perceived by that individual as a constitutionally protected personal and idiosyncratic point of view. When individuals start to perceive that their points of view have constitutional validity, they start to take those views and themselves very seriously. And from there it's only a short leap to intolerance, to the kind of Pavlovian urge to impose your views on others and, more important, to exude the fumes of fundamentalist moral absolutism. In short, we've come full circle back to the puritanism of the 1950s, only now there are more truths demanding compliance and competing for primacy. And the voices are louder and more urgently strident.

But what makes the new fundamentalism in my view more frightening than the old fundamentalism is the way it merges with the two other emerging Isms in the nineties, producing a neurotic national psyche. We are forgetting, it seems, that nothing, not even rights, is absolute, and as a result, we are losing our balance as a country.

Federalism is the name we have given to the political relationship of ten provinces with one another and with a central government. The roles and rights in this relationship were distributed by Sections 91 and 92 of the BNA Act, interpreted by the courts and eventually circumscribed by the Charter.

The very same trends we have seen since the 1950s in fundamentalism have also been at work in federalism. The 1950s were quiet for federalism; the 1960s were turbulent, with Quebec waking up to its rediscovered identity; the 1970s saw articulate expressions of increasing identity awareness on the part of all the provinces; and by the 1980s the lines were drawn, the expectations more or less fixed, with each side certain that its position was the right one and therefore entitled to acceptance and implementation. Adding the Charter, with its alluring language of entitlements, to this aerobic stretching exercise by governmental muscles exaggerated the perception of provincial governments that their expectations, if converted into the language of rights, could be realized.

As we enter the 1990s, we learn that a new federalism is gripping the land. And what is the new federalism? No one knows yet, but it has enough appeal that it has already spawned synonyms: asymmetrical federalism, renewed federalism, decentralized federalism, to name just a few. And nobody knows what they mean either. What it will be about, however, we do know. It will be about the kind of relationship ten provinces want with one another and with the central government; in short, the issues of the old federalism with louder and more urgently strident voices.

Part of what makes the discussion about the new federalism sound so shrill is the discussion we're having about the new pluralism. Pluralism represents the attempt at peaceful co-existence by disparate groups who by choice or necessity are interdependent. It implies that each group is equal and acknowledges that each group is different. Examining trends from the 1950s, we find a burst of immigration adding to the existing collection of ethnic, racial, linguistic and religious groups; the beginning of human rights laws to protect them from discrimination; and a general concern about how to fit everybody in or whether they would fit in even if we could find places for them. Many of these minority groups added their voices to those of the reawakened female ones in the 1960s, and spent the 1970s adding, among others, francophones outside Quebec, disabled people and aboriginal people to the discussion table. By the 1980s, as was true of the debates over our other two Isms, lines had been drawn, sides taken and expectations forcefully articulated.

When the Charter was introduced to this Ism, rights truly became capitalized, and people started capitalizing on their rights. This rights frenzy produced an interesting phenomenon. As groups and the individuals in them spoke with increasing confidence of their rights, bolstered by the Charter and inspired by the Supreme Court of Canada, more and more people outside these groups started asserting their right to be free from pluralism. People we used to call biased now felt free to raise insensitivity and intolerance to the level of a constitutionally protected right on the same plateau with the rights of minorities, or women, or aboriginal people. We have started to think that all rights are created equal; and, speaking of *Animal Farm*, we have even started to think that animal rights may be equal to human rights. This, it seems, is the new pluralism: disparate groups seeking equal status, and disparate individuals seeking to take status away from them. In other words, the old pluralism, but more of it. It is the old competition between "equal" and "equality," and between individual and group rights.

The fact is that, unlike the Americans, we in Canada were never concerned only with the rights of individuals. Our historical roots involved as well a constitutional

271

appreciation that two groups, French and English, could remain distinct and unassimilated, and yet theoretically of equal worth and entitlement. That is, unlike the American model, where individualism promoted assimilation, the Canadian system has always conceded that the right to integrate based on differences has as much legal and political integrity as the right to assimilate. A melting pot if necessary, but not necessarily a melting pot.

So those who want freedom from pluralism, who assert that groups and the individuals in them have no right to a unique identity or to protection from enforced assimilation, are contradicting history. Individual and group rights in Canada have not been either/or propositions. We acknowledge both. We accept a notion of equality that respects differences, and we understand that there are different meanings to equality under each rights regime: one regime gives primacy to the individual, and the other gives primacy to the individual's group. That is why it is important to appreciate the difference between civil liberties and human rights; otherwise, we will throw ourselves hopelessly into analytical anarchy over which approach applies when, especially under the Charter.

Civil liberties represent the theory of individual rights developed by Locke and refined by Mill, whose premise was that all individuals are equal in their right to be free from arbitrary state intervention. Every individual has the same presumptive right as every other individual to individual autonomy, subject only to those limitations that the state can justify as reasonable.

In human rights, on the other hand, we are talking of individuals in their capacity as members of groups that are disadvantaged for arbitrary reasons. Here the state is asked, indeed required, not to abstain but to intervene, to protect individuals from discrimination based on group affiliation. Equality here means not that everyone is the same, but that everyone has the same or an equal right to be free from arbitrary disadvantage caused by ignoring or inappropriately taking into account differences we attribute to individuals who are members of groups.

There is a difference between treating people equally, as we do from the perspective of civil liberties, and treating people as equals, as we do in questions of human rights. For purposes of the former, we treat everyone the same; for purposes of the latter, we treat them according to their differences.

The reason in human rights that we do not treat all individuals the same way is that not all individuals have suffered historic generic exclusion because of group membership. Where assumptive barriers have impeded the fairness of the competition for some individuals, they should be removed, even if this means treating some people differently. Otherwise, we can never correct disadvantage, chained as we would be to the civil libertarian pedestal of equal treatment of every individual.

There is nothing to apologize for in giving the arbitrarily disadvantaged a prior claim in remedial responses. Nor need we endorse all claims with equal righteous vigour. Success in eradicating disadvantage will be measured by the extent to which, over time, those who were inappropriately underrepresented take their representative place throughout our systems and institutions, not by the extent to which everyone was treated the same.

Similarly, we should not be embarrassed to admit that yelling "Fire!" in a crowded theatre is fundamentally different from yelling "Theatre!" in a crowded firehall; or that teaching Holocaust denial is different from teaching about the Holocaust; or that promoting racist ideas is different from promoting race. The harmful impact is different and so, therefore, should be our attention. The issues in each equation are not and should not be of equal weight on the scales of justice. Intellectual pluralism does not and cannot mean the right to expect that racism or sexism will be given the same deference as tolerance.

Yet this is what the new pluralism seems to tolerate: a variety of groups and a variety of views about them, all perceived to be of equal legitimacy and weight. On the one hand we find different groups trying to integrate their distinctiveness into the mainstream, and on the other hand we find other groups trying to keep them or their distinctiveness out by setting homogenizing terms and conditions at the gate. Just like the old pluralism but multiplied and with louder and more urgently strident voices.

The intensity is what is new about all these renewed Isms, an intensity born of a deep fear of change, and an intensity that has turned the national conversation into a series of monologues and harangues. Too many people think they know what they're talking about and, worse, won't listen to anyone else. We're locked in old struggles, wearing old scars as uniforms and using old vocabulary as weapons.

If we don't start afresh to try to figure out what these troubles are really about, with more accurate and less provocative terminology, we won't know what the issues are. If we don't know the issues, we won't know what questions to ask. If we don't know what questions to ask, we won't be able to figure out what our common objectives are. And if we don't know what our objectives are, how in the world can we figure out the strategy for getting there?

Labels like fundamentalism, federalism and pluralism, old or new, are irrelevant to the national debate. This is not about moral purity, it's about whether anyone should be allowed to impose his or her truth on anyone else. This is not about the distribution of powers in Sections 91 and 92, it's about whether our political institutions are sufficiently responsive. And this is not about individual versus group rights, it's about whether some people are being arbitrarily disadvantaged. It's not even about what we have in common, because what we have in common is our diversity.

We don't need labels, or semantic smoke-screens, just some real tough thinking. Instead of drafting a separation agreement with words like "irreconcilable" in the preamble, we should be drafting a new social contract with words "tolerance" in the preamble about our differences. We need a presumption of goodwill, a healthy dose of patience and good ears. And we need them soon.

Women and
Constitutional Process

Mary Eberts

*Mary Eberts is a Toronto lawyer who has been active for
years on the interface between the Constitution and
women's rights.*

For those who lack true equality, like women, questions
of process can never be separated from questions of
substance. The lack of substantive equality, including full
participation in the institutions of democratic
government, has a profound effect on one's methodology
and on the demands which that methodology makes on
the democractic process. The relationship of process and
substance can be seen in one of the first constitutional
changes to be accomplished by women, namely winning
the vote and the right to hold public office. That
relationship has continued throughout the past decade, as
women have attempted to influence the outcome of
recent constitutional deliberations.

Serious constraints affect women's participation in
policy making at all levels. In July 1916, Nellie McClung
predicted that it would be many years before there were
women legislators in Canada. She was prescient. Women
are still in a minority in elected assemblies at the federal
and provincial/territorial levels, in cabinet and in the

Senate. They do not have a strong foothold in the organizational hierarchy of the national and provincial political parties. This exclusion from a major direct role in representative institutions is paralleled by women's exclusion from other key locations of decision-making power. Women are seriously under-represented in the ranks of the senior civil service and in the judiciary. They are in a minority in senior positions in the academy, in business and in trade unions.

Such exclusion means that women must influence from the outside the development of legislation and other policy affecting their interests. For the most part, they are not direct actors in the formulation of policy options by the bureaucracy and the academy, in the shaping of a legislative agenda by cabinet or in the deliberation upon that agenda by legislatures. Though they have the franchise, women have still had to concentrate on lobbying and advocacy (in court and out of it) to persuade male decision makers to sponsor and accept initiatives to further women's equality.

An important means of advocacy has arisen since 1970: advocacy units created within and close to government that address the impact of government policies and programs on women, educate government and the public on equality issues and serve as advocates on behalf of women. Advisory Councils on the Status of Women, which exist in most jurisdictions, are funded by government but operate for the most part at arm's length from it. In addition, departments responsible for the status of women, with a cabinet minister, deputy minister and staff, exist in several jurisdictions. The creation of these bodies, described in general terms as government "machinery" to promote the advancement of women, was recognized in 1985, at the World Conference to Review and Appraise the Achievements of the United Nations

Decade for Women, as an important means of promoting women's equality.

Because few women are established in the élites traditionally included in the process of "élite accommodation," which has been the foundation of much of Canadian policy making, women's appeals to legislators have been for the most part public and explicit. Many powerful élites can wield their influence quietly and unobtrusively, but women's position on the margin means that they must much more often seek to influence policy in the public forums available to them. While this public role is less effective than the matter-of-fact ways in which those with established power can influence the development of policy, it allows women to be perceived as playing a highly visible role in policy discussions. This visibility can be used to blunt their effectiveness; arguments against allowing well-organized "special interest" groups to dominate public debate on the Constitution have been heard, for example, from several directions on the right in recent months, including the prime minster himself as well as those influential in business circles.

One of the fundamental problems of being an outsider to the policy process (whatever the field) is the lack of capacity to influence both its timing and its agenda. Those external to a process find themselves reacting to it, on someone else's timetable. For women and women's groups who are reacting to agendas and timetables set by male-dominated institutions, the difficulty is compounded. In many areas, male priorities are clearly not women's priorities; not being able to change the ordering of priorities, women may question whether it is a wise use of their scarce resources to respond at all. If little time is provided for a response, the careful consultative consensus-building process of voluntary organizations, where much of women's work to influence policy is undertaken, cannot be accommodated. Again, a choice is forced: to participate in the manner characteristic of male élite organizations — namely, empowering a small élite cadre to make decisions for the group — or to refrain from participating altogether. At this point in their development, many women's organizations are trying to become more inclusive, in response to criticisms from immigrant and visible-minority women and women with disabilities about the dominance of these organizations by white, élite women and their agendas. This process requires more consultation, not less; more time to reach shared positions on issues of concern to women, not demands to render up quickly some views on what men consider important.

The fact that women are, for the most part, outside the central corridors of the policy process has had a major impact on their participation in the constitutional debates. Moreover, this is not the only policy area in which their participation is as unpaid volunteers, responding to someone else's agenda. Indeed, the neo-conservative agenda of the federal government over the past seven years has ensured that the drain on women's volunteer time and resources has increased, as they have struggled to respond to the disintegrative effects of government policies on programs of value to women.

In a kind of dreadful, but inevitable, coincidence, that neo-conservative agenda has now clearly emerged as part of the constitutional discussions themselves, so that women's groups whose capacity to cope has been stretched by its previous effects must now address the question of how they can prevent it from being entrenched in the Constitution. And although the reaction to the failure of the Meech Lake Accord has produced more formal opportunities to "participate" in the process of constitutional deliberation, in reality women are just as far from meaningful participation as they ever have been, as the following review of recent developments will highlight.

Women's first taste of the contemporary constitutional renewal process came in 1978. In the dying moments of a first ministers' meeting, Prime Minster Trudeau proposed to concede to the provinces jurisdiction over marriage and divorce. The concession had not been requested by the provinces. It was greeted with alarm by women's groups, which had been lobbying throughout the seventies for reforms to family property and support laws; they realized that a return to decentralization in the area of divorce would threaten the continuation of a uniform law on divorce and make enforcement and variation of support orders in a federal system even more difficult. Once the proposal had found its way into the formal machinery and documentation of intergovernmental relations, however, it took months of lobbying by women's groups to halt its momentum.

Once again in 1980, a federal initiative resulted in the large-scale mobilization of women's efforts to influence constitutional reform. As part of its patriation initiative in 1980, the federal government tabled a proposed Charter of Rights and Freedoms. Part of a "people package" of amendments, the Charter was intended to enlist the support of ordinary Canadians in favour of patriation, and in favour of entrenchment of a bill of rights in the Constitution, thus permitting the federal government to short-circuit provincial opposition to these measures.

Women had not been involved to any great extent, as civil servants or as politicians, in the development of the 1980 version of the Charter. The federal Advisory Council on the Status of Women, chaired at that time by Doris Anderson, played a significant leadership role in educating women about the implications of constitutional renewal generally and of the proposed Charter, by means of working papers, mail-outs and speeches. Its resources, added to the resources of voluntary women's groups like the National Action Committee and the National Association of Women and the Law, helped to produce a very effective showing in favour of strengthening the Charter before it was entrenched in a patriated constitution.

Public presentation at the Special Joint Committee hearings on the Constitution in 1980, as well as private meetings with experts in the Department of Justice and political contacts with Liberal cabinet ministers and their key staff, produced some changes to the Charter's equality guarantees (now Section 15) and other provisions when the package came back to the House of Commons in January 1981. Although expertise and "inside" contacts were influential in this lobbying process, a major factor behind the success of the effort was the broad support for a stronger Charter demonstrated by grass-roots women. These efforts on behalf of women joined those on behalf of disabled persons, members of visible minorities and others to demonstrate broad popular support for effective equality guarantees in the Charter.

The changes introduced to the draft Charter were not, however, fully responsive to the concerns that had been expressed before the Special Joint Committee. Other amendments raised new concerns. When these reservations were raised, it became apparent that the government's tolerance for women's advocacy had reached its limits. The minister responsible for the status of women, Lloyd Axworthy, told a forum of women convened to debate the new draft that they should "trust us" and not press for further change. When the appeal to paternalism failed, government loyalists on the Advisory

Council engineered the cancellation of a conference that the council had scheduled to study the proposed Charter.

It was at this point that the grass-roots appeal of the Charter and of entrenched equality guarantees became manifest. Volunteers organized the Ad Hoc Conference of Canadian Women on the Constitution, which took place in Ottawa on February 14, 1981. It was an enormous effort, explicitly aided by the opposition parties and unofficially aided by civil servants and Liberal women like the new minister responsible for the status of women, Judy Erola. A series of resolutions emerged from the conference; these were then taken to Parliament and government officials by the women and their supporters, resulting in the text of Section 28 being included in the Charter. This provision specified that all the rights in the Charter are extended equally to males and females.

The proponents of this basic declaration had hoped that it would be set at the head of the Charter, as a declaration of fundamental principle. Instead, it is now to be found near the end, with various interpretive sections. There has as yet been no authoritative interpretation of its meaning and effect, although it has frequently been called upon in women's equality arguments before the Supreme Court of Canada and other courts. The fate of this cardinal women's demand is emblematic of what happened throughout the process to the positions formulated by women. In order to accomplish anything at all, women's concerns had to be slipped into an existing framework and thus were stripped down to the few points upon which consensus could be achieved, not only among women but also between women on the one hand and politicians and officials on the other.

The survival of even the few equality gains thus won by women and other disadvantaged groups was imperilled by events later in 1981. The decision of the

Supreme Court of Canada in the Constitutional Reference case in the summer of 1981 sent the federal and provincial leaders back to the bargaining table; the court found that although there was no legal requirement for unanimity in these circumstances, a sturdy constitutional convention existed in favour of unanimous consent for a step as serious as patriation. The resulting compromise included in the Charter an "override" provision, known as the notwithstanding clause, allowing a government to declare certain provisions of the Charter inapplicable to legislation for periods of up to five years. The record is unclear on whether the framers of this November Accord actually agreed in their all-night session in November 1981 to include both Section 15 and Section 28 under the override. Whatever their intent, by the time the first drafts of the accord were made public, both sections had been made subject to it. Thereafter, the politicians stayed very loyal to the work of the drafters, and a national lobby was needed to lift Section 28 out from under the override. Efforts to have Section 15 similarly excluded were unsuccessful. Once again, the volunteer work of grass-roots women and women's leaders was key to this successful lobby, although the federal and provincial Advisory Councils also participated to good effect.

No account of women's place in constitutional development would be complete without mention of an important initiative taken by the women's community between passage of the Constitution Act, 1982, including the Charter, and the publication of the text of the Meech Lake Accord in the summer of 1987. This key development was the advent of women's equality advocacy under the Charter of Rights.

Up until the Charter of Rights, which conferred rights on individuals and arguably groups vis-à-vis the state, constitutional litigation had dealt entirely with the rights of governments. The major constitutional decisions dealt with the division of powers between the federal and provincial governments; whenever these decisions dealt with individual or group rights, they did so as a by-product of determining the rights of governments. This intergovernmental litigation, highly technical and obscured from popular consciousness, was mostly done by male counsel before male courts.

The Charter's equality guarantees, in particular, gave rise to the need for a different approach to litigation. Legislation would still be defended by the governments that enacted it, but challenges to its constitutional validity under the Charter would come from the individual or the group possessing the rights affected by the legislation. The women who had worked so hard to have equality guarantees included in the Charter had no wish to leave the interpretation of those guarantees to largely male courts, at the instigation of male plaintiffs. Yet experience had shown that individual women on their own would have difficulty gathering the resources necessary to sustain lengthy and complex litigation against a government adversary.

In order to marshal those resources, so that litigation for women's equality could be pro-active and purposeful, women across Canada established the Women's Legal Education and Action Fund (LEAF) to litigate women's equality rights under the Charter. LEAF was the first such advocacy organization formed specifically to give particular communities control of the litigation agenda affecting them. The Canadian Disability Rights Council and the litigation activity of the Canadian Ethnocultural Council were soon to follow. All three of these communities had been instrumental in securing the Charter's equality guarantees, and all meant to use them to prompt review of government legislation.

The record of the first few years of quality legislation established some important benchmarks, which would influence the response of women and other disadvantaged groups to the Meech Lake Accord. The landmark decision of the Supreme Court of Canada in *Andrews v. Law Society of British Columbia* in 1989 established that the court would interpret the equality guarantees as those who had sought them intended: in order to promote equality. The court has also recognized that the Charter should not be used as an instrument for the powerful to roll back the few legislative gains made by the disadvantaged, and it has applied in the equality context the same rigorous standards it uses to determine whether violations of other sections of the Charter are justified.

Just as important as these substantive gains, the techniques employed by disadvantaged groups to do their Charter litigation have enhanced the sense of democratic participation experienced by members of those groups. Recognizing that the cases they take forward will have an effect on equality rights for all disadvantaged groups, the major litigants in the equality field have adopted a consultative style of making decisions about what cases to take and how to conduct them.

These developments in equality litigation have had two important effects on the constitutional process. First, the substantive rulings have confirmed the determination of the disadvantaged to press forward in their quest for substantive equality and substantive democracy, by affirming their worth in a way that is binding upon governments. For the first time, women and other disadvantaged persons have not had to depend entirely on the goodwill or internal political priorities of politicians to establish a point: principled argument, even without a mass showing of grass-roots support, can carry the day against the wishes of a hostile or indifferent political majority.

Second, the process of litigation used by the disadvantaged, even though carried on largely by volunteers and in straitened financial circumstances, has been striving to create the substantive democracy that its participants are denied in mainstream political life. Participants in this democratization of litigation, however imperfect it yet may be, know that it produces good results, because it permits the position put forward to be more truly representative of the diversity of the community and of its needs. Knowing that such an inclusive process is a sound process, and feeling entitled to it because of the court's affirmation of their dignity and their place in the legal scheme of things, women and other disadvantaged people reacted very negatively to the high-handedness of the Meech Lake Accord process.

The political leaders who framed the Meech Lake Accord and presented it for speedy ratification seem to have neglected these important developments in the equality-seeking community since the passage of the Charter. It seems to me that they also underestimated the force of developments in the aboriginal community since the Charter's passage, developments that had, in a comparable fashion, fostered a sense of intolerance for the old élitist ways of arranging Canada's constitutional affairs.

Hence it was that the framers of the accord presented Canadians with a document that stressed in its preamble "the principle of equality of all the provinces" without mentioning the principles of equality enshrined in the Charter; that required the Charter to defer to the recognition of Quebec's "distinct society"; that made it virtually impossible for the two geographical areas of

Canada with the largest aboriginal population to achieve provincial status; that made no mention of promoting equality for minorities in its provisions dealing with government institutions like the Supreme Court and the Senate; and that promised to erode national standards in new shared-cost programs.

Those who were concerned about these and other effects of the accord were quite clearly, and often, told that the only option before them was to agree to it in the interests of keeping Quebec within Confederation. In a way somewhat reminiscent of the response to those who criticized invocation of the War Measures Act in 1970, those who dared to point out the flaws in the accord were either dismissed as fools or vilified as Confederation wreckers. The only forum for dissent that offered itself was participation in legislative hearings in those provinces that had left their minds somewhat ajar, if not wide open, on the question of ratification: New Brunswick and Manitoba. In other jurisdictions that held hearings in spite of their public commitment to the accord — like Quebec, the federal government, Ontario and P.E.I. — participation in the hearings posed a real dilemma. If one participated, one contributed to the creation of an illusion of public debate; if one did not, then governments could point to an absence of dissent. Many groups participated wearily and somewhat hopelessly, in order to register criticisms of the process and to ensure that there was no silence that could be taken as consent.

In the result, the expressions of concerns by grass-roots women had little to do with the derailing of the accord. In reacting to the government initiative of the Meech Lake Accord, women learned in 1987 and after that it is easier to steer and embellish such an initiative, as they had done in 1980 and 1981, than to oppose one. But as in 1980–81, the outcome of the drama was decided more by actions of the main federal and provincial players than by the submissions of the organized grass-roots. In all fairness, perhaps the only thing that the women of English Canada did, in recurrently voicing their opposition to the price at which the accord ensured Quebec's affirmation of Confederation and the process used to bring it about, was to contribute in some small measure to the unfolding of the process that allowed other key events to take their course.

That role was played at considerable cost to women's national voluntary groups, because large numbers of women in Quebec gave their public support to the accord. The national women's groups that went forward with positions on the accord were all careful to affirm the principle of re-including Quebec in Confederation, and their cautious suggestions for changes to make the accord more palatable were worked out in consultation with their Quebec members. However, their statements were portrayed as the voice of English Canada; proponents of the accord stated flatly that women outside Quebec really had no business offering comment on whether women's rights would be hurt by the accord, because Quebec women felt no such peril. For English-Canadian women, who value the opportunity to work with Quebec women on matters affecting all women, the politics of the Meech Lake Accord was often agonizing, as well as fruitless.

There was widespread consensus on the part of legislative committees studying the Meech Lake Accord that the process used to put the Meech Lake Accord before the country was seriously flawed; even governments admitted this. The lack of advance consultation, in particular, was acknowledged to be a major contributor to public unease about the process; greater responsiveness to public commentary concerning the draft proposal was also seen as desirable. In the wake of the failure of Meech, these criticisms resulted in a wealth of committees being appointed by governments at the federal and provincial level to harvest comments about the future of Confederation.

Whether these committees will provide any real participation for women and women's groups in the design of new constitutional arrangements is open to doubt. The memberships of the major governmental task forces and commissions, like Spicer and Bélanger–Campeau, do not represent women or other disadvantaged persons in proportion to their presence in the population. Legislative committees, too, reflect the under-representation of women and minorities in elected assemblies; the private think-tanks reflecting upon Confederation, like the "Group of 22," are similarly under-representative of women. Even where the architects of such committees recognize the need for minority representation, as in the Northwest Territories, making only a small number of minority seats available may mean "competition" for them between women and other minorities.

Even if measures are taken now to improve the access of women and other disadvantaged persons to the real processes of decision making about the Constitution, it will be difficult for them to steer the process to a satisfactory outcome, as they did in 1980–81. In 1980–81, a vast amount of grass-roots energy was required to accomplish some of the limited objectives women had formulated; today there is much more at stake and the scale of the discussions is less manageable. In 1980–81 there was also, at the level of the federal government, some congruity between government objectives and minority objectives, a congruity that seems unlikely in the present circumstances: while recent federal government budgets emphasize cost-cutting to national programs that women's advocates claim will put national standards at risk, women's groups in English Canada emphasize the importance of national standards and the continued vigour of national social programs. It can be predicted, then, that if the participation of women in this round of constitutional talks follows the old pattern of being reactive, voluntary and marginal, it will have more of the hallmarks of the dispiriting Meech Lake Round than of the more productive Charter Round.

Yet women as stakeholders have an enormous interest in the outcome of these discussions. Women's groups have overwhelmingly supported the objective of maintaining Quebec in Confederation and have acknowledged its distinctiveness, even during the Meech round. Moreover, the agenda of decentralization seems in the forefront of the upcoming discussions, and women as significant "consumers" of social spending have long been interested in the maintenance of national standards and appropriate levels of spending. Women and other disadvantaged persons have, as well, a strong interest in the maintenance of strong equality guarantees in the Charter of Rights, guarantees that have a national dimension: recent studies suggest that provincial legislation, perhaps more often passed without accommodating the range of interests influencing the national government, has more often been found to be contrary to the Charter than legislation passed at the federal level. And given their continuing exclusion from the major institutions of democratic government, women and other minorities may well wish to revive, in this round, their interest in constitutional means to ensure greater representativeness of such institutions. These are only three subject matters in which women have a strong interest. If the whole structure of Confederation is at issue, it is hard to imagine that there would not be many more.

With a challenge and an opportunity of such magnitude, it would indeed be unfortunate if women were once again relegated to participation in the process only as unfunded volunteers, reacting to an agenda determined by others, at a pace and on occasions permitted by others. A scramble to inject something of women's interests into a process staffed by white males, going on behind closed doors, is a poor way to have to participate in the forging of the future of one's country.

Up until now, Confederation has been a child with only male parents. If there are to be mothers of Confederation, or Reconfederation, certain firm measures must, in my view, be adopted. To begin with, each government involved in the process should make particular efforts to see that women and women's interests play an integral part in the development of its position. This will not happen by staying with the established cadre of advisers, most of whom are male. It will happen only if governments incorporate into their planning detailed consultation with organized women's groups and if they retain as advisers people who understand and appreciate the social and economic agenda of these groups. In addition to searching out women's perspective for all government positions, it is essential that women have the capacity to formulate, as a community, what they want to see for the future of Confederation. This process has already begun as a volunteer activity; the National Action Committee on the Status of Women formulated a position at its national conference in the spring of 1991, and five thousand grass-roots women met in various places on the tenth anniversary of the first Ad Hoc Conference in February 1981 (called "Equality Eve") to discuss their hopes for the future of the country. Common to both groups is an emphasis on maintenance of national standards for social programs, and emphasis on the role of a strong central government in this goal. In keeping with the traditions of women's voluntary constitution making, this emerging vision also stresses the social agenda of women: emphasis on interdependence and inclusiveness rather than separation and élitism, and creation of a positive, violence-free environment and a real measure of economic security.

This beginning of consensus building, on a volunteer basis, would benefit from the provision of resources for more research, consultation and discussion. It is important that the process continue the efforts to acknowledge the interest of all women, not just élite women, in constitutional renewal. Government funding for this process, as part of governments' constitutional budgets, would mean that these resources would not have to be diverted from essential social services and advocacy now provided or financed by women's volunteer activities. Sufficient funding should be provided to allow women and other disadvantaged groups to formulate their own consensus agenda for the constitutional future. This commitment of resources for development should then be matched by a genuine commitment to take these views into account, by allowing participation at the "table" where the real constitutional bargains are hammered out. Long-time activist Ursula Franklin points out that when people are not included in the process of planning change that will affect them, they react, counterplan and avoid or frustrate the majority's hoped-for result. Some proponents of the Meech Lake Accord doubtless consider that this is just what happened in 1990 and before. To avoid that result, surely it is wiser to include us all in the planning for our common future than to entrench our inequality by excluding us once again.

Federalism and Social Legislation: Past and Present

Michiel Horn

Born in Holland and raised in British Columbia, Michiel Horn is a professor of history at Glendon College, York University, and author of books on the Great Depression.

"Just at the very time when the exigencies of the economic situation call for drastic action, for increased international co-operation and for a planned internal social order, we find ourselves with cumbrous legislative machinery and outworn social doctrines." The time was the late spring of 1931, the occasion the annual meeting of the Canadian Political Science Association, the speaker a young professor of constitutional law at McGill University, Frank R. Scott. Canada was in the grip of the Great Depression, which remains to this day the most serious economic crisis of the century. However, the structure of Canadian federalism and its endemic conflict between levels of government made it almost impossible to grapple with this calamity.

Sixty years after Scott spoke, Canada is in an economic slump that may turn out to be the deepest since the 1930s. It is also in a constitutional crisis that threatens the country's very existence. A very large number of voices in Quebec are calling for sovereignty and independence;

even Quebeckers who identify themselves as friendly to the Canadian connection want a high degree of decentralization as the price to be paid for Quebec's continued partnership. Elsewhere in Canada, notably in Alberta and British Columbia, there are echoes of the demands in the Allaire report that the powers of the central government be reduced and those of the provinces increased.

Given Quebec's challenge to Confederation, it is not surprising to hear some people assert that we must decentralize in order to "save" the country. Those who make the assertion assume that decentralization will induce Quebec to remain in Canada. They also imply either that after decentralization Canadians would be no worse off than they are now (and might be better off), or that they would be so badly off, should Quebec separate, that they should be prepared to pay a high price in order to induce it to stay. These propositions require careful analysis.

Leaving aside the matter of what Quebec may decide to do, what is the status of the other propositions? All assertions about how Canadians will fare under one or another constitutional regime are based on guesswork, but some guesses are better informed than others. The historical record can provide relevant information. Of course, some can use history to prove whatever they want. The relentlessly tendentious account of Canadian constitutional history prefacing the Allaire report is a case in point.

In the search for enlightenment the record of the past, particularly that of the 1930s, provides a rich source. Some of the problems that beset Canada in the 1930s are similar to those of the present day. More important, the attitudes that shaped the roles of the federal government and of the provinces from the 1940s into the 1970s, and the social policies that emerged, owed much to the Depression experience.

During the downturn of 1929 to 1933 virtually all Canadians worried about the economy. Some of them worried, too, about the worsening fiscal situation of government at all three levels, and about the ability of the Canadian federal structure to cope with unprecedented economic and financial strain. Alberta's default on a debenture of $3.2 million in March 1936 highlighted the crisis, but several other provinces were also very close to insolvency. In 1937 concerns that the Dominion's credit might be in danger if additional provinces defaulted led W.L. Mackenzie King's government to appoint the Royal Commission on Dominion-Provincial Relations (the Rowell–Sirois commission).

Simply put, the ability to pay did not coincide with the need to spend. Many municipalities and several provinces lacked both the capacity to tax and the ability to borrow that would have enabled them to meet their obligations for social spending, including education, even at the low levels of the 1930s. In an increasingly industrialized and urban society the need for social services was growing, and a market economy could not provide them equitably if at all. Yet it was difficult to see how most of the provinces could meet the need.

The federal government had greater capacity to tax and ability to borrow than the provinces. For most of the decade, however, Ottawa was unwilling to assume increased responsibilities. One important reason was the size of the national debt. The debt, both direct and that of the Canadian National Railways, stood at $3.8 billion in 1930 and rather more than $4.8 billion by 1937. By contemporary standards these amounts were large: federal net current revenues were $314 million in 1930 and $464 million in 1937. Servicing the debt took 47.5

per cent of net revenue in 1930; it still took 36 per cent in 1937 when Ottawa had increased its revenue, most notably from sales taxes.

Another reason for Ottawa's reluctance to act was the dominance of Gladstonian principles of public finance. "Balancing the budget" was a principle enjoying quasi-religious status even though it was utterly unsuitable to the economic conditions of the early 1930s. Keynesian notions of counter-cyclical budgeting were in the air, but outside academe few Canadians had heard of them, let alone accepted them. No minister of finance did so until the end of the decade. All levels of government tried desperately to reduce expenses during the downturn, which only made the Depression worse.

As well, social legislation, especially unemployment relief, seemed to offer small electoral reward for a high financial cost. In any case, Mackenzie King refused to admit in early 1930 that unemployment constituted an emergency serious enough to require action by his government. His successor after the election of July 1930, R.B. Bennett, was willing to go a bit further than that and introduced emergency legislation to assist the provinces, on a shared-cost basis, in coping with the effects of unemployment. But at a Dominion-provincial conference early in 1933, he rejected a proposal that Ottawa assume a greater portion of the burden of unemployment relief.

That year his government did authorize the establishment, under the supervision of the Department of National Defence, of work camps for unemployed single men. This took a load off the provinces, particularly those in the West. Like emergency loans to the western provinces, this federal initiative was intended to prevent provincial defaults that might in turn affect the Dominion's credit rating.

In 1935 Ottawa invaded several areas of jurisdiction

belonging to the provinces, passing legislation establishing maximum hours of work, minimum wages and unemployment insurance. It is unclear whether Bennett's "New Deal" signalled a commitment to a more interventionist role for Ottawa. In 1935 Bennett spoke of the need to reform capitalism. Two years earlier, however, he had said that "all forms of social insurance were largely incompatible with the spirit of freedom." He was nevertheless willing to introduce a scheme of unemployment insurance, he added, but only because of Canada's commitments under the conventions of the International Labour Organization, and only if the provinces would tell him how much they would contribute even before he presented them with a scheme! No wonder that in 1933 the proposal went nowhere.

When at last he did move, he had some support. The socialist academics in the League for Social Reconstruction (LSR), among them Frank Scott, approved Bennett's use of the treaty-making power to expand the role of the central government, even though they doubted his credentials as a reformer and were unimpressed by most of the measures proposed. At the same time, significant elements of the Canadian business community favoured Bennett's reforms. They saw them as a necessary price to be paid for the survival and growth of capitalism, a price made more acceptable because much of the cost would come out of the pockets of working-class Canadians.

Those who were concerned primarily with the domestic economy, such as bankers and manufacturers, tended to be friendlier to Bennett's reforms than those who sought to export their products, notably executives in resource industries. The former, being in industries that sought to sell goods and services to Canadians, were understandably more concerned to bolster domestic purchasing power. As well, being federally regulated or supported, they were less inclined to worry about encroachments on provincial rights.

Some critics interpreted Bennett's reform program as a belated effort to save his party from electoral defeat rather than as a genuine effort to overhaul capitalism. But whether the skeptics were right is probably irrelevant in light of what happened in 1937: the Judicial Committee of the Privy Council in London ruled that most often the New Deal measures were beyond the constitutional power of the federal government. Both before and after that decision Mackenzie King, returned to office in 1935, showed no eagerness to expand Ottawa's authority.

The 1937 rulings confirmed that the constitution of Canada made positive social action by Ottawa difficult. Even a problem such as unemployment, manifestly country-wide in scope, remained under provincial jurisdiction. Most provinces lacked the money to mitigate the effects of unemployment or to cope with other problems of an industrializing and urbanizing society, but social welfare was their responsibility. Ottawa might make a financial contribution, as it had undertaken to do in 1927, under defined conditions, in the case of provincial old age pension plans. But it was up to the provinces to act.

In the inter-war years most provinces ignored as much as possible the need to act in the social realm. Even Ontario, richest of the nine, did little to promote the cause of social welfare. This was true whether the government was that of the Conservatives Howard Ferguson and George Henry or the Liberal Mitchell Hepburn. The latter's social conservatism owed not a little to his solicitousness on behalf of the mining industry. Like other resource industries, the mining sector was close to provincial politicians, in Ontario and elsewhere. This was no accident: Crown lands (Prairie lands before 1930 excepted) were within the jurisdiction of the provinces.

Quebec did even less than Ontario. L.-A. Taschereau, Liberal, and Maurice Duplessis, Conservative-turned-Union Nationale, shared a firm belief in laissez-faire and the importance of attracting foreign investment into the resource sector. Their governments allowed the poor, the municipalities, the educational systems and other non-business elements to look after themselves as best they could. Public assistance for the strong, free enterprise for the weak: the pattern was already well established.

Reformist provincial premiers were little in evidence. British Columbia's T.D. Pattullo was the chief exception. His Liberal government, elected in 1933, actually went so far as to try to introduce public medical insurance. The attempt was abandoned because of opposition from the medical profession and business groups, and because of concerns about costs. Pattullo did call, along with other provinces, for the transfer of fiscal capacity from Ottawa to the provinces. He argued that the Dominion should withdraw from the personal income tax field, which it had "invaded" during the 1914–18 war. He also asserted that Ottawa should compensate for the operation of the tariff structure, biased as it was against provinces that lacked extensive manufacturing industry.

A major drawback of Pattullo's approach was that it could not be generalized. It would have worked for Ontario and might have worked for B.C. and Quebec; it could not have worked for the Prairie or Atlantic provinces. It would be unworkable for a majority of the provinces even today.

Some commentators recognized the limits of provincial action. Only the federal government enjoyed the potential to tax and borrow enough to pay for social programs, they argued. Among those who counselled an expanded role for the Dominion government were the publicists of the LSR, the Co-operative Commonwealth Federation (CCF) led by J.S. Woodsworth, as well as reformist Liberals such as Brooke Claxton, Paul Martin and Norman McLeod Rogers (after 1935 King's minister of labour). In time such Liberals, aided by like-minded people in the public service of Canada, did much to advance the role of the positive state. But the LSR played a key role in making the case for a central government with augmented power and responsibility.

The LSR's view of Canadian federalism found its clearest expression in the brief the organization presented to the Royal Commission on Dominion-Provincial Relations in 1938. Written mainly by Frank Scott, the document had the title "Canada One or Nine: The Purpose of Confederation." One of its main points, still relevant today, was that political power in Canada was divided — "Today, for considerable sections of the Canadian people Ottawa has become almost the seat of a foreign power" — while *economic* power had become increasingly centralized. "There have grown up in Canada new centres of power and authority, not part of the formal constitutional structure yet capable of shaping the destinies of the country in a manner that parallels, if it does not indeed exceed, the power of government." One result of the concentration of economic power was a growing maldistribution of income and wealth. "It is the duty of governments in Canada to remedy these evils and to check these trends. The only government capable of attempting this vitally important task is the federal government. There is a vested interest in this concentrated wealth which only a national government is strong enough to control." Provincial autonomy had become an unaffordable luxury in the era of huge corporations. The provinces could not meet the social needs of the Canadian people.

Scott said to me that the commissioners gave the LSR brief a kind reception. But there is very little evidence in their report, published in 1940, of the LSR point of view. The Rowell–Sirois report, published in 1940, proposed that responsibility for unemployment and old age pensions be transferred from the provinces to Ottawa, but only after demonstrating at length that there were serious disadvantages in not following this course. It left other important matters, such as health services and education, to the provinces. "Mere importance of a service," the commissioners asserted in discussing health care, "does not justify its assumption by the Dominion." The commission favoured fiscal centralization, but chiefly in the interest of redistributing tax revenue. All provinces should be able to "provide adequate services (at the average Canadian standard) without excessive taxation (on the average Canadian basis)" but none would be compelled to do so.

Little in the Rowell–Sirois report was acted on. The Dominion government obtained unanimous provincial consent in 1940 for transferring unemployment insurance to its jurisdiction and introduced a scheme the next year. Thereafter federal governments virtually ignored Rowell–Sirois. In spite of some provincial opposition, Ottawa introduced family allowances in the closing stages of World War II, partly to stave off an electoral threat from the CCF. The federal government made grants to the universities in order to allow them to cope with the flood of veterans after the war and followed this up in 1951 with a scheme of direct grants to universities in recognition of their important national role. In 1951, too, it gained provincial assent to federal control over old age pensions. The Hospital Insurance and Diagnostic

301

Services Act of 1957 was yet another move into the field of social legislation.

In the 1960s the federal government used its fiscal power to introduce a shared-cost system of comprehensive, country-wide health insurance. In part this was a triumph for the tradition of reformist Liberalism, which reached its apotheosis during the prime ministership of Mike Pearson. But it also owed a lot to the Pearson government's minority position. This gave considerable weight to the members of the New Democratic Party, successor of the CCF. Earlier in the decade, a CCF-governed Saskatchewan had pioneered medicare.

It is ironic that in 1966, the very year Parliament passed the health insurance bill, Ottawa began its long retreat from federal support for higher education. It announced that direct grants to Canadian universities would be replaced by a shared-cost scheme to be administered by the provinces. Eventually, in the Established Programmes Financing arrangement of 1976, Ottawa withdrew from the shared-cost feature of hospital insurance and medical care as well as higher education. The consequences for higher education have been calamitous. Left to the not-so-tender care of provincial politicians, Canadian universities have been sliding steadily backwards.

The experience of the universities indicates the difficulty most provincial governments have in safeguarding what should be seen as national institutions and programs. They have had a measure of difficulty, too, in looking after the health and welfare of their people. When acting autonomously, the provinces were relatively inactive in the social sphere well into the 1960s, some because they feared the costs, others because they were reluctant on ideological grounds to expand programs.

Saskatchewan, governed from 1944 to 1964 by the CCF and more recently by the NDP, and British Columbia, where the CCF was a potent opposition, were willing to act. Other provinces were less so. For example, most of them adhered only reluctantly to the national medicare program.

Such facts are surely not lost on today's advocates of decentralization, whether in Ottawa, in the provincial capitals or in the boardrooms of Toronto, Montreal and Vancouver. The neo-conservatives who in recent years have set the tone for policy making in the English-speaking world have little respect for the welfare state or the principle of universal access to higher education. The gospel of competitiveness conveys the message, implicitly or explicitly, that Canada cannot afford the present level of social services (or even of wages).

For some people, decentralization is attractive primarily because it is expected to lead to a reduction in social expenditures. Perhaps the surest way of ensuring that Canadian social services will be watered down is to assign all of them to the provinces while abandoning the attempt to maintain nation-wide standards.

Federal budget making in the recent past has seen not only a shift in federal government taxation from income to consumption (the Manufacturers' Sales Tax was raised in stages by 50 per cent before being replaced by the Goods and Services Tax) and the effective end to the universality of some social programs (children's allowance and old age security payments are "clawed back" from high- and middle-income earners), it has seen also the freezing or capping of transfer payments to the provinces for post-secondary education, health care and social assistance to the poor. The argument for all three policies has been the need to reduce the budgetary deficit. But there are other, and to Conservatives more compelling, reasons. As minister of finance, Michael Wilson was clearly convinced of the "need" to reduce taxes on the wealthy and on corporations even more than of the need to reduce the deficit. It is also apparent that many members of the government and of the business community believe that Canada's social programs act as a drag on our economic performance. Never mind that our programs generally lag behind those available in the European Community. In social services as in levels of income tax, Canadian Conservatives take as their standard for comparison the United States, of all the rich countries the most backward in its social welfare policies.

Some critics of Ottawa's recent fiscal manoeuvres have charged that the intention is to transfer the federal deficit to the provinces. But the minister of finance likes provincial deficits no better than he does the federal deficit. The objective of federal budgetary policies is to encourage the provinces to spend less, even in the midst of a serious economic slump. Public-sector employees constitute one target for cuts; social programs another. And Ottawa is likely to get what it wants from the provinces, with the exception of NDP-governed Ontario.

First of all, most provinces don't have the fiscal resources to adequately maintain health care, higher education or social assistance if funding from Ottawa is reduced. Second, the social commitment of most provincial governments, including those of "haves" such as Alberta and British Columbia, has been unimpressive. Many provincial politicians are preaching the virtues of belt-tightening as earnestly as any federal Tory.

So federal government policy is tending towards decentralization for reasons that have little or nothing to do with the constitutional crisis. But this tendency will probably be reinforced in any new constitutional proposals emanating from Ottawa during the next twelve to eighteen months. Canadians should be aware of the social and economic implications of this trend: the freeing of corporations from costs and conditions of operating in Canada that they regard as hindering international competitiveness. Today as in the 1930s, saying "power to the provinces" is close to saying "power to the resource and export industries." Their interests are emphatically *not* synonymous with those of the many low- and middle-income Canadians who benefit from the welfare state, incomplete and imperfect though it may be.

The claim that Canadians will ultimately be better off as a result of decentralization must be treated with profound scepticism. But what of the argument that Quebec will remain within Confederation only if more federal power is spun off to the provinces, and that this justifies the dilution in social programs that decentralization will entail?

Some will find this argument persuasive; I do not. No one can know with certainty what Quebec will do. But sovereigntists have made it clear they will not be satisfied with half-measures that deny sovereignty to Quebec. It will be a sad outcome if, having agreed to a transfer of federal power to the provinces, we find that this fails to satisfy majority opinion in Quebec. The main beneficiaries of our willingness to compromise would turn out to be global corporations whose interest in the well-being of Canadians is minimal.

In these difficult times we cannot risk a further decline of power at the country's political centre. Even if Canadians were to be certain that further decentralization would keep Quebec within Canada, they might justifiably conclude that the price is not worth paying. And to those who observe that in recent years the central government has not acted in the interests of most Canadians, there is an obvious retort: work to elect another political party!

Part IV

The Future

Quebec's Rendezvous
With Independence

Thomas R. Berger

Thomas R. Berger is a former politician, judge and royal commissioner. He practises law in Vancouver. This essay first appeared in Canadian Forum.

What should English Canada's response be as Quebec moves towards its rendezvous with independence?

Since the death of Meech Lake, we have heard repeatedly that Quebec knows what it wants, that English Canada must get its act together and come up with a response to the proposals that Quebec is making for fundamental constitutional change.

The flaws in Meech need not be reiterated. What was to have been Quebec's round became the provinces' round. To obtain the provinces' agreement to Quebec's five points, the federal government agreed to enlarge the powers of all the provinces. The Meech Lake Accord gave Quebec — and all the provinces — more than they had at first sought.

We are told that the Meech process was flawed, too, that what is needed is a new process. Of course the Meech process was flawed. The first ministers did not use the amending procedure provided in the Constitution Act. The result was that amendments requiring the consent of only seven provinces could not be proclaimed because they had to be unanimous, and amendments that required unanimity but that were subject to no time limit had to be passed by June 23, 1990. By this means the first ministers laced themselves, and the country, into a constitutional strait-jacket.

Meech's death alarmed Canada's political establishment. We were told that Quebec would treat the rejection of Meech as a rejection of Quebec, and that this would mean the end of Canada as we know it. The defeat of Meech, it is said, has revived the dragon of Quebec nationalism. If only we had not rejected Meech, the cause of Quebec independence would have no following in Quebec today.

This just won't wash. We would have been in worse condition if Meech had passed. By rejecting Meech we preserved the Supreme Court as a national court and we made sure that Senate reform was not translated into nothing more than a repository for provincial, instead of federal, hacks and mediocrities. (There have been exceptional appointments, such as Carl Goldenberg and Eugene Forsey, but these have not fundamentally altered the institution.) We thwarted a transfer of powers to the provinces that would have undermined federal programs and institutions. And the passage of Meech would not have accommodated Quebec nationalism, let alone the Quebec independence movement.

If Quebec nationalism is on the rise, it is surely because of a widespread sense of linguistic and cultural solidarity, not a reaction to the rejection of Meech. Does anyone really believe that if Meech Lake had been adopted, Quebec nationalists would have been satisfied? That believers in independence would have been satisfied? Of course not. And why should they have been? Quebec nationalists believe that Confederation must be fundamentally restructured if Quebec should remain in Canada. Of course, *indépendantistes* do not think Quebec should remain in Canada under any circumstances. If Mr. Parizeau wins the next election, he is going to hold a referendum. Would the passage of Meech Lake have made any difference? No, it might have spared us Mr. Bourassa's referendum, but not Mr. Parizeau's .

Now the prime minister and the Canadian political establishment are telling us that we must respond to the Allaire report and the Bélanger–Campeau report; according to Keith Spicer, this was the purpose of his Citizens' Forum, to respond to proposals from Quebec, "no matter how radical" they may be.

I disagree. It is time to take stock of what Canada means to English Canada (by that I mean Canadians outside Quebec) and not to rush into another round of constitutional talks. At any such talks, as at Meech Lake, there would be no one to speak for Canada. Certainly not Mr. Mulroney. He is a deal maker, not a nation builder. The premiers speak for the provinces, not for Canada. All that will occur will be further concessions to the provinces, further undermining of Canadian federalism. Although this may send the premiers home happy, it will be catastrophic for Canada as we know it.

The idea of Canada is an idea that will keep us together even if Quebec should opt for independence. The Meech Lake debate revealed the strength of that idea. English Canadians had a greater commitment to that idea — a greater faith in that idea — than our leaders did. That is why Meech failed; not because of cranky opposition by the people of English Canada to the distinct society clause. They sensed — even if they did not understand the details — that Meech Lake was another chapter in the Mulroney government's dismantling of Canada's federal system.

311

Traditional Canadian deference to our political establishment was absent during the Meech Lake debate. Although everyone from Brian Mulroney to Stephen Lewis urged us on, the people of English Canada rejected this creation of their political leaders. And we were right to do so.

Soon Mr. Mulroney will propose an even more drastic transfer of federal powers. But this will appease no one in Quebec. Not even the Conservatives will agree to transfer the multitude of federal powers claimed for Quebec in the Allaire report. For *indépendantistes*, independence will always beckon. Quite rightly. We Canadians believe in the self-determination of nations. It is too late to argue that Quebec is not a nation. If Quebeckers decide that they want to be independent, to establish their own nation-state, that is for them to decide.

It is time we took Quebec's movement for independence seriously. Mr. Mulroney and others seek to establish an equivalence between western alienation and the demands of Quebec. Each is said to be a form of regional discontent, curable by transferring federal power to the regions. But they are antithetical ideas. It is true that western politicians ask for more powers. They always have and they always will. But the only proposition they have advanced that has popular support across the West is Senate reform. And Senate reform is intended to give the West greater influence in the government of Canada, whereas independence is intended to put an end to Quebec's connection with the government of Canada.

Western alienation is not an issue of the same order of magnitude as Quebec independence. To equate these stale cries for political aggrandizement to Quebec's call for national independence is to magnify the one and to trivialize the other.

In fact, the departure of Quebec would by itself

reform the Senate. The principal complaint of those seeking reform of the Senate is that it does not act as a counterweight to central Canada's dominance of the House of Commons. If Quebec leaves, central Canada, which now has forty-eight senators, would be reduced to Ontario's twenty-four. Western Canada would have twenty-four senators, the Maritimes twenty-four, and Newfoundland six. The Northwest Territories and the Yukon would each have one. There would remain as well six of the eight appointments made to pass the GST. From there it is only a step to an elected Senate, for the principal opponent of an elected Senate is Quebec. With Quebec gone, the way would be open.

But westerners should not think that a reformed Senate would change Canadian life. Populations and markets are smaller in the western provinces than they are in the large, populous provinces of Ontario and Quebec, with their great metropolitan centres. That is why central Canada is the financial and commercial hub of the country. A reformed Senate would not change that. It has been the federal spending power, transfer payments, equalization payments and regional development policies that have addressed the inequities produced by these economic tendencies. And these federal powers and programs must be preserved. Those who think that Senate reform can alter geography and demographics are bound to be disappointed.

Of course Quebec is a distinct society (it is puerile to suggest that each of the other provinces is a distinct society in the same sense in which Quebec uses the term); Quebec's distinctiveness ought to be recognized in the Constitution. The Civil Code gives it a distinct legal system. The French language is predominant in Quebec. Quebec has its own pension plan. It collects its own income tax. It has a special arrangement with Ottawa regarding immigration. Premier Bourassa himself has said that Quebec's *de facto* distinctiveness should be recognized *de jure*. But does this recognition require a wholesale reconstruction of the Constitution? Does the ordinary Quebecker sleep uneasily because Mr. Bourassa has not centralized in Quebec City the laundry list of governmental powers in the Allaire report? I don't believe it.

This brings me to sovereignty and independence. Here we are entitled to ask, once again, exactly what *does* Quebec want? Sovereignty-association is an attempt to have it both ways. What must be understood is that we are talking about independence. Sovereignty, if it is more than a slogan, must mean independence.

Premier Bourassa has gone well beyond demands for shuffling bureaucratic control from Ottawa to Quebec City. Quebec Liberals want control over such a long list of powers that theirs is no longer a claim for expanded provincial powers, but a claim of a different order of magnitude; in truth, it is a call for independence. For the proposals in the Allaire report will never be accepted by Canada.

Quebeckers should now call their political establishment to account, just as we did in English Canada. In English Canada we have a healthy scepticism of our politicians It may be that Quebeckers regard their political leaders as charismatic figures, and their slogans as talismans of Quebec's destiny. But I doubt it. I think Quebeckers want to know what independence is all about. For Quebec it must be a moment of truth, unobscured by soothing sounds from English Canada about accommodating Quebec in some absurdist confederal state.

Quebeckers should now require their politicians to explain the meaning of the rhetoric that, with the complicity of the prime minister and the leaders of Canada's other national parties, pervaded discussion of Meech Lake. Quebec's political establishment must flesh out what independence means.

Premier Bourassa has said that, whatever happens, Canada and Quebec must have a common currency, central bank and customs union. And a common Parliament. Mr. Parizeau disagrees; he rejects a common Parliament. But he says an independent Quebec will continue to use the Canadian dollar as its unit of currency, that there must be a joint central bank and a customs union.

At the end of the day every spokesman for independence, when pressed, wishes to retain the Canadian dollar, to have a joint central bank and a customs union. On these fundamental economic questions Mr. Parizeau fudges the true meaning of independence as much as Mr. Bourassa does.

We rejected Meech Lake because it impaired the powers of our central government. Why would we now go further than Meech did? An independent Quebec would be truly independent. *But so would Canada.* Why would we agree that control of our central bank and our currency, of fiscal and monetary policy, should be shared with another country?

An independent Quebec would have to choose: true independence, its own currency and its own central bank. If it wished to retain the Canadian dollar as its unit of currency, it would have no control over its own fiscal and monetary policy, certainly less influence over fiscal and monetary policy than it does now. This would be the shadow of sovereignty, not the substance. Yet this question, like so many others, has been avoided by *indépendantistes*.

Is Quebec's political establishment prepared to acknowledge that independence can only be achieved after protracted negotiations? Will they disclose to Quebeckers that there can be no separation without tears? And will they tell them that independence means independence, not some confederal contraption devised by the same convocation of politicians and bureaucrats that came up with Meech Lake?

Is independence simply a vehicle to enable Quebec's politicians to hold the same offices as they do now, but with more expansive titles? Or do they believe in true independence? If they do, they should have the courage to say so. Or are Quebec's political leaders, and its political establishment, as empty-headed as English-speaking Canada's proved to be?

When East Germany decided to join West Germany, what was the *sine qua non* of union? A common currency. The same central bank. A customs union. But this is precisely what Quebec's leadership insists an independent Quebec must have, *after independence*. Granted, the two Germanys had a common language; English-speaking Canada and Quebec do not. But this reveals the true issue — how to protect the French language.

So Quebeckers will no doubt think hard about any scheme hatched by their political establishment. Parades and demonstrations are all very well, but what, in terms of new political and economic arrangements, does independence mean? Wherein lies the true expression of linguistic and cultural solidarity?

Does Quebec really want to be a nation-state, an independent country, in a continent dominated by the U.S. monolith? What chance would Quebec have as a French-speaking redoubt, more and more inward-looking? An independent Quebec would have to be a fortress Quebec, with ever more stringent restrictions on the use of English. If Quebeckers get a good look at independence, they may well re-examine the Canadian option, for the survival of their language and culture is better assured within Canada than without.

An independent Quebec would be leaving behind the sizeable French-speaking populations of Acadia and eastern Ontario. And what of the minorities within Quebec? Even if Quebec were to achieve independence, she would at once be faced with the very questions that now confront Canadians: the rights of a great linguistic minority with a rightful claim to be considered a founding people, the claims of the aboriginal peoples, and the place in the new state of a multitude of ethnic and racial minorities.

Quebec must sooner or later have its rendezvous with independence. And it is a mark of respect for that right of choice to permit it to be made without English Canadians wringing their hands over the fact that the choice is being considered. There is no need for us to be fussing over them, coming up with half-baked constitutional proposals designed to postpone that moment of choice. And it is wrong for the prime minister or any of our leaders to offer to build constitutional half-way houses in which Canada, if it is to survive, with or without Quebec, cannot agree to take up residence. English Canada must take independence seriously. But so must Quebeckers.

Suppose Quebec opts for independence. By that I mean true independence. For Quebeckers and Canada's political leaders must understand that English Canadians will not countenance the dismantling of the federal institutions and federal programs that we have built over the past century.

So what will happen? I think English Canada will stay together. Of course the departure of Quebec will be an enormous loss. But the idea of two peoples, two linguistic communities, will survive — the Acadians and the French-speaking population of Ontario, together with other French-language minorities, will have a claim on Canada's traditions of bilingualism. The Constitution and the Charter will still be there to protect them. The idiotic idea that the Charter enshrines English Canada's individualist notions of our polity, but does not recognize collectivities, and that Quebec rejects the Charter on that ground, could only occur to anyone who has never read the Charter. It protects both. And not only by express acknowledgement of the rights of linguistic minorities, aboriginal and treaty rights and our multicultural heritage. In fact, it was the notwithstanding clause of the Charter that allowed Mr. Bourassa to enact his sign law despite the ruling of the Supreme Court that it was unconstitutional.

With Quebec gone, will Canada be a Pakistan of North America, with the Maritimes inevitably breaking away, as Bangladesh did from Pakistan? Such comparisons are trivial. A better one would be the United States, which is a Pakistan of North America: it has forty-eight contiguous states, and Alaska with Canada's land mass in between (not to mention Hawaii). Alaska shows no sign of leaving the Union because of the distance it lies from the lower forty-eight. I lived in Alaska for two years in the mid-1980s. Alaskans, like Canadians, believe they have good reasons to remain where and as they are.

For in the midst of the despondency that afflicts our political establishment, let me bring you the good news about Canada. Look around the world. Is there another country where you would prefer to live? Haven't we, here in the snow and scenery, built a nation-state worth preserving? We in English-speaking Canada believe in a public sector that helps to knit the country together through transportation and communication, linking the vast spaces of the land. We have our network of social programs, the centrepiece of which is medicare. We have our national institutions, such as the CBC, designed to keep our country together. These are not just artifacts. Behind each there is an idea, the idea that there must be a government of all Canadians and federal institutions to serve all Canadians.

We have avoided the extremes of wealth and poverty that disfigure U.S. society. We believe in government intervention to assuage the condition of the weak and to ensure Canadians everywhere a decent standard of living. We have even provided for it in the Constitution. Under the Constitution Act, 1982, the Parliament and the provinces are committed to promoting equal opportunities for the well-being of Canadians, furthering economic development to reduce disparity in opportunities and providing essential public services of reasonable quality to all Canadians.

We are the kinder, gentler nation that George Bush spoke of in 1988. "Peace, order and good government" is a phrase of which we should not be ashamed. It has spared us the lawlessness that is the hallmark of life in the United States.In our own time Canada has become a haven for people from all over the world; we have the highest proportion of refugees per capita of any country in the world.

It is said that this is not enough, that there must be an overarching national ideal, arising from a stirring encounter in our history. This is exactly what we do not have. And we are better off without it. We have been able to do without mindless patriotism. We are not ruled by a triumphant ideology. We could be the nation-state of the twenty-first century, in which the citizen's own identity does not have to be authenticated by a spurious nationalism.

All of these features of our national life would have been altered by Meech Lake, and they are still at risk. But this is not all that is in jeopardy. A deal cobbled together to keep Quebec in will undermine our federal institutions, threaten the capacity of the federal government to protect minorities and certainly make it impossible to settle outstanding questions of aboriginal land claims and aboriginal self-government. We cannot throw everything we have built over the side simply to keep Quebec on board.

I suppose it will be said that I am anti-Quebec. I am not anti-Quebec or indifferent to Quebec's aims. I opposed the denial of Quebec's veto in 1981. (In an article I wrote for *The Globe and Mail* in November 1981, I urged the restoration of aboriginal and treaty rights to the draft constitution to be submitted to Westminster. This act of *lèse-majesté* led to my departure from the bench. In the same article I also urged the restoration of Quebec's veto.) I favour continuation of Quebec's special status. I am in favour of Quebec's right to independence. I think that an independent Quebec would be entitled to insist upon its present boundaries (but only after Canada had discharged the fiduciary obligations it undertook to the native peoples of northern Quebec in 1870 and 1912).

But I want to ensure that, whatever happens, the principles of Canadian federalism remain intact.

If Quebec votes against independence in a referendum, where would that leave Quebeckers? Well, they would still enjoy special status. Pierre Trudeau rejected the idea of special status for Quebec. But Quebec has had special status since 1774. To pretend that Quebec is juristically a province like the others is a barren notion, putting constitutional form ahead of historical substance. Mr. Mulroney believes not in special status for Quebec, but in special status for all the provinces — a decentralized idea of Canada not shared outside Quebec. This is what led to the constitutional débâcle of June 1990.

I want to see Canada survive, with Quebec. Staying together is important not only to ourselves. If people of differing languages, cultures, races and religions can live together harmoniously within a great federal state, perhaps they may learn to live together harmoniously in the wider world. In Canada we have democratic institutions, the rule of law, an educated populace. If we can't find a way to live together, what peoples, what nations can? Quebec, like English Canada, has a stake in the survival of these ideas in the world.

I think the people of our country, including Quebec, will decide that the Canadian adventure should not be ended. There should be special status for Quebec, but not a Constitution turned inside out simply to keep Quebec in. And as Quebeckers make their choice — independence or no — they should not think that they can turn away from Canada and yet remain within it.

There is no foregone conclusion to our constitutional journey. Quebeckers have the right to choose; I hope that they choose Canada, but whether they do or not, we want to preserve the idea of Canada and the institutions that have brought us this far.

An Emergency Operation for the Constitution

Tom Kent

Tom Kent's knowledge of constitutional issues and federal-provincial relations was gained as principal assistant on policy to Prime Minister Lester Pearson and as a federal deputy minister.

Canadian democracy must find the best way to reach decisions about the recasting of our federal structure of government, and it must do so in 1992. The timing is dictated by the understandable impatience of the people of Quebec and the calculations of their premier. Robert Bourassa knows where the best deal he can ever hope to get for the government of Quebec would come from: from the present Mulroney government, whose survival until 1993 is, to say the least, doubtful.

There is no profit in resenting the pressure thereby put on the rest of us. Prolonged uncertainty about the place of Quebec, in or out of Canada, would hurt us all. Moreover, our political system is in need of major repair whether or not Quebec stays with it. Left to themselves, the politicians we elect but distrust would go on evading that need. We can be grateful to Quebec for forcing its recognition.

This sense of opportunity is valid, however, only if we make sure that Prime Minister Mulroney and Premier

Bourassa are not allowed to repeat the gamble with the country's future that they attempted in the Meech Lake affair. Brian Mulroney may be deluded into thinking that another deal with Quebec would restore his political fortunes; he could campaign as the saviour of national unity. Politicians and commentators of all political sympathies, including Conservatives, should make it clear to him that the attempt would be another misroll of the dice. Even in the unlikely event that most of the premiers would again go along with it, a Mulroney-made deal with Quebec would be voted down in the rest of Canada. Far from saving him and Mr. Bourassa, it would be the perfect present for Parti Québécois leader Jacques Parizeau. Quebec would again feel rejected, and it would be the last time; separation would follow.

The disaster would not be attributable primarily to distrust of Mr. Mulroney, deep and widespread though that is. The basic cause is that Quebec's strategy for pursuing its constitutional goals challenges, from the start, Canada's existing institutions. Mr. Bourassa wants to negotiate with the federal government, but what he is demanding is a response to Quebec's claims from the rest of Canada, what Quebeckers commonly label, inaccurately, "English" Canada.

No federal government, elected to run the federal affairs of the country as a whole, has any right, legal or moral, to represent one part of the country in constitutional negotiations with another part. The disqualification of the present government is particularly obvious because it is led by a Quebecker and depends on its Quebec caucus for its survival. However, while a replacement might not be as deficient in moral authority, it would still have no entitlement to respond to Quebec on behalf of Canada outside Quebec.

The nine provincial premiers might aspire to fill the

vacuum, if Mr. Bourassa would relent and talk to them. Certainly they have a role. The only democratic mandate of a premier is, however, to run provincial affairs in his or her province. Premiers are not elected to be national statesmen. Their natural bias is towards increasing provincial power, their readiest agreement is in fed-bashing. Even if they are agreed, the nine collectively have no more right than the federal government to be the constitutional representatives of "English" Canada as a whole.

In short, Quebec's challenge is to an entity — whatever we call it — that has no institutional form without Quebec. To respond to Quebec, the rest of us have to go outside the present political process. This would be true even if we were entirely satisfied, for normal purposes, with that process and with the federal and provincial politicians who operate it. The need for special procedures has already been recognized, in a small way, by the establishment of the Spicer commission; it has given a kind of official recognition to public attitudes. But the larger process we require has yet to be got under way and must be directed to the making of definite decisions next year.

It is widely agreed that the errors of 1987–90 must not be repeated. First, though Quebec is again the immediate driving force, a response to Quebec will not be valid if it is only that. There are other deep discontents that require constitutional redress: of the aboriginal peoples, of western Canadians, of the large majority of Canadians who have no faith in our political processes. The rest of Canada will not now be satisfied with constitutional reforms directed only to the conciliation of Quebec.

Second, the process must be open. It cannot again be centred on secret meetings of first ministers. There must be opportunity for widespread public discussion before conclusions are formulated. That is the universal view. There is now wide acceptance of a further step. When conclusions are proposed, they should be subject to final judgement by direct popular vote; this time the whole country, not Quebec alone, will require a referendum.

It should be emphasized that a constitutional referendum in no way implies espousal of the same procedure to determine public policies. We choose a government to run our public affairs for a period during which it makes thousands of policy decisions. At the next general election, it stands or falls according to its performance as a whole. To pick out particular policies for decision by referendums would destroy our system of government.

The Constitution, however, is different. It establishes the fundamental rules under which politicians must operate while they hold office. The politicians should not make their own rules. Those should come directly from the people by referendum. This is a democratic principle that we have neglected, because of the nature of our emergence from colonial status.

Agreeing to correct the deficiency by a referendum on major constitutional change is the easy part of the decision. The difficult part is to settle on the question or questions to be submitted to referendum. That also should be a democratic process, involving the widest possible public discussion. In order to hear as many voices as possible, we must begin without delay. We should therefore not be unnecessarily ambitious. The process that will serve us best in 1991–92 may not be the ideal for future constitutional changes. We might even hope eventually to rejuvenate our politics so thoroughly that we could trust governments to frame appropriate questions for constitutional referendums. But that day is not now. Public confidence requires a special procedure.

The crucial step is to create a special body charged with considering what constitutional arrangements would reflect the wishes and serve the interests of most Canadians. There are plenty of precedents from other countries for such a constituent assembly. In the desperate final stage of the Meech affair, something of the kind was suggested as the way to develop a proposal for reform of the Canadian Senate. And in the Bélanger–Campeau commission, Quebec has already used the procedure, though in a more élitist format than would appeal to most Canadians.

The early talk has been of a national assembly. Newfoundland premier Clyde Wells is a principal proponent, which underlines the improbability of Quebec agreeing to attend. Quebec has taken its position and awaits the response from the rest of Canada. Premier Bourassa cannot be expected to retreat so far from his negotiating stance as to participate in a constituent assembly.

Indeed, the plain fact is that Quebec's involvement in the initial phase of the assembly would probably work against, not for, eventual agreement. One of the main reasons why moderate opinion in Quebec has moved towards separatism is that federal Canada seems so disorganized, leaderless, uncertain. The Meech affair was a painful demonstration. The rest of Canada is unprepared to deal with a Quebec that thinks it knows much better what it wants. A nation-wide assembly at this point would only underline the contrast and, probably, widen the gulf.

We will not be rejecting Quebec if we join in its acknowledgement of this situation. To be effective, a constituent assembly should now be established, without apology, for the rest of Canada. Quebec should be invited to send official observers, of course, and the hope would be to move on to a nation-wide assembly. But Canada must first prepare itself.

The disillusionment with present politics suggests that the assembly should have a direct mandate from the people; that is, it would be created by a special election. But this would take time we don't have, and there are even greater obstacles.

Though a special election could be conducted without formal identification of the party affiliations of the candidates, in practice most would have party connections and certainly constituency associations would have preferred candidates for whom they would campaign. An election theoretically confined to constitutional issues would in fact take on much of the character of a general election. The Mulroney government would, on present evidence, suffer a massive rebuff. Its authority for running the normal affairs of the country, diminished already, would be impaired almost to destruction. Whatever one thinks of the Mulroney administration, it is entitled under our present constitution to try to restore its reputation over the life of this Parliament, until the fall of 1992, or even until 1993. In these circumstances it is unrealistic, to say the least, to ask the present government to agree to a constituent assembly by direct election.

One alternative that might appeal to Mr. Mulroney is to appoint an assembly of prominent persons. With consultation, such an assembly could be made representative of all the main interest groups in society — labour and business, farmers and fishermen, ethnic groups and regions, political parties, aboriginal peoples.

The objections to this idea are not of practicability but of principle. Our concern with the fundamental law of our society, with the Constitution, is the common concern we all have as citizens, not as people with various origins, occupations, particular interests. People chosen to represent the things that differentiate us would be, disproportionately, representatives of élites. All would come to the assembly to defend and promote particularities. They would reach agreement, if at all, by trade-offs. That is not the way to build consensus on a workable constitution embodying our common concerns as citizens of Canada.

Further, to retreat from an elected to an appointed assembly would run counter to the intensifying demand, as horizons widen, that people should have more say in the affairs that affect them. This is the democratization, in the fullest sense, that is a growing force around the globe. We should not be facing the opposite way when we remake our constitution. If the condition of the Mulroney government makes direct election of an assembly impracticable, as I acknowledge with regret, we should still preserve the principle that the qualification for representing citizens is to have been elected by citizens. So the acceptable alternative to direct election is an assembly of members of Parliament and of provincial and territorial legislatures.

For this there are excellent precedents: our own Constitution of 1867, like those of the United States and Australia, was created through meetings of delegates from the pre-existing legislatures. To adopt a similar procedure now would respect democratic principle while getting around Mr. Mulroney's problem; indeed, it would surely be welcome to most of his caucus and particularly to his surviving supporters in western Canada.

My proposal therefore is that most of the members of a constituent assembly should be elected, from among themselves, by MPs and MLAs; the associations of aboriginal peoples should also choose some delegates; these original delegates should then elect a smaller number of additional members who would bring special knowledge and experience to the assembly's deliberations.

The assembly must not be larger than is necessary to give it the credibility of broad representation. My estimate of the size is 150. The starting point for the calculation is that the legislatures, provincial and territorial, could not be adequately represented by fewer than a total of sixty delegates. The problem is their distribution among provinces. The smaller provinces could not accept representation by population for the purpose of constitution making. Nor, however, could Ontario, with nearly half the population of Canada outside Quebec, accept equality of provincial representation — which would give a resident of Prince Edward Island seventy-two times more influence on the future of Canada than a resident of Ontario. Some compromise between provincial weight and provincial equality is necessary. But any new formula for that purpose would be suspect. There would be concern that it might become a precedent for the future balance of power. In effect, one of the contentious issues about a new constitution — the composition and power of an elected Senate — would be brought into play before the assembly to draft it could even be set up.

The essence of my proposal is that, rather than prejudge issues, we should start from what we have. For our national affairs, representation by population in the House of Commons (with a few anomalies, notably P.E.I.) is qualified by regional equality in the Senate. The combined total of MPs and senators, from Canada outside Quebec, is 300 (excluding the senators specially appointed to pass the GST). I suggest that the sixty provincial and territorial delegates to the assembly should be divided in the same proportions as the present totals of MPs and senators. That is, each province and territory would have, in the constituent assembly, a number of delegates equal to one-fifth of the combined number of MPs and senators that it now has in Ottawa. This would produce the following distribution: British Columbia, seven; Alberta, six; Ontario, twenty-four; Saskatchewan, Manitoba, New Brunswick and Nova Scotia, four each; Prince Edward Island, two; Newfoundland, three; Northwest Territories and Yukon, one each.

The number of MPs in the assembly should be fewer than the total of MLAs but appreciably more than the number of Ontario MLAs; forty would be reasonable. They could be chosen by party caucuses, in ratio to party strengths (excluding Quebec) in the House of Commons. The same principles would apply for delegations from the legislatures.

Presumably those chosen would include some ministers, former ministers, party leaders, even first ministers. A few at least of these would be among the best-qualified delegates. A large proportion of office holders would, however, lessen the credibility of the assembly — particularly if they jetted in by special planes replete with aides. Moreover, it is crucial that the assembly be expeditious, and therefore it might occupy a great deal of the time of its members. Consequently, while ministers could not be excluded, their eligibility as delegates could be conditional on taking leave of absence from their offices for the duration of the assembly; it could be unpaid leave as far as their ministerial emoluments were concerned, though of course they would remain MPs or MLAs. The weight of ministerial representation in the assembly might then be reasonably contained.

The aboriginal peoples have special claim to constitutional change and are little represented in

Parliament and the legislatures. Like the smaller provinces, they are entitled to weight in the assembly more than proportionate to their numbers in the population. Ten members might be appropriate.

The 110 members so far suggested would not be strong in constitutional expertise. To support them by allowing for bevies of advisers, no doubt offering conflicting advice according to the delegations they served, would detract from the openness of the assembly's proceedings. Rather than participation by whispers and back-room meetings, it would be better to round out the assembly by indirect election. The original 110 would be empowered to co-opt, as their first act, 40 people distinguished by their knowledge or experience. Election by majority vote of the 110 should ensure that most of the additions would be people of national status, enhancing the breadth of view of the assembly.

A few names can be suggested as illustrations. The most obvious is the recently retired Chief Justice, Brian Dickson. Some former premiers — the names Davis, Blakeney, Lougheed come to mind — would be strong candidates. Consideration might also be given to a few retired federal politicians, a category that could include a senator or two. Experience in the third level of government — particularly that of some city mayors — would be highly desirable. Leading constitutional lawyers, political scientists and historians should be drawn from the universities. It is to be hoped that the assembly would be broadminded enough to welcome Preston Manning, whose Reform Party does not have present standing in Parliament but will undoubtedly be of some significance after the next election.

The Meech affair put an end to constitution making in private conclave. The assembly should hold all its discussions in public. Private committees would be needed, but they should be required to report the attendance and conclusions of each meeting at the next session of the assembly. The appropriate location for most of the work would be Winnipeg, the city most central to Canada.

Tight deadlines are necessary. Certainly the first phase of the work will need to be completed before winter next leaves the prairies. That phase is to develop the guidelines for a federal constitution that, in the judgement of most of the assembly, would best serve the kind of society in which most Canadians outside Quebec want to live.

This constitution would certainly give a larger role to the federal government than most Quebeckers want. There may be some federal responsibilities that other Canadians would be happy to have moved to their provinces, but in some fields where jurisdiction is at present muddled we would be better off if the federal role were predominant. The regulation of financial institutions and environmental control are two obvious examples. Indeed, it seems probable, and certainly in my view it is to be hoped, that the consensus of Canadians outside Quebec would involve, on balance, more strengthening than weakening of federal responsibilities for economic affairs.

In that event, the second phase of the assembly's work will be the most testing. A high degree of wise realism will be required in order to suggest terms on which a more independent Quebec, particularly in social and cultural policies, could still have a significant part in a federation satisfactory to the rest of Canada.

The third phase of the assembly's work will require it to appoint an executive committee to discuss its proposals with representatives of Quebec in the summer of 1992. The outcome will determine the nature of the fourth phase. At best, if there is some agreement in principle, a full Quebec delegation would join the assembly. There would no doubt be more detailed discussion of the tax system and the political structure appropriate to Quebec's partial involvement in federal affairs. The latter would require innovations of some difficulty, but they could undoubtedly be devised if there were genuine will to do so fairly. The now-national assembly could then frame the questions to be put to all Canadians in a referendum.

Alternatively, if the executive committee had to report to the original assembly that no satisfactory agreement with Quebec was possible, the assembly's final task would be to frame the question to be put to the people of a continuing federal Canada, while Quebec would no doubt conduct its own referendum.

In either event, the referendum or referendums as such would not change the constitution. The existing amendment process requires action by Parliament and the legislatures. If, however, a clear popular consensus had emerged from the assembly-referendum process, the politicians could not fail to embody it in the necessary legal form.

The decisions of the next twelve months will be embodiments of the will of Canadians only if they are reached in the open, after wide public discussion. The existing federal government, the provincial governments, the various legislative bodies, cannot by their separate procedures or their negotiations provide a publicly acceptable focus for constitutional considerations and decisions. A special body with no other purpose, in the nature of a constituent assembly, is essential to legitimacy. Further, the assembly's conclusions will be too fundamental to the future of Canada for their validation to be restricted solely to legislators. They must pass the test of a referendum clear enough to ensure that the legislators collectively serve the public will.

Most of us will hope that this method produces a recast federalism in which Quebec takes a continuing part. But if it does not, we will still surely go on to build the future of a new Canadian federation.

Canada Cannot Be Held Together by Taking It Apart

Bryan Schwartz

Bryan Schwartz is a professor at the Faculty of Law, University of Manitoba, who frequently writes and comments on constitutional policy.

It's been a year or so since the Meech Lake Accord collapsed, and we are currently in the "fog of negotiations" again. The participants, including many Quebec politicians, are not entirely sure what they want and are temporizing with the usual posturing, bluffing, threatening and stalling. No one can possibly know how the game will be played out. Much still depends on the choices of senior politicians, who themselves are not sure what they are going to do and who will react in unpredictable ways to persuasion, the movement of their own thoughts and external political pressures. The attitude of the people may count for something more than it did during the Meech round. The "civilian population," however, also contains many people who are conflicted, uncertain or amenable to persuasion.

With all of this confusion and uncertainty, the tempting course will be to make substantial concessions to Quebec's current demands. Doing so may create the appearance that peace and unity have been maintained.

Unfortunately, no matter how we respond to Quebec, we may already be close to the point of no return in the denationalization of Canada. "Denationalization" here refers to more than impairing the authority of the federal government. Not that the federal government can stand any more diminution; a leaked report by a committee of federal deputy ministers recently pointed out that Canada is already more decentralized than Switzerland. By "denationalization," though, I mean the erosion of the whole ensemble of programs, symbols, institutions that make up the life of the national community.

We in the rest of Canada should be lucid and resolved about a few key points. First of all, the Constitution is not the underlying cause of Quebec separatism, and amendments will not "solve" it. Quebec has prospered, economically and culturally, under our evolving constitutional arrangements. If the Québécois wish to separate, it is first and foremost because they have a sense of national identity as Québécois and will wish to affirmatively express that in a state of their own.

An additional factor fuelling current separatist feeling in Quebec is the sense of "humiliation" that has largely been created and fostered by the prime minister. In order to "sell Meech," Prime Minister Mulroney and others promoted the myth that patriation was a stab in the back for Quebec. (As many observers have reported, the prime minister actually favoured the 1982 deal as it was proceeding.) Mulroney went on to portray the possible rejection of Meech as amounting to another rejection of Quebec. In order to peddle his remedy, Mulroney helped to create the disease. Quebec's resulting sense of affront should not now be addressed by a package that further denationalizes Canada.

As the Québécois become psychologically separated from the rest of Canada, there is a decreasing advantage to the rest of Canada in Quebec's continuing to participate, as an "insider," in the life of the larger Canadian nation. It is true that the transition costs of separation would be considerable; even with the best of goodwill (and the rest of Canada should exhibit that) there would be economic uncertainty and reduced investment while Quebec's ascension to statehood is negotiated. But such costs would be temporary. The costs of two embittered or indifferent partners staying together would be ongoing. Quebec should not be threatened with dire consequences if it separates. A state held together by fear is not worth preserving. On the contrary, both sides will make a far more constructive and rational choice if the rest of Canada resolves that it will accept the right of the Québécois to form their own state and determines to negotiate the terms in a fair-minded and constructive manner.

There are worse things than Quebec's detaching itself from Canada on a map of the world. The things that define and impart value to a community are the ways in which it enriches the welfare and spirit of its citizens. We would almost all want a Canada enlarged and enriched by the willing participation of the people of Quebec in a strong national community; but if Quebec's attachment to the federation is only legal, not emotional, the mere fact of sharing the same coloured blotch on a map counts for nothing.

We are already too far down the path to the denationalization of Canada, and we cannot afford to go any further. A strong national political community is needed to counter-balance powerful natural forces of disintegration — which include geographic expanse, ethnic and linguistic division and the assimilative pull of the United States. A long history of judicial decisions and political arrangements has left us with a highly decentralized state already. The U.S.–Canada Free Trade Agreement diminished or eliminated a number of areas of federal authority and is sure to accelerate economic integration with the U.S. The federal government of recent years has been busy off-loading responsibilities on the provinces, selling off Crown corporations and undermining the unifying effect of national institutions such as the CBC. The national community is not a millionaire that can blithely remove the gold rings from its fingers. Canada is more like an independent carpenter, just getting by, who is being asked to give away the tool kit. We should not be misled into surrendering the hammer with the consolation that we get to keep the nails and screwdriver.

In any case, separation cannot be "bought off" in the long term by further concessions to Quebec. The diminution of the remaining bonds of nationhood would accelerate Quebec's psychological separation from the rest of Canada. The more Quebec is *de facto* a sovereign state with economic links to the rest of Canada, the easier it will be, emotionally and administratively, to formalize the arrangement.

According to the Spicer commission, Canadians outside of Quebec have a strong commitment to having a nation and, although they would prefer to have Quebec in, are not prepared to grant special privileges to Quebec or seriously impair the authority of the national government. Earlier polls have shown that Canadians overwhelmingly would want to stick together if Quebec separated. It is quite likely that most Canadians will accept that it is better to have two healthy nations than one divided and embittered one.

The politicians are another matter. When push came to shove, almost all of the senior ones were prepared to ignore public opinion and proceed with Meech. Some may have acted primarily out of genuine conviction. Others may have been influenced by self-interest; for provincial premiers, signing Meech meant simultaneously looking and feeling like nation builders or new Fathers of Confederation, while at the same time grabbing a great deal more power. The prime minister's intimidation techniques also had considerable success; he attempted to pressure potential hold-outs into submission by isolating them from their constituents and by suggesting that they would be held personally responsible for disastrous consequences unless they went along.

Unless the rest of Canada holds firm this time, then, a denationalist "megaMeech" deal is a distinct possibility. Here's a preview of some possible Mulroney razzle-dazzle.

The federal government may tell us that we must break away from "rigid centralism." The reality is that we are already one of the most decentralized states in the world.

The federal government may say it is "empowering the provinces" and "bringing government closer to the people." The reality is that federalism works best when it is balanced. There is much to be said for the intimacy and accessibility of local government. But there is much to be said as well for a strong national government. It can protect minorities from local excesses; it can provide a larger framework in which people can achieve bolder aspirations; it can give all of us a real voice in the world or in the face of powerful special interests, such as big business, where ten small communities would be impotent.

The federal government may say it is eliminating "wasteful overlap and duplication." The leaked report by federal deputy ministers has concluded, however, that there is very little outright duplication. There are many areas in which federal and provincial governments handle different aspects of the same policy area; but in a healthy federation, competition between governments helps to check abuses and improve performance on both sides. In areas of divided jurisdiction, a citizen can appeal to the other order of government against oppression and injustice. It should not be assumed, moreover, that the elimination of "waste" involves decentralization. Large economies of scale can be achieved by having one national government administer a policy, rather than nine or ten separate bureaucracies.

The federal government may tell us that the Constitution is 125 years old, and that Mulroney is bringing us "a constitution for the twenty-first century." The reality is that the Constitution has been formally changed many times since 1867. Moreover, our constitutional tradition, inherited from Great Britain, has always been of gradual change without formal amendments. Over the years, we have developed many new procedures and institutions without formal amendments; we have built everything from the Bank of Canada to the Supreme Court of Canada to the CBC to medicare. Yet these institutions affect the fabric of day-to-day life. There is much work to be done in renewing the country. But the task is best done by focusing on particular areas and proceeding at a measured pace, with full consultation, and with the possibility of revision later on.

The federal government may tell us that it is building the "Canadian economic union" and that the prime minister is helping to make us "internationally competitive." The reality may be that Canada will still end up less integrated than the European Economic Community. Provincial governments have tended to resist internal free trade; all that is left of Trudeau's economic union initiatives from the Patriation Round is the mobility rights section of the Charter, and it is shot through with qualifications. Quebec has traditionally been resistant to any loss of sovereignty. In any event, the "economic union" that will be emphasized will be free movement of goods and services; the Mulroney government is unlikely to be interested in assuring the social welfare aspect of the union, such as the ability to retain and revise national medicare. (Meech included an attempt to buy off public opposition by preserving some existing federal programs; but it is vital for the federal government to have the authority to act creatively in the future.) And our "international competitive" position will not be enhanced by leaving us with a federal government that cannot act decisively to manage the national economy, to invest in human resources or to conduct a unified foreign policy.

Watch out for some fancy footwork on the Senate. The federal government may propose a triple-E Senate in which the "equal" part refers to four equal regions. Quebec will be one of them, all of western Canada another. Or perhaps Quebec senators will be offered special voting status within the Senate. It is almost certain that the Mulroney government will not offer western Canada a Senate package that gives it significantly more power at the expense of Ontario and Quebec; it is more likely to offer an expensive gewgaw that preserves the domination of Canada by the centre.

Mulroney has learned from last time not to antagonize certain constituencies. He may well offer aboriginal people whatever rhetorical, political or legal recognition they desire. Perhaps the federal govenment will attempt to use the pro-aboriginal component of the deal to stifle criticism of the overall package. Aboriginal people should indeed achieve a reasonable measure of self-government, but they should be accommodated within a federalist philosophy — one that balances local and national control. Such a balanced proposal requires thought and consultation; it is unlikely to emerge as part of Mulroney's gift-wrapping for a corrosive proposal.

"Assymetry" is a buzzword we are likely to hear. We will be told that the existing Constitution already contains differences in the power among provinces. Yes, it does contain some differences; there are some institutional differences (some provinces guarantee denominational school rights, some do not) and different standards of official bilingualism (New Brunswick is officially bilingual, Quebec and Manitoba have a lesser measure of it). But the catalogue of powers assigned to each province is essentially the same. Furthermore, differences in the powers given to different provinces are not necessarily positive factors to be built on; they can just as well be seen as historical anomalies that depart from the general principle of equality.

The form of "assymetry" we may be offered could be called "buffet federalism." Each province will be offered powers in areas such as culture and telecommunications; some will choose to take them, some not. Bilateral negotiations, between Ottawa and the province choosing to accept powers, would determine the terms and conditions.

Assymetry is objectionable in principle unless strict safeguards are applied. The principle must be "pay as you go," not "profitable separatism." These safeguards are that every increase in the authority of a province ought to be accompanied by a proportionate reduction in its authority in the national government and its share of federal revenues. If Quebec wants to exercise control over telecommunications at the provincial level, then its federal politicians should have no say whatsoever over telecommunications for other Canadians. Otherwise, we have reverse imperialism. The representation of Québécois in the federal public service should also be reduced in a proportionate fashion. Furthermore, Quebec should not be subsidized for receiving the share of federal money that it would have obtained if the federal government still exercised policy control. Instead, federal taxation of Quebec residents should be reduced, and the provincial government should be strictly responsible for raising the revenues needed to run the program.

The immigration deal signed in December 1990, between Quebec and Canada, suggests that assymetry is liable to amount to "profitable separatism." The federal government surrendered more control than ever to Quebec over immigration. It completely withdrew from providing settlement services for immigrants. In pointing to a similar promise in the Meech Lake Accord, Prime Minister Trudeau objected that immigrants come to Canada, not to the "distinct society" or "western alienation." In return for the privilege of abandoning even more of its power to set immigration policy to Quebec, the federal government provided Quebec with a promise of $332 million worth of funding over five years. So Quebec, with 25 per cent of the population, was promised more than 30 per cent of the immigrants and generous federal funding. How's that for profitable separatism?

The immigration deal is not an accident. When it comes down to bilateral dealing between Ottawa and Quebec, the latter is bound to do very well. About a quarter of the seats in the House of Commons are from Quebec, federal governments of recent years have included hard-line Quebec nationalists, and the threat of separation gives governments additional leverage. Ontario is also likely to do well in bilateral negotiations; it can afford to run its own programs, and its political clout is massive. The "losers" in a regime of bilateral negotiations are likely to be smaller provinces. Unable to afford to run their own programs, and with little political clout in Ottawa, their bargaining power is poor.

The smaller provinces are in fact far better off under nation-wide, formula-funded programs. The fact that such programs apply to all provinces will help to ensure that the necessary political support exists for their continuation. Formula-funding means that small provinces will not be pushed around or exploited in bilateral negotiations, and that the larger provinces, including Quebec, will not unduly exploit their political power.

"Buffet federalism" will be attractive to people like Prime Minister Mulroney because it permits decentralization to take place gradually, through obscure intergovernmental agreements, rather than in one comprehensive, high-profile deal. The people of Canada should reject it for the same reason. We need more open constitution-making. "Buffet federalism" maximizes the importance of the back-room deal.

Instead of these dangerous steps in the direction of denationalization, whether done openly and directly or covertly through "buffet federalism," I support the following measures.

Constitutional reform should proceed in incremental steps. Each formal change should take place only after careful deliberation and full consultation all along. Formal methods of change should be used sparingly. We should experiment with ordinary legislative and administrative arrangements that are open to revision.

The next step should not be a massive and rushed restructuring of Canada. A more modest package might be attempted. It would address one or two provincial concerns but would also contain several elements that build the national political community or ensure greater regional equality. The package would not be presented as the "solution" to all of Canada's problems, let alone Quebec's. It would be portrayed instead as a demonstration that gradual and measured constitutional reform is possible.

Debates over symbolism and rhetoric should be avoided. If Quebec insists on formal acknowledgement of its distinctive character, then the rest of Canada should insist that the recognition be placed in the context of a commitment to building Canada as a whole, and of recognizing other elements of its diversity, including aboriginal peoples and multiculturalism. (Such a "Canada clause" was proposed by the federal government in 1980, and again by Manitoba's three political parties in 1989–90.)

Progress must be made towards freeing up the Canadian internal market. Trade within Canada must be at least as free as trade within the European Community or trade between Canada and the United States. But building the common market must be accompanied by a commitment to national standards of medical care, pensions and educational opportunities. The federal government should be given the financial and political role of defining, financing and enforcing the minimal standards. The national programs would contribute to a sense of shared nationhood. They would produce not only a gentler society, but potentially a more "competitive" one; public investment in human resources can, if done wisely, produce a more productive society. The federal government should be recognized as having a role not only in social welfare, but in developing post-secondary education, research and employment training.

Provincial equality should be better guaranteed. As

David Kilgour has suggested in *Inside Outer Canada*, Canada should borrow from the Australian constitution and entrench the principle that all provinces and parts of provinces must be treated equally with respect to federal taxing and spending measures. Overseeing the principle might be entrusted not only to the courts but to a reformed and elected Senate. It should have substantial authority, but not enough to paralyse the House of Commons. As Gordon Robertson, a pro-Meecher, has acknowledged in *A House Divided*, there is a clear consensus among Senate studies from all quarters that each western province should have at least 50 per cent of the seats held by each of Ontario and Quebec. Anything less would prevent the Senate from acting as a counter-balance to the domination of Canadian politics by the centre.

On the process front, the best course would be to hold a morally binding referendum on the text of any package before it is submitted to the legislatures for formal ratification. Only if the people have the final word is there any reason to believe that politicians will respect anything the people have to say along the way. There is already a long history of constitutional committees and task forces who solicit opinions from the public and then proceed to "interpret" that input in accordance with whatever is demanded by the higher-ups. A referendum on general principles is not good enough; a proposal can be understood and evaluated only when the specifics are provided. It is no valid objection that referendums require "yes-no" answers, whereas compromise is needed. Sooner or later must come a "yes-no" ratification vote; the only question is whether legislatures will proceed with them without polling the people.

The Canadian nation has always been a product of political will, not natural cohesiveness. Maintaining a sense of shared purpose and effective national government always requires us to overcome natural forces of disintegration. Accelerating and entrenching the evisceration of our remaining sense of shared national purpose should be as easy as taking a financially troubled company and guiding it into formal bankruptcy. The far more demanding and proper task would be to try to maintain and enhance the legitimacy of national government, institutions and programs.

Our search for nationhood should be tempered by realism in both remembrance and hope. We should not be nostalgic for what never was; the federal government has never been sufficiently even-handed, honest and efficient. "National unity" has too often been maintained by telling different stories in different parts of the country, and turning over the pork-barrel where the votes are needed and words are not enough. We must show those who would dismantle the federal government that a better alternative would be to improve it. We cannot expect the natural forces of disintegration to disappear, even if the federal government retains its ability to deal with them. Maintaining national cohesion will require an ongoing expenditure of energy and patience. We have to remember that no state has any intrinsic value; Canada is worth preserving only for the good things it delivers to the individuals within it. A "national unity" that is maintained by stifling the economic, political or cultural opportunities of individual Canadians is unworthy of loyalty.

It is tempting to see resistance to denationalization as futile. But resignation in the face of the inevitable is one thing; giving up in the face of the merely probable is another. If the will can again be found, among enough politicians and enough of the people, it may be possible to maintain a Canada that is worthwhile. It would be a community whose national structure is strong enough to permit its people some real control over their own political and economic lives, wise enough to make long-run investments in human resources and decent enough to protect them from tyranny, whether public or private.

The Economic Consequences of Quebec Sovereignty

Patrick Grady

Patrick Grady is a partner in Global Economics Ltd., an Ottawa economic consulting firm. He was formerly a senior official in the Finance Department.

Quebec sovereignty has many possible dire economic consequences for Canada and especially Quebec. Few would deny that to date Canada has been an economic success story. Although Canada has a small population, it has the seventh-largest economy in the world. Our standard of living is the second-highest after the United States. Canada is richly endowed with resources and has a diversified industrial economy. Immigrants from all over the world flock to Canada, drawn by our prosperity. Quebec has flourished economically in Canada, and Quebeckers have shared in the bountiful income and wealth generated by the Canadian economy.

We must have been doing something right. Certainly there are ways we can do better, but there are also ways we can do much worse. Separating Quebec from the well-functioning Canadian economy is unquestionably a way to do worse.

Since Quebec separation is looming ever larger on the horizon and it threatens the economic success we have achieved, both Canadians and Quebeckers need to understand fully its economic consequences. Negotiating issues, transition costs and long-run economic impacts must all be considered to gain a proper appreciation of the economic consequences of Quebec sovereignty.

Quebec is an integral part of the Canadian economy. Even if Quebec were to separate, flows of goods and services, capital and labour would have to be maintained in both directions. This would require some accommodation on both sides, but Quebec would be wrong to assume that it has Canada over a barrel with no choice but to negotiate economic association on Quebec's terms.

Sovereignty-association seems to be the preferred option of many Québécois for economic relationships with the rest of Canada. It has the attraction of preserving the continued free circulation of people and goods between Canada and Quebec. The two pillars of sovereignty-association are a customs union and a monetary union. The former has nothing to recommend it, from a Canadian point of view; the latter is dubious at best.

A customs union would not be in Canada's self-interest. It would require Canada to give up control over our external tariffs. It does not make economic sense for Canada to retain duties as high on clothing, textiles and footwear as those now imposed by the federal government for the benefit of Quebec, where more than half of the industry is centred. The textiles and clothing industries, which are the largest and most important of Quebec's "soft" industries, are able to operate only behind high tariff walls and then only after being propped up by protectionist international agreements.

There would be other contentious trade issues from Canada's perspective that would have to be resolved. Quebec's dairy farmers supply almost half of Canada's milk at inflated prices under the shield of supply management marketing boards. Hydro-Québec, benefitting from a long-term contract, sells Churchill Falls power from Labrador to the United States for a huge profit while paying Newfoundland only a pittance. Neither of these situations would be allowed to continue.

In a Canada without Quebec, the traditional western Canadian support for freer trade and grievances over the treatment of the resource industries would be more influential in the determination of national trade policy. The Ontario–Quebec axis in support of manufacturing would be broken with the departure of Quebec.

A free trade agreement would probably be about as far as Canada would want to go to accommodate Quebec. And this would not be an act of magnanimity. It might be in Canada's interest. Under a free trade agreement, there would probably have to be border control points between Canada and Quebec. Even in the European Economic Community there are still border controls on the flow of goods to enforce rules of origin and commodity taxes. But Quebec–Canada free trade is no foregone conclusion. At the moment, Quebec sells a great deal more to the rest of the country than it buys from the other provinces. That favourable situation might well change in the event of Quebec secession. Most of what Quebec sells to the rest of us could be bought elsewhere — in many cases at considerably lower cost.

If a customs union would not work, a monetary union between Quebec and Canada seems almost as unlikely. It would certainly be hard to sell in the rest of Canada. English Canada could be expected to embrace the idea only reluctantly, if at all, and not to yield much control over monetary policy to a sovereign Quebec. Other provinces would find it very difficult to accept Quebec representation on the central bank if they are excluded. Early reaction suggests that Jacques Parizeau's view of what would constitute a "fair" apportionment of policy influence in a monetary union would be unacceptable.

Perhaps the only way that Quebeckers might be able to persuade English Canadians of the need for a monetary union would be to appeal to their pocket-books by trying to convince them that common currency would be necessary if Quebec is to stay strong enough to assume its share of the Canadian-dollar-denominated public debt. The lack of a monetary union would be more troublesome for Quebec than for Canada. The smaller and more open an economy and the less diversified, the less the benefits from a floating exchange rate in fostering adjustment and the higher the costs in increased transaction costs and volatility. The Bank of Canada has already gained the confidence of the international financial community for the stability of the Canadian dollar. Quebec would have to earn such confidence for its new currency. The only short cut to confidence would be to peg the Quebec piastre, or whatever it would be called, to either the Canadian or U.S. dollar. But such a link could hardly bring Quebec the monetary independence it craves.

In the actual division of the $380-billion national debt, Quebec would have the upper hand and Canada would have to make sure it did not get short-changed. The debt is an obligation of the government of Canada; persuading Quebec to assume its one-quarter proportional share, based on population, would not be easy.

Currently, we are getting mixed signals from Quebec on the debt-split issue. Jacques Parizeau, the PQ leader, said in Toronto in December 1990, "We will ... haggle for a few weeks before we come to something like a quarter." But one of the background studies of the Bélanger–Campeau commission argued that Quebec's share of debt should be only 18.5 per cent based on federal assets and revenues in Quebec. For Quebec, this would make the difference between an almost balanced budget and a huge deficit. In fact, a strong and inflammatory case could certainly be made that, as a long-time net beneficiary of transfer payments, Quebec's equitable share of the national debt should be considerably *larger* than its proportion of the population.

There also seems to be some resistance in Quebec to the idea of replacing federal bonds with Quebec bonds. The preferred option in Quebec is to leave the federal debt as it is and to reimburse the federal government for the interest. This has obvious advantages for Quebec in avoiding an increased risk premium for Quebec government securities. It would also strengthen Quebec's hand in future negotiations as it would give Quebec the option of threatening to withhold payments if the bargaining were not going its way.

A related issue would be the division of national assets. Presumably those federal government assets such as buildings and land that have a fixed location would have to be transferred. A great many federal assets in Quebec were, of course, created for the benefit of the whole country — harbour, canal and navigational facilities, broadcasting and other communications installations, defence industries and CFBs, rail and air systems, to name the most obvious. These could not merely be transferred. Mobile assets would be subject to even more disagreement. Breaking up commercially viable Crown corporations would be controversial and if not done carefully could lead to declines in output and employment.

Almost as tricky as the debt and assets questions would be that of the federal public service, which would have to be cut back sharply if Quebec were to separate. While some public servants in Quebec would be hired by the Quebec government, many others would find themselves out on the street. They would include many of the 25,000 Outaouais residents with federal jobs in the National Capital Region. Unemployment would rise until displaced public servants could find new jobs. Property values in Ottawa could take a real shellacking and Hull could become something of a disaster area. Nor would there be much hope of Canadian assistance in making the abrupt transition; any "foreign aid" that Canada grants to Quebec could not come close to the scale of Ottawa's current largesse towards the province today.

Another likely cost for an independent Quebec would result from the probable end of bilingualism in Canada. Canada has operated as a buffer between French-speaking Quebec and English-speaking North America. An independent Quebec would have to deal directly with the United States without the accustomed support from Canada. French documentation and labelling would no longer be obligatory for suppliers of goods to Canada, eliminating one small non-tariff barrier to trade and one large irritant to some admittedly intolerant English Canadians (no more French to be forced down unwilling Canadian throats with the corn flakes). The Quebec economy would have to bear the full cost of preserving and protecting French on its own, and the specific economic cost would be compounded as many foreign exporters simply wrote off the shrivelled francophone market in North America.

Perhaps the most divisive issue of all, and a costly one, is the territorial boundary of a sovereign Quebec. With the transfer of Hudson's Bay Company lands to the province of Quebec under 1898 and 1912 federal legislation, Quebec's territory has grown since Confederation from 193,000 square miles to 595,000 square miles today. The added territory includes a part of James Bay and its hydro-electric facilities, which have been central to the development strategy of a succession of Quebec governments. In the not unlikely event that an international arbitration decided that the District of Ungava (as of 1912) should revert to Canada, not only would the power generators be on Canadian soil, that soil would be contiguous with Ontario; hence transmission lines could be built through Ontario without Quebec's permission. Future electric power revenues for Canada would more than offset compensation paid to Quebec for the existing plants. Again, although Quebec has made a claim to much of Labrador, based on its rejection of the 1927 decision of the Judicial Committee of the Privy Council settling the Canada–Newfoundland boundary, reversal of that decision by arbitration is extremely improbable.

There would be nothing like a territorial dispute with a very costly outcome for Quebec to turn negotiations over sovereignty sour. This would almost guarantee an acrimonious, expensive and mutually destructive split.

The costs incidental to bitterness are seldom considered. The consensus among Quebec economists and businessmen as reflected in the Bélanger–Campeau report is that in the long run there are no economic costs of sovereignty and that the short-run transitional costs can be minimized if both sides to the split are rational. This consensus is based more on wishful thinking than on facts.

The process of separation would be very costly. A strong central government in the rest of Canada and a Quebec government with sound economic policies would be necessary to control the damage. Even so, economic disruptions and hardship would be great. Many people would move from Quebec to Canada, adding to the flow of 200,000 anglophones who have left Montreal over the last fifteen years. Confidence in the Canadian and

Quebec economies would be shaken. Capital would flee Quebec and become nervous in the rest of the country until reined in by high interest rates. Stock markets would dip and maybe even crash. In some sectors, business investment plans would be shelved pending the resolution of the uncertainty. There would probably be at least a mild recession in Canada and probably a worse one in Quebec. And this assumes that the present economy would have had a chance to recover fully from the current recession.

In English Canada, in addition to the dangers of Balkanization, we would have to be very careful to guard against a nationalist backlash that could result in the introduction of interventionist and protectionist policies and an increase in fiscal deficits. These could transform the short-term economic costs of Quebec independence into long-run permanent losses. For its part and to its credit, Quebec seems to be committed to pursuing market-oriented and fiscally responsible policies regardless of the resolution of the current crisis. Quebec has been one of the biggest boosters of the Canada–United States Free Trade Agreement and is supportive of a trilateral pact with Mexico. Such outward-looking economic policies might strengthen its hand to weather the economic storms of separation; but those storms would not be short-lived.

Once through the transition period, both Quebec and Canada would continue to be hurt. It would take a long time to make up for the investment lost during the transition phase. Investment loss stemming from plant location decisions might never be made up. In addition, there would be the dead-weight loss from the time and effort that the best brains and talents in the country would have to spend reorganizing and sorting out our affairs. This time and effort would be much better put to use working to improve our international competitiveness and other pressing domestic problems.

In the longer run, Quebec would probably continue to be much harder hit than the rest of Canada. For one thing, Quebec might have difficulty negotiating its own favourable free trade agreement with the United States given the much higher degree of government intervention in the economy in Quebec than in the United States and the rest of Canada. In any event, the external position of Quebec would be weak, and structural adjustment policies of the type that the World Bank likes to impose to overextended developing countries would be required to strengthen the current account. Consequent social security cut-backs could be necessary to stabilize the finances of a new state of Quebec.

The Quebec economy would exhibit several weaknesses, exacerbated by independence, and these should not be ignored. On the fiscal front, Quebec would lose the benefit of net fiscal transfers from the federal government. According to André Raynauld in a recent study for the Conseil du Patronat du Québec, the federal government spent $27 billion more in Quebec than it received in taxes between 1981 and 1988 after correcting for the deficit and public debt charges. The budgetary deficit of the Quebec government would increase to well over $10 billion if Quebec were to take over the existing federal structure of revenues and expenditures.

Public debt as a proportion of GDP would rise from 29.0 per cent of GDP in 1990–91 to a dangerously high 98.5 per cent if Quebec's almost $110-billion share of federal gross debt based on population were factored in. Quebec would have a larger gross public debt than any of the seven largest industrialized countries except for Italy. Of the smaller OECD countries, only Belgium and Ireland would have higher gross debt. A sovereign Quebec would definitely be a country with high public debt — critically high if proportional refunding of previous net transfer payments were factored in. International and domestic lenders could be expected to exact an interest premium from the Quebec government to compensate for the greater risk of lending to a high-debt sovereign Quebec, as indeed they are already doing in anticipation of possible sovereignty.

If Quebec were to lose the benefit of federal fiscal transfers (and even repay some) and to assume its full quarter share of the federal debt, taxes would have nowhere to go but up. Fiscal belt-tightening would become the order of the day as structural adjustment policies were adopted to redress Quebec's weak external position. Without question, this would compound any shocks to the Quebec economy that might result from free trade negotiations with the U.S.

If Quebec became a sovereign state, there would be a renewed exodus of the head offices of Canadian corporations out of Quebec. Quebec's business and entrepreneurial base would be further eroded. Canadian Crown corporations such as Canadian National Railways, VIA and Air Canada would have no reason to be headquartered in a foreign country. Private firms such as Imasco, Montreal Trustco and Power Corporation that own Canadian financial institutions that are subject to restrictions on foreign ownership would, under existing legislation, be required to move their head offices or divest. Similar restrictions apply to federally regulated telecommunications firms or their holding companies such as BCE Inc., Bell Canada and Teleglobe, airlines such as Air Canada and broadcasting companies such as Astral Inc. Other major firms such as Canadian Pacific, Seagrams Corporation and Alcan and many smaller firms too numerous to name might also decide to move.

However, while a sovereign Quebec would be much worse off than as a Canadian province, it cannot be denied that Quebec would still be a viable economy. It would not be the smallest country in the OECD Measured by GDP in U.S. dollars in 1989, converted at the average exchange rate, Quebec would only be slightly smaller than Austria and larger than Denmark, Finland or Norway. In terms of population Quebec would fit in among the same countries. Quebec's GDP per capita, measured by U.S. dollar purchasing-power parity at $17,207, would place it third among OECD countries — behind the United States and Canada. Yet such an estimate presupposes more favourable outcomes of bilateral negotiation with Canada and of arbitrations than may seriously be anticipated. A sovereign Quebec would have adjustment problems, but they would not be insurmountable if business, labour and government were induced by a crisis environment to work together for the greater good of a newly sovereign Quebec. Quebec Inc. once more into the breach.

The problems for Canada itself, while far less ominous, would not be negligible. The rest of the country would be worse off in the longer run as a result of Quebec separation, but maybe not greatly. Key to the economic well-being of the rest of the country would be the need to resist centrifugal forces and to retain a strong central government capable of managing the Canadian economy. Nevertheless, any reduction in access to the Quebec market would obviously still have some costs. Ontario and the Atlantic provinces would be most affected by any disruption in trade flows because of their greater dependence on trade with Quebec (8 to 9 per cent of manufacturers' shipments from Ontario and the Atlantic provinces go to Quebec). The Prairies and British Columbia would be virtually unaffected (only 3.8

per cent of manufacturers' shipments from the Prairies go to Quebec and only 1.7 per cent from British Columbia).

The sharing of the public debt would be a critical determinant of the long-run impact of the separation of Quebec on the rest of Canada. For the impact to be relatively minor, Canada would, of course, have to make sure that Quebec assumed its full share of the debt; Canada would also have to fight very hard for equitable settlement of boundaries, federal assets, compensation for past net benefits from transfer payments to Quebec and a guaranteed transportation corridor to the Maritimes.

The most serious disadvantage of Quebec separation for the rest of Canada would be the potential loss of international influence and prestige and the weakening of our bargaining position in international negotiations. This could harm our trade and other international economic relations with the United States and other major trading partners. But the significance of our weakened international position should not be overstated. Canada without Quebec would still be the seventh-largest country in the OECD and would retain its status as a member of the G-7 economic summit nations.

On the positive side, Canada would benefit from the end of net fiscal transfers to Quebec from federal government transactions with the Quebec government and residents. With the recipient of almost half of current equalization gone, the cost of fiscal transfer payments to less well-off provinces would be much more affordable for the deficit-strapped federal government. The longer-run economic impact of Quebec sovereignty on the rest of Canada would be conditioned as much by the policy responses of the Canadian government as by the direct impact of the act of separation itself. If Quebec could pull together in adversity, why could the rest of Canada not do likewise?

Beyond doubt, the economic costs of the separation of Quebec would be high. Pointing them out is not to blackmail Quebec. Rather it is to try to warn Quebeckers of the possibly dire economic consequences of their political choices. If successful, such a warning will spare much needless economic pain. If not, we will have to pull together to make the best of a bad situation. If we have to establish economic relations with a sovereign Quebec, we must keep our emotions under control and be guided by self-interest and not spite. An emotional response would only make a bad situation worse. Damage control would be the name of the game.

Pros and Cons of Separation

Thomas Walkom

Thomas Walkom has a doctorate in economics from the University of Toronto and writes a column on Ontario politics in The Toronto Star.

In purely economic terms, Quebec's separation from Canada will cost both sides. This seems to be a given; only the amount is in question. But there are other elements involved in the national question. If the polls are right, Quebeckers seem willing to pay a percentage point or two of their standard of living to achieve something they consider more important. That is why, one suspects, the economic argument — up to now the mainstay of the federalist position in Quebec — ultimately cannot work.

True, the scare strategy may succeed again this time around. Prime Minister Brian Mulroney and his constitutional lieutenant, Joe Clark, may be able to persuade Quebeckers that mid-recession is a bad time to leave, that the costs of dislocation will simply be too high. But that would merely put off the moment of truth, transfer it to a different point in the business cycle. For Quebeckers want to develop their own nation. If they can't do that inside something called Canada, they will leave — and they seem willing to pay an economic price to do so.

Outside of Quebec, such questions have not been addressed. There is no sense yet in the rest of Canada of what the country should look like. The most crucial question for Canada — would it be better off without Quebec? — is being asked only on the fringes. Within the mainstream, there is much official hand-wringing over the prospect of Quebec's separation. But there is no fall-back. What does Canada do if Quebeckers (and it is their choice) decide to leave? Will separation cripple Canada economically? Politically? Can the country exist as a nation without Quebec? If so, at what cost?

Expect to hear more about the financial costs. Most of the key federalist politicians in the rest of Canada — Mulroney, Clark, Ontario premier Bob Rae, Alberta premier Don Getty — are heading for something that can be loosely described as Meech Plus — that is, an accommodation with Quebec that will give that province at least as much as the abortive Meech Lake constitutional accord, and probably more. The country didn't buy Meech Lake even when these politicians warned it was the price of unity. To sell Meech Plus, Mulroney, Rae et al. feel they will have to convince Canadians that Quebec separation hits the rest of the country in the tender spot — the pocket-book.

They argue that separation will interfere with trade and investment, that even if individual westerners or Ontarians don't like Quebec much, the companies they work for will be hurt by dismemberment. This is not an unimportant argument. To a large extent, the original project of Confederation was sold to the British North American colonies in terms of mutual economic self-interest. But economics alone has never addressed the central problem in this country: Can French and English Canada together form one coherent nation?

As the constitutional debate reheats, Canadians

outside of Quebec may find themselves looking with favour on Parti Québécois leader Jacques Parizeau's solution to this question. Parizeau says that both Canada and Quebec would be far better off if the two separated. What if he's right?

In fact, English and French Canada have strained at each other since the beginning. To read the Confederation debates of 1865 is to be reminded that federalism was seen from the start as a means of separating two nations, not uniting them. The reality then, however, was that central Canada — Ontario and Quebec — was one economic unit centred on Montreal. For the Fathers of Confederation, the trick was to maintain that central economic unity while allowing the French and English halves of Canada to go their different ways.

The answer was Confederation. In Canada West (Ontario), Confederation was seen as a way of countering French, Roman Catholic control. The new central parliament (the only parliament that John A. Macdonald, George Brown and their confrères thought would count) was to be chosen on the basis of population. And in 1867, rep by pop favoured the English. In Canada East (Quebec), the reverse argument was made. The Quebec provincial government, Bleu politicians insisted, would be a powerful body committed to preserving French in North America.

In short, the central Canadian contradiction was glossed over but never resolved. Canada — the Canada of Ontario and the Maritimes — was to be a new nation in North America. But in Quebec, Canada was to be simply an entity, a safety zone. The real nation, Quebeckers were told, would remain French Quebec.

Now, 124 years later, the same ambiguity bedevils the country. Quebeckers are shocked and insulted when they hear other Canadians denying their province's distinct nationality. And the rest of the country simply cannot comprehend why Quebeckers have so little feeling or interest in Canada beyond their own provincial borders.

Programs such as bilingualism have helped overcome French-English animosities within the country. (Bilingualism has also increased these animosities, but that, I would argue, is a short-term effect. The enthusiasm with which anglophone parents adopted French-language immersion schooling demonstrates that over time the notion of Canada as at least a symbolically bilingual state could have worked.) However, bilingualism did not address a related but analytically separate issue, the Quebec–Canada question. Bilingualism was designed to make francophone Quebeckers comfortable in the rest of Canada. But that, it appears, is not what Quebeckers wanted. They wanted to be at home in their own home, literally *maîtres chez nous*.

Perhaps Parizeau is right. Perhaps the idea of creating a country containing two diametrically opposed notions of nationhood was doomed from the start. Perhaps it would have been better had the original relationship been defined as one of sovereignty-association or special status. But that is not the question now. The question now is what happens if Quebec leaves.

First, look at the abstract economics of the issue. In a world where politics didn't matter, Quebec independence shouldn't be a problem — if it were combined with economic association. Goods, capital and labour would continue to flow freely between Quebec and Canada, or at least as freely as they do now. The Canadian dollar could continue to be used in Quebec. True, this joint Canada–Quebec dollar could be affected by the fiscal policy of the newly independent state. But, in theory at least, this effect should be no greater than at present.

Provinces (as the brouhaha over the 1991 Ontario budget shows) are already largely fiscally independent.

There would be an increase in duplication of state services; the new Quebec would have to expand to carry out its new sovereign functions. But this burden would fall on Quebec alone. Indeed, since Quebec is a net recipient of federal equalization grants, the rest of Canada should theoretically be better off with separation.

In 1978, following the election two years earlier of Quebec's first Parti Québécois government, the Ottawa economic forecasting firm Informetrica Ltd. was commissioned by *The Toronto Star* to study the effects of separation. The study, carried out by Carl Sonnen, now vice-president of the company, came up with an intriguing conclusion. Sonnen looked at four scenarios: the status quo; sovereignty-association; movement towards a unitary state (with special status for Quebec); and devolution of power to all provinces.

The scenario he referred to as movement towards a unitary state might better have been called binationalism: Quebec would be given special cultural status; all provinces, including Quebec, would surrender economic authority to Ottawa; all provinces except Quebec would surrender important cultural powers in fields such as education to Ottawa. In Sonnen's study, this binational option came up tops. He reckoned that real per capita disposable income for all Canadians would double by the year 2000.

Sonnen's worst scenario was devolution, where powers were decentralized to all provinces. Under this scenario, income would rise by only 56 per cent over the period. Sovereignty-association was considerably better (income up 67 per cent across Canada and Quebec). But the status quo would have seen per capita income rising by 77 per cent. So sovereignty-association would cost, but it would not be as bad as radical decentralization.

Sonnen says the general outlines of that 1978 study are still applicable today. In 1990, he told the *Star* that, based on rough estimates, separation would cause Quebec living standards to drop by 4 to 8 per cent. The rest of the country would experience a smaller decline, 3 to 6 per cent.

But even the economists who carry out these studies recognize that they rest on shaky assumptions. The world is not an abstract place. Politics, blood and emotions count. Once we enter this world, there are no longer safe and secure econometric models; there are no numbers.

Consider the phase referred to, in the bloodless language of economists, as the "transition" — the arguments over boundaries, debts and assets. Who gets the Montreal Post Office? Who gets the St. Lawrence Seaway? Who maintains responsibility for Quebec natives — Quebec? Canada? The natives themselves? What happens to the small anglophone communities of west Quebec or the small francophone communities of eastern Ontario? Who gets Labrador? Who gets the Ungava? Should there be a transit corridor — such as the one that linked the former West Berlin to West Germany — set up between Ontario and New Brunswick?

Quebec sovereigntists see these as practical, solvable questions. Keep present boundaries; divide debts and assets in the same proportions. After all, Norway and Sweden separated without great difficulty in 1905. But consider the other examples of history: Greece and Turkey; India and Pakistan; Slovenia and Yugoslavia.

The idea seems absurd here in peaceable Canada. But emotions are dangerous to play with; once lines are drawn it is hard to retreat. Pierre Berton's history of the War of 1812, *The Invasion of Canada,* demonstrates this point. As Berton shows, the war began initially with little enthusiasm on either side; Canadians and Americans were, after all, much the same people. But once the first blood was shed, the war became ugly. The bitterness along the border persisted for at least fifty years after war's end. In Canada at least, it may still exist.

Similarly, recall the attempt by the U.S. southern states to separate. Here too were two fundamentally similar societies, with little desire on either side for conflict. Not until four months after the South seceded did the firing on Fort Sumter occur. It was this shot — the actual instigation of violence — that turned a relatively peaceful constitutional crisis into bloody civil war.

The point here is not to argue that a unilateral declaration of independence by Quebec will lead to civil war. It is to point out that the so-called transition to sovereignty can be more wrenching, politically and economically, than anyone now can anticipate.

Suppose though that the transition is accomplished. Do Canada and Quebec simply enter the period of benign sovereignty-association, where economic ties continue unabated? Again, in the theoretical world of economics, this should happen. But in the theoretical world of economics, there are no nation-states at all. In the real world, politics enters the equation.

First, it seems clear that an independent Quebec will move quickly to ally itself intimately with the U.S. Quebec nationalists, from Pierre Bourgault to Robert Bourassa, have made this clear. This enthusiasm for the American embrace may puzzle English Canadians, many of whom are used to seeing the U.S. as public enemy number one. However, the generation that controls Quebec still smarts from the province's all-too-recent quasi-colonial status *vis-à-vis* English Canada. Emotionally, for French Quebeckers, the enemy is still Westmount and Toronto, not Washington. Many Quebeckers seem to have no fear that their new state might be overwhelmed by linking it more tightly to the U.S.

On the one hand, they are right. The French language provides a barrier against America, a barrier that the rest of Canada has always lacked. Ontario, bombarded by U.S. television sitcoms and police shows, feels defensive about the U.S. Quebec worries less about this. On the other hand, though, Quebec complacency towards the U.S. is naive. Even now, a Quebec that is already sovereign in most cultural fields feels threatened by English Canada. A nominally independent Quebec will be threatened far more when it moves directly into the American orbit.

Some federalists have argued that the U.S. might not accept Quebec — might, for instance, freeze it out of the existing free trade deal. That too is naive. Washington will have no interest in isolating a major territory on its northern border. An independent Quebec may not end up trading freely with Canada. But it will trade freely with the United States, no matter what Ottawa says.

As well, an independent Quebec will quickly be invited by the U.S. to join NORAD, possibly NATO and perhaps the Organization of American States. The incentive for quick action will be an old one: to prevent European meddling. France is one of the few old-time imperial powers with continuing imperial ambitions — witness its aggressive posture in the South Pacific and its continuing intrigues in Africa. Sectors of the French government would not be averse to signing a defence treaty with an independent Quebec. Washington will not want French paratroopers along the St. Lawrence; it will get in there first.

For Canada, this means that Quebec independence not only breaks the country in two. It creates a new state that will be an integral part of the U.S. economic and defence systems — right in the heart of Canada. Already, Quebec sovereigntists are saying that if Canada refuses to allow the new country to use the Canadian dollar, it might adopt the U.S. one. Again, don't expect the Americans to object.

None of this is particularly heartening. And it should give pause to those who feel Quebec separation would be a non-event in Canada. But let's return to the original question. Suppose a long and difficult transition. Suppose a level of mutual bitterness that created even more economic barriers between Canada and Quebec. Suppose that trade, investment and labour no longer flowed as freely across the Ottawa River. Suppose a Quebec that, functionally, became a kind of French-speaking Puerto Rico or American Samoa to the United States. What would the effect of separation be on the rest of Canada? Could the country, as a country, survive?

In economic terms, the answer is yes. There has been much loose talk about the importance of Ontario's economic ties with Quebec. Donald Creighton's image of the Empire of the St. Lawrence has been resurrected. It is said that, even were Quebec to become independent, Ontario would have no choice but to align itself with its old pre-Confederation partner. In fact, this is used as an argument to explain why Canada cannot exist without Quebec. In a post-separatist world, it is said, an Ontario forced to choose between Quebec and a new, truncated Canada would choose Quebec. Its own economic interests would force it to.

What is not realized is that the Empire of the St. Lawrence is dead. Ontario's main trading partner is not Quebec but the U.S. Indeed, Ontario trade with all Canadian provinces has been steadily declining over the last ten years. The Montreal–Toronto axis of money and power no longer exists. Or, at least, it is not fundamental.

Talk to any Toronto businessman. His external reference points are New York and Cleveland or perhaps London and Tokyo. Not Montreal. Ontario will lose if Quebec goes, but it will not lose much, not in purely economic terms. The West will lose even less.

Once again, the question of costs and benefits of separation must go beyond economics. They are also political and psychological. To tear a chunk from the heart of the country — a country that already is unclear about the reasons for its existence — would be profoundly traumatic. This is why the Maritime provinces, particularly New Brunswick (with its 33 per cent Acadian population), are so nervous about the prospect of separation. Once a country starts unravelling, the process is hard to stop. Witness the Soviet Union. If Quebec were actually to leave, many unthinkables would start to be thought.

Should Alberta and British Columbia form their own nation and set up their own direct deal with the U.S.? Should Ontario? Ontarians now assume they should pay equalization to poorer provinces in the Atlantic and the West. Most don't even think about it. If Quebec were to go, though, they might reconsider the premises of equalization.

Confederation itself was by no means a populist democratic event. Far from it. The politicians of the day worked hard to make sure there would be no direct vote by the people of British North America on the project. They knew they might lose. Indeed, in New Brunswick, which could not avoid an election, the pro-Confederation government did lose in the first round. However, once it was rammed through, Confederation was an energizing concept. It was assumed that bigger could become better, that the colonies were at least moving in the right direction.

Deconfederation, by contrast, is psychologically demoralizing. To many Canadians outside of Quebec, separation will confirm what they had already suspected: that Canada is an impossibility. And this is the real cost, the real threat to Canada of Quebec leaving. For too long, this country has been unable to define itself clearly. Perhaps the separatists are right when they say that the great Canadian experiment of trying to unite Quebec and Canada has contributed to this fuzzy self-image. But whatever the reason, it exists. The shock of Quebec's leaving threatens to turn fuzziness into a terminal condition.

For Canadians outside of Quebec, the most frustrating aspect of this is that it is all essentially outside our control. Sure, we can participate in a constitutional process. We might even come up with a scheme that, for the time being at least, Quebec can buy. But the final decision of whether to go or stay is not ours. It is Quebec's. The terms of separation depend on both sides, but not the act of separation itself. Yet in the rest of Canada, there seems to be no attempt among political leaders to create a fall-back position, a what-if. Instead, politicians, in an effort to persuade Canada to support a Meech Plus solution, emphasize how crucial Quebec is to Canada.

Crucial or not, if Quebec does go, we will have to think of something else. And to prevent the real possibility of disintegration of whatever is left of Canada, that thinking should start now and should embrace at least five principles.

• It is worth continuing a country called Canada that contains all of the territory outside of Quebec.

• This Canada will have to take into account regional

differences at the political centre, in order to accommodate the West. In practical terms that means immediate movement to some form of a triple-E Senate.

• The new Canada will continue to follow the principle of regional equalization enshrined in the Constitution Act. That is needed to reassure the Maritimes.

• The new Canada will continue as a federal state with a strong national government.

• The new Canada will include constitutionally protected native self-government.

As well, there is more thinking to be done. I would argue, for instance, that under new arrangements, Ontario should move immediately to become officially bilingual. This would reassure the largest francophone population outside of Quebec. It would also make the point — as does the recognition of native rights, as would the continuation of certain British traditions — that Canada is a country with its own history.

However, none of this will happen automatically. It requires work and thought. Quebec's departure — if it happens — will not be a happy event for Canada. But if the rest of us prepare, we might be able to draw some good from it. Perhaps it will even shock Canadians outside of Quebec into figuring out why they want to bother with this country. If we don't, however, we are finished. Not because of the economics of separation, nor because Quebec is so central to the national psyche, but because of the sheer trauma caused by the surgery of separation itself.

A Second Sovereignty

Richard Gwyn

Richard Gwyn is based in London as international affairs columnist for The Toronto Star; *from 1973 to 1985 he was the newspaper's nationally syndicated Ottawa columnist. He is the author of many books, including a biography of Pierre Trudeau,* The Northern Magus.

In the March 1991 issue of *Saturday Night*, Rick Salutin beat me to my punch. "Maybe the time has come for Canada to get out of Quebec," he wrote. I would say the same thing a bit differently, if less succinctly. Quebec's ascent to sovereignty in some form or other is sufficiently probable that the rest of Canada must now set out to define its own sovereignty; either this, or accept that it is likely to vanish. Other Canadians, that is, must do as Quebeckers have done.

To voice such a thought is treasonable to national unity as conventionally defined. But to suppress it is a form of treason to the 20 million or so Canadians outside Quebec who want to continue to be a distinct society above the forty-ninth parallel, one that is more collectivist and civil, if less egalitarian and dynamic, than the society that fills up the rest of North America. The Canadian sense of solidarity — our identity — resides in our conviction that a society's highest goals should be those of fairness and equity rather than those of efficiency and excellence (the pursuit of which, let's face it, is impeded by fussing about fairness). It is this idea, inherited from the Loyalists, of Canada as a "better America" that is now at risk. Unless other Canadians anticipate Quebec's ascent to sovereignty first by figuring out who they are and then deciding what they must do to continue to be so, they could vanish into the American maw.

In fact, rather than treasonable, the act is merely an infringement of the politically correct rules of the existing national unity debate. These hold that any discussion of sovereignty by other Canadians will provoke Quebeckers into asserting, protectively, their own sovereignty. Aside from the fact that Quebeckers are doing this anyway, the assumption itself belongs to yesterday's national unity agenda. While the self-justifying reason for other Canadians to define their own sovereignty is to provide themselves with the means, political and institutional, to survive, alone if necessary, the side-effects of this exercise could be entirely creative. On the intermittent occasions when other Canadians talk to Quebeckers today, they do so defensively-aggressively. Once they've figured out who they are, they ought to be able to talk to Quebeckers as psychic equals, a balance long absent from the relationship. A restored psychic balance could turn today's dialogue of the deaf into a conversation between partners who respect each other and, better yet, understand each other.

"Sovereignty" is of course one of the most slippery words in the political lexicon. Whatever it means, almost everyone wants to be sovereign today, from the Slovenes and Croats and Slovaks to the Walloons and Flemings and Catalans, from the Tamils and Sikhs to the Kurds. Just why race — to avoid the euphemisms of culture and language — should be so important amid the contemporary global economy is a good question. The global economy itself has to be a good part of the answer. By eroding the ability of nation-states to protect their citizens from being buffeted by the wide, cruel world, globalism has heightened the importance of ethnicity as a protective, collective shield.

In such a context, it would be more surprising if Quebeckers weren't seeking sovereignty than that 60 per cent should now tell pollsters that this is what they want. It is relevant that continental free trade has made the Canadian market less and less important to Quebec in the same way that the European Community has made that of Spain less important to Catalonia and that of Britain to Scotland. Relevant also is that abundant evidence now exists — Denmark, Austria, Singapore, let alone Luxembourg — that the small can be economically beautiful. Lastly, it matters to Quebeckers' self-esteem that today being small no longer necessarily means being parochial. Far from "retreating into their wigwam," as Pierre Trudeau once warned would be nationalism's consequence, Quebeckers have never before been so outward-turned and at the same time never so turned away from Canada. Witness the Quebec premier's welcoming of possible free trade with Mexico in contrast to the Ontario premier's terror of it.

This isn't at all to say that Quebec will go tomorrow. All constitutions are flexible: Canada's skin is almost infinitely stretchable. Our leaders and their experts undoubtedly can think up a fix. "Assymetric federalism" might do the trick. "Massive decentralization" might prompt other Canadians to applaud the constitutional conjuring act by giving them a share of the rabbits.

The problem is that while a new deal could be done, it could never be a done deal. Quebec negotiators could sign their names only in pencil — not out of duplicity, but out of honesty. The imperative of survival compels

Quebeckers always to retain the option of full sovereignty. They now possess almost all the necessary attributes of a fully fledged nation-state, owing this to their own determination and daring but also in part — life just isn't fair — to the contributions of other Canadians. They may never go all the way, but they always may because they always will be able to. In this sense, the problem isn't so much Quebec as Canada. Inherently and inescapably, it must remain forever on trial, incomplete, in harm's way.

The Meech Lake affair was about as close to a political crime as it's possible to get without consciously setting out to commit one. Hence the edge of anger in this essay — from a distance I have watched my country reduced almost to national impotence and international risibility.

To proclaim that Canada is now falling apart is to record a truism. Amid the deconstruction, though, something new is stirring, an instinctive response to an overwhelming challenge. One new event in the country is the assertive, confident way in which Quebeckers are reacting to their "rejection." To blame this on other Canadians' rejection of Meech Lake, though, is facile, besides being self-serving. It reduces the latest manifestation of Quebeckers' historical evolution to a fit of pique.

Instead, the defining difference between pre-Meech and post-Meech is in the rest of Canada. Other Canadians no longer feel guilty about Quebec. They are convinced, or so they tell the pollsters and the Citizens' Forum answer-phones, that the Confederation on offer — federal, bilingual, multicultural, with state-to-person and person-to-person relationships governed by the Charter of Rights — meets all of Quebec's legitimate needs, including that of being distinct. Beyond this there's no give, because other Canadians have concluded that the giving of more will not alter the ultimate demand.

At some point during the Meech debate, the realization took hold among other Canadians that for Quebeckers, *mon pays* meant, and could only ever mean, only Quebec. For much of English Canada's cultural élite, the moment of truth was the free trade debate. That Quebeckers voted for free trade was not the point; so did westerners. The point was that throughout the prolonged period during which other Canadians engaged in a fundamental debate about their future — as painful and as polarizing a debate as the one Quebeckers went through during their 1980 referendum — Quebeckers had no idea what was going on, nor did they give a damn about it. There was no awareness, no interest, no respect. English-Canadian cultural nationalists, the same types who tend to be Parents for French activists, simply stopped caring about Quebec. For others, the consciousness-raising "click" was of course Quebec's rejection of national bilingualism.

None of this is intended to allocate any blame here or there. Instead, it's an attempt to move the debate towards a new agenda. Which isn't to say that those who burned the fleur-de-lys in Brockville were not a bunch of louts.

For the best of reasons, some Canadians would not want to take part in any new debate. For them, a Canada without Quebec still within its skin — no matter if only nominally — would not be their Canada but a bland, one-dimensional nation. Others would regard a Canada that had "lost" Quebec as a country of losers from which they would want to escape as quickly as possible into the nation of winners so conveniently next door.

What's so striking is how few Canadians say they want to escape. Throughout the crisis, the "American option" has scarcely been mentioned. There is a widespread anger at the passing, or degrading, of national symbols such as the CBC and VIA Rail, which keep us from becoming more like Americans.

Even more striking, Canadians know who they are, or say they do. "A very clear consensus exists in all parts of the country about the individual and social values which define Canada," reported the Citizens' Forum in March. These were tolerance, compassion, peaceableness, all very self-flattering and in some instances perhaps fantastical since Americans are probably more welcoming of newcomers nowadays, including the flood of Hispanics and Asians, than Canadians are.

The qualifications don't blunt the point. A will to survive exists that is extraordinarily strong. In many respects, financial, economic, constitutional, political, Canada is in terrible shape today. Yet according to a mid-winter poll by Decima Research, 92 per cent of Canadians ranked Canada as "the best country in the world to live in" — the highest ranking they've ever collectively given their country.

To sharpen the point, a sense of solidarity seems to exist from coast to coast. The founding slogan of the Reform Party — "The West Wants In" — represents a complete flip in western attitudes (on the Prairies certainly if not in British Columbia); in the seventies the West wanted to be left alone to decide its own affairs; in the nineties, it wants to crash into the centre to help shape the affairs of the nation. On behalf of Newfoundland, Clyde Wells is making the same claim.

The real point of all this is that other Canadians are already sovereign psychologically, as are all peoples who are convinced that they are distinct. But in conspicuous contrast to Quebeckers, they lack *political* sovereignty, in fact or in prospect. A measure of sovereignty does devolve onto them as citizens of Canada. But this is attenuated by Quebec's counter-claim to internal sovereignty. This has to be one of the reasons why so many Canadians have opted out of the pan-Canadian enterprise in recent years, limiting their identity to that of their province, their region, their ethnic group.

Here, surely, resides the source for a good deal of the unfocused grumpiness of so many Canadians. They know that something is missing. They can't put their finger on it and each time they try are told that they are traitors to national unity.

Thus, most Canadians were deeply offended by the spectacle of their constitution being rewritten by "eleven white males in the back room." Yet Quebeckers uttered not a peep of complaint about this process. This isn't to say that Quebeckers are less democratic but rather that their concept of democracy is a collective one, while that of other Canadians is an individualistic one in which, in the idealistic if impractical limit, everyone should be heard. Somehow, this complaint by other Canadians that the existing constitutional process offended their political culture got turned into their being, yet again, offensive to Quebeckers. Similarly, the reason for the anger of many other Canadians at Quebec's exemption of itself from the Charter of Rights in order to impose unilingual signs has been insufficiently appreciated: to many other Canadians, the Charter of Rights has become a summary description of Canadian citizenship.

In his *Saturday Night* article, Salutin argued, "It's as if the rest of country has become more ... open, alert, *interesting* — like Quebec in an earlier phase." He's on to something important. Outside Quebec, today's political rage is populism. Its first manifestation — ignored by the political establishment — was the dispatch by ordinary Canadians of 40,000 letters, an all-time record, to Meech "dissident" Clyde Wells. Its subsequent manifestations range from the election of the New Democrats in Ontario to the late-blooming popularity of the Citizens' Forum (because it actually listened to people) to the extraordinary success of the Reform Party. According to the pollsters, ordinary Canadians feel "empowered," feel that their leaders have made a mess of things and they could do a whole lot better.

So let's follow the people and let them have at it. Since Canadians say they know who they are, this "it" need not involve yet another search for identity. Rather, other Canadians need to be released from the confines of yesterday's constitutional agenda — generous, imaginative, idealistic in its day but now overtaken by history — and set free to try to conceive of reforms, even total rewrites, of existing political structures and conventions so as to realize better their distinctive political culture.

To describe is one thing. To prescribe is quite another. All kinds of tricky questions about the process, the procedures, the rules of representation now raise their nagging heads. The best way to get across a minefield is to follow the footsteps of someone who's already made it across. This is why other Canadians must now do what Quebeckers have already done.

Collectively, Quebeckers now have a pretty good idea of what it is they really want. What's instructive is the way they've gone about reaching this conclusion. They've conducted their internal debate amid a lot of heat. But it has always been informed by a cool, clear light. This has been the light of self-interest, as defined by their imperative need to survive. As individuals, Quebeckers follow different paths, but they are all facing in the same direction. Even Trudeau and René Lévesque were reaching from opposed directions towards the common goal of Quebec's fulfilment. Today, it's irrelevant whether the demand for twenty-two areas of jurisdiction made by the supposedly federalist Quebec Liberals in the Allaire report can be labelled more accurately a (last chance) federalist solution or a sovereigntist one (on the instalment plan).

What Quebeckers do want, of course, is sovereignty-association. An old concept, but now honed to a new precision. Thus sovereignty is seldom now invoked as necessary for cultural and linguistic survival; few Quebec nationalists any longer express angst that these are threatened, and most certainly not by English Canadians. Instead, sovereignty's principal justification has become economic survival: only by escaping from the encumbrances, delays and compromises inherent in any federal system (Canada as a trans-Atlantic Yugoslavia) can Quebec become a globally competitive economy.

Similarly, association's purpose appears to have changed. Other Canadians still tend to assume that it is sought so Quebeckers can have their separatist cake while still eating their federalist subsidies. Certainly Quebec dairy farmers, in their brief to the Bélanger–Campeau commission, seemed to have that trick in mind. But the real trick being attempted is to resolve the problem that while Quebec undoubtedly could cope with *being* independent, the process of *becoming* independent could cripple it. The transition costs, such as those involved in disentangling the national debt, could be ruinously high. It's entirely possible that other Canadians will be so consumed by rage and spite that they will cut off their own noses in the hope of nicking Quebec's throat. By contrast, association, perhaps up to the level of a binational parliament, would make possible sensible and mutually beneficial deals. On a joint army, say, and a joint currency. Also, on a swap of a corridor to the Maritimes for federal properties in Quebec. As a bonus, a Canada–Quebec condominium might be able to retain its membership in prestigious bodies like the annual Western summit.

It won't be easy for other Canadians to copy Quebeckers. Not so much because we aren't homogeneous like them, although that's a considerable complication, but because defining our decisions by the rule of self-interest will be a novelty to us. We are guilt addicts.

So other Canadians will simply have to take a deep gulp and accept that, this time, nice guys won't even finish at all. They will vanish. If we want to survive, we will have to act self-interestedly, unsentimentally and without apology, in the way all survivors do.

For a start, Quebec's ultimatum that it must receive "definitive offers" within a year or so or proceed with its referendum on sovereignty should be ignored. It just isn't in the self-interest of other Canadians to fit their search for sovereignty into someone else's — self-interested — timetable.

This edge can get a lot sharper. It's plainly in the interests of other Canadians that those Quebeckers who may want to remain Canadian — the Cree of northern Quebec are an obvious example — know well in advance of any Quebec referendum that they will be able to exercise the same right of self-determination that Quebeckers are claiming (quite validly) for themselves. The objective here isn't to be provocative. It's to be honest. Quebeckers need to know that a Canada bent on survival will insist on the restoration (assuming that this is what the people there want) of a territory that would restore to Canada the psychologically vital attribute of still stretching unbrokenly from sea to sea.

Less sharply, but still pointedly, English Canadians should renounce the title that has come to be hung on them by default. It's a relic of yesterday's constitutional agenda. They should call themselves *Canadians*. It's an honourable title. Best of all, like Québécois, it's an unapologetically un-hyphenated one.

From this point onwards, Canadians should talk to themselves — not to disregard Quebeckers, still less to reject them, but to find themselves. The forum for this exercise in self-discovery is self-defining. It must be a constituent assembly, made up of some combination of newly elected members to give it legitimacy and of appointees from the legislatures and federal Parliament to give it continuity. As a personal preference, creative artists could be among the assembly's most creative members: the forum would be debating a people's soul, and whether it exists; our artists, whether on canvas or in print or on film, have held up mirrors to that soul, or idea, or dream.

Several important figures, such as Bob Rae and Clyde Wells, have come out in support of a constituent assembly. But they have not cited, because they cannot, the real reason why a constituent assembly is now needed so desperately. This is because it would be an entirely new political entity.

The central and irrevocable fact about Canada's existing political institutions is that they have failed us. Whether this has happened because of a particular personality — Mulroney, to be specific — or because the national unity debate has become stale and flaccid with repetition, or because this debate has too seldom extended beyond a small élite (too many of them Montrealers or over-specialized experts in such arcana as the Fulton–Favreau formula) is neither here nor there. The cardinal and palpable fact is that our existing institutions have lost their moral authority.

A new basis for political legitimacy not only is needed, but is hungered for. Hence the contemporary popularity of populism. This is most unusual within Canada's deferential political tradition. It is unique in the sense that earlier populist outbursts — the United Farmers, the CCF, the Créditistes — were concerned with tangible economic issues rather than today's almost inchoate political concerns.

Customarily, populism has short legs. It rises up full of righteous wrath, then gets confused or co-opted. This may not happen this time. Canada may be going through a milder version of what has happened in Eastern Europe. There, at some magical moment, everyone switched from taking for granted that the Communist system was immutable to saying out loud, "Of course I knew all along it couldn't work." Canada may have arrived at the same kind of discontinuity, a development that can be compared — to reach for an analogy closer to home — to the Depression years when everyone, even R. B. Bennett, suddenly said, "Of course capitalism as it is can't work."

This new version of populism has a long reach, if not long legs. The rage is directed not merely at the government but at the entire governing class of bureaucrats, constitutional experts, mainstream media commentators, and also at para-government institutions such as the Business Council on National Issues, recently so influential in the free trade debate. It's as if nothing and nobody is trusted except the new — like Bob Rae, Clyde Wells, Preston Manning. (Joe Clark is an exception, not least because his own political creed is populism.) Within such a political context, it's self-destructive to treat yesterday's bit of guilt-tripping — that for other Canadians to seek to define their sovereignty is to drive Quebeckers towards sovereignty — as an inviolable taboo.

To break any taboo is risky. But the effect can be

liberating and creative. Other taboos, every bit as encrusted, may suddenly be seen to be mutable, even disposable.

Consider that hoariest taboo of all, the monarchy. Today, to voice even the slightest doubt about it is to provoke a storm of criticism, for "giving in" to Quebec, quite aside from being rude to the Queen. The fact is that Canadians need to debate — as could happen only without Quebeckers present — the effect upon their maturity of clinging forever to the coat-tails of someone else's head of state; they need also to debate the costs of the enforced immaturity of the post of governor general, which, overshadowed by the monarchy, can never become a true symbol of national unity and a role model for particular forms of excellence.

Consider also that ever-popular remedy for all constitutional ailments — "decentralization." Under Quebec's watchful gaze, it can be applied only one-dimensionally, by transferring jurisdiction to the provinces. This isn't decentralization, it is "provincialization." If the real purpose of the exercise is to move power to the people, this may well be done best by enlarging the authority of those closest to them, municipalities and townships, perhaps even city-states.

The list of dubious taboos can be extended almost indefinitely. The triple-E Senate is the least arguable example. By bringing the regions directly into the centre, it could make Canada into a real confederation for the first time since 1867. But Quebec will veto any change that would reduce its proportional representation. If other Canadians want to gather together at the centre, why on earth should they foreclose this option for the sake of a "partner" whose own need, quite validly, is always to draw further away?

Education is another example. Whether it needs more

discipline or more money, it clearly needs to be more than it now is if Canada is to be globally competitive. All provinces, not just Quebec, jealously guard their jurisdiction. Maybe — a thought not worth introducing so long as Quebec is around the bargaining table — our provincial educational parts could be expanded into a larger whole by implementing national standards and by concentrating resources upon centres of excellence.

Multiculturalism, of course. Quebeckers have never accepted its statutory proclamation that "there is no official culture, nor does any ethnic group take precedence over any other." Many Canadians now have their own objections to official multiculturalism, mainly that national solidarity is being shattered by a salvo of hyphens. Quebec's absence from the debate would have only an indirect effect: ethnic interest groups would no longer be able to claim that subsidized multiculturalism is owed them in exchange for bilingualism.

There is bilingualism itself. If that other great Canadian achievement, medicare, is now open for debate, so also can this one be. The 300,000 families now immersing their children in French can't all be wrong. Neither can all those who regard official bilingualism as a Procrustean bed into which they have to fit, and from which they often are rejected. It has to be within the wit of Canadians to figure out reforms that will turn a perception of bilingualism as an imposition into an appreciation of it as an opportunity.

Last and far from least is the question of a new deal for native peoples. One of the new things all Canadians appear to agree on today is that a debt of guilt is overdue to be paid to Indians and Inuit. Quebeckers just don't feel the same way, perhaps because, as minorities often are, they are self-obsessed (hence their slogan, *pure laine*). While solutions aren't easy to find, one imaginative idea, for a pan-Canadian province of native peoples, would be vetoed automatically by Quebec. By themselves, Canadians might figure out how to discharge their well-merited guilt, not least because native leaders would be full participants in a constitutional assembly.

Little of this may happen. Once alone by themselves, other Canadians may discover that they don't have that much to say to each other — that they really are "others," their identities derived almost entirely from their province or region or ethnic group. This would confirm that the existing élite (despite all the barracking of it) has indeed read the country correctly and been following the correct constitutional policy. This policy amounts to trying to get Canadians to stay together by arranging things so that they have as little as possible to do with one another. It's the view of Canada as "a community of communities" or, rudely, as a "nation of shopping centres." It doesn't create a country. But it does buy time for it to muddle on.

Or the entire exercise could turn out to have been unnecessary. Quebeckers, unnerved by the recession, may decide this is not the time to make a long leap, let alone a final leap. Other Canadians, bored to death by the subject, may accept gratefully any shuffling of constitutional phrases that ends their need to think about it — for a while at least.

But the dare may be taken on the wing. Canadians, not wanting to become Americans, and realizing that the end product of today's constitutional policy has to be not so much national dismemberment as national pointlessness, may cohere into a real nation. At the entirely attainable best, Canadians will apply their populist rage creatively, figuring out new political structures and conventions that would reflect more accurately the character of their political culture and make them feel *maîtres chez nous* in their own country. Then, having talked themselves out, they would be able to talk to Quebeckers, with self-assurance and without rancour.

The constitutional consequence of such a dialogue could be a kind of Belgium. It's scarcely a role model for racial harmony. But it still exists, is still a single nation-state, and both of its constituent nations are now confident about their survival. So far as Canada is concerned, though, the flaw in this solution would be that the country would have a huge hole in its middle where once there was Quebec.

But nothing ordains that Canada must become a Belgium of two contiguous but unconnected nations. The initial reaction of Quebeckers to a withdrawal of other Canadians into a constituent assembly might be shock, although *La Presse* approves of "English Canada defining the broad lines of what it really is." Their succeeding reaction might well be pleasure at discovering that those with whom they've been partners throughout their entire history were not, as some Quebeckers appear to believe, a formless mass of "others," without definition and conviction. If Quebeckers were too self-obsessed to notice when other Canadians put themselves through the hell of debating whether continental free trade might cause their extinction as a distinct society, they most certainly would be self-interested enough to notice a debate among other Canadians about what they should do if Quebec leaves.

The consequence of attention being paid could be the filling up of the real hole within Confederation — the vacuum of mutual respect. Quebeckers, realizing that other Canadians do care about their survival, might come to care quite deeply about their "kin." Other Canadians, realizing that Quebec is their best possible tutor, might come to care deeply about those they were emulating. It's

188

by no means impossible that both sides would recognize that Confederation, pretty much as it is, is about as good an arrangement as can be invented for each partner's survivalist needs, the only real change being that mutual respect would have become Confederation's glue in place of the frayed adhesive of *féderalisme rentable.*

This may be reaching too far. The basis for an effective partnership can be found much closer to each of our grasps. The simple truth is that Quebeckers and Canadians need each other. Neither of us has anybody else. Necessity could be the mother of commitment.